Reversing Relations with Former Adversaries

Reversing Relations
with Former Adversaries

U.S. Foreign Policy after the Cold War

Edited by C. Richard Nelson
and Kenneth Weisbrode

With a foreword by James N. Rosenau

Published for the Project on U.S. Relations with
Cuba of the Atlantic Council of the United States

University Press of Florida
Gainesville Tallahassee Tampa Boca Raton
Pensacola Orlando Miami Jacksonville

#37353997

Copyright 1998 by the Board of Regents of the State of Florida
Printed in the United States of America on acid-free paper
All rights reserved

03 02 01 00 99 98   6 5 4 3 2 1

Library of Congress Cataloging-in-Publication Data

Reversing relations with former adversaries: foreign policy after the cold war /
edited by C. Richard Nelson and Kenneth Weisbrode;
with a foreword by James N. Rosenau.
p. cm.
"Published for the project on U.S. relations with Cuba of the Atlantic Council of the
United States."
Includes bibliographical references and index.
ISBN 0-8130-1545-6 (cloth: alk. paper)
1. United States—Foreign relations—1989–. I. Nelson, C. Richard. II. Weisbrode, Kenneth.
III. Atlantic Council of the United States.
E840.R44 1998
327.73—dc21 97-34113

The University Press of Florida is the scholarly publishing agency for the State
University System of Florida, comprised of Florida A & M University, Florida
Atlantic University, Florida International University, Florida State University,
University of Central Florida, University of Florida, University of North Florida,
University of South Florida, and University of West Florida.

University Press of Florida
15 Northwest 15th Street
Gainesville, FL 32611

Contents

FOREWORD

We live in a time of profound, persistent, and pervasive change. Restless publics, expanding markets, ethnic sensibilities, weakened governments, and dynamic technologies are transforming world affairs. No less powerful are the numerous tensions that result when processes of globalization generate localizing reactions or when bureaucracies and people resist change and cling to established goals and conventional means of achieving them. Many challenges have arisen since the end of the cold war, challenges posed by new political equations and unfamiliar situations.

These conditions call for clarity in our understanding of the dynamics of change. Neither the attitudes of citizens nor the foreign policies of officials can be solidly grounded without an explicit conception of what is meant by change, how we know a transformation when we see one, and how we differentiate between the appearance and the reality of new orientations in courses of action. But clarity is not easily achieved. Not only are the processes of change marked by uncertainty and obscurity, but so are we prone to allow long-standing assumptions and patterns of thought to govern our appraisal of what is transpiring both within and among societies. As the chapters of this book make clear, for example, it took U.S. officials considerable time to overcome their habitual modes of reacting to the Soviet Union and to acknowledge that deep-seated transformations were at work in that society. For all the intelligence reports at their disposal, they still had enormous difficulties surmounting their time-tested premises as to the source of Soviet behavior.

How, then, to begin to conceive of change in world politics? How to distinguish between enduring transformations and those that are temporary? How to trace likely outcomes of those change dynamics that are slow to evolve? And, from the perspective of policy makers, how to nudge both evolutionary and abrupt changes in desirable directions or at least prevent them from making situations worse? While some of the answers to these questions are explicit in the essays in this book, others are implicit and serve as a stimulus in trying to differentiate types of change.

One useful approach to the problem of delineating transformational dynamics and distinguishing them from momentary shifts is to follow the lead of the French historian Fernand Braudel by making a three-way division based on the time span involved. First is the short run, what Braudel conceives of as a "world of events." Next is a middle range of time, "conjunctural time," in which trends unfold slowly over ten, twenty, or even fifty years. Finally, there is the very long run, Braudel's *longue durée*, which covers centuries and involves the broadest patterns and structures. One can readily think of examples of each of these types of change, but the task gets more difficult when one appreciates that short-run changes may not be reflected in conjunctural time and that the latter, in turn, may not be sufficiently durable to be registered in the longue durée.

Until recently, foreign policy makers had perforce to focus on the world of events, leaving changes that occurred in conjunctural time to social scientists and those that marked the longue durée to historians. There seemed little choice. Much as those in the policy-making community wished for time in which to anticipate long-term trends, the demands of immediate events seemed overwhelmingly urgent. What might Saddam Hussein or Fidel Castro do next? Or what might result from Deng Xiaoping's new policies or Gorbachev's endeavors to shift the direction of Soviet policy? Such are the questions that have preoccupied American officials. And for good reasons: The immediate events cannot be ignored or postponed; they do have consequences, and they need to be either encouraged or countered.

Yet, as these essays make clear, immediate events are culminations of conjunctural trends, and as the pace of change accelerates, such trends can no longer be ignored. In a world marked more by change than by continuity, the long term is as important to policy planning as is the world of events. Put more forcefully, in a world where military preoccupations have given way to economic and social concerns, where nature is withering in the face of human exploitation, where population growth swells the ranks of those below the poverty line, and where governments and states are increasingly unable to meet the needs of their peoples—to mention only a few of the underlying long-term processes stirring beneath the surface of daily events—neither officials nor publics can afford to confine their attention to today's crisis or tomorrow's challenge. Now they must extend their analytic horizons well into the future if they are to avoid the many catastrophes that arguably may be the final link in causal chains now being fashioned in every region of the world.

And, indeed, this need for expanded attention to a lengthened shadow of the future has come to be appreciated in the policy-making community. Consider, for example, this excerpt from a lengthy account of the turn in this new analytic direction:

> Environmental threats like the beautiful water hyacinths choking Lake Victoria and the desert sands eating away the sparse pastures bordering the Sahara are some of the issues deemed urgent today by American foreign policy makers in much the same manner as military sites alarmed policy makers several decades ago.

> These days, intelligence officials are being asked to look at softer targets—those flowers and sand dunes—to shed light on this decade's hot wars. Through this optic, Somalia and Rwanda can be interpreted not as spontaneous outbreaks of clan warfare or ethnic violence, but as conflicts nourished by the underlying strains of hunger, drought and a lack of arable land in Somalia, and huge population growth and population density in Rwanda.[1]

Viewed in the context of long-run considerations, it follows that reversals of course on the part of foreign adversaries are among the most important changes that need to be probed and grasped. From an American point of view, such reversals are greatly to be desired. They represent movement toward a more cooperative and peaceful world. And reversals also call for deep causal inquiry if they are to be encouraged and the perpetuation of adversarial relations avoided. But such inquiries cannot be confined to a focus on the adversary's underlying circumstances and how these might be affected by policies from abroad; inquiries must also focus on the readiness of the United States to adjust to reversals of course by adversaries. The American public needs to overcome what I call enemy deprivation and to give policy makers leeway to explore new terms for an emergent relationship with former adversaries. Likewise, policy makers need to overcome their long-standing assumptions and to heed the import of dynamics unfolding across conjunctural time in the social, economic, political, and environmental life of current or potential adversaries.

It is the great virtue of this book that it highlights the problems and opportunities inherent in the transformation of adversarial relationships.

Here, in several case studies of recent situations, readers will find sensitivity to the delicate links that form the causal chains. Here they will encounter the diversity of factors that enter into the politics and economics of transformations in international relationships. And here readers will be compelled to ponder the severe limits within which the United States can bring about moderation and progress in the orientations and policies of former (and in the case of Iraq, current) adversaries. Above all, readers will come to appreciate yet again that the complexity of causal chains requires patience—deep patience that eschews unduly simple solutions—if the course of events is to be marked by ameliorated tensions and expanded cooperation.

James N. Rosenau

NOTE

1. Steven Greenhouse, "The Greening of U.S. Diplomacy: Focus on Ecology," *New York Times,* October 9, 1995, p. A6.

ACKNOWLEDGMENTS

The editors wish to thank David C. Acheson, president of the Atlantic Council of the United States, for first inspiring our work on this subject, and Alfred D. Wilhelm Jr., executive vice president, for his encouragement. Additional appreciation goes to the members of the Atlantic Council's working group on U.S. relations with Cuba; its chairperson, Sarah C. Carey; and its financial sponsors, the Ford Foundation, the Tinker Foundation, and the U.S. Institute of Peace. Finally, a special debt of gratitude is owed Burt Sapin, whose intellectual guidance and pleasant colleagueship made completion of this project possible.

1

Introduction

BURTON M. SAPIN

This book investigates the process of reversing relations with former adversaries—when that process has not involved a major war that brings about the change. Such a reversal has been a particularly noteworthy characteristic of the cold war and post–cold war international environments, and it has clear relevance to future developments as well.

In spite of the great importance and high visibility of past reversals of relations and the continuing appearance of new cases, this subject has received relatively little systematic analysis, either for purposes of academic illumination or for practical policy implications. Thus, when the Atlantic Council embarked upon its major study of possibilities for restructuring U.S. relations with Cuba, it seemed logical to search for guidelines by reviewing past cases of reversals in relations. This book is the product of that decision.

Traditionally, the new relationship has usually been the product of either a dramatic internal change in one of the adversaries or a serious military conflict between the two. Among the most notable of the latter in the twentieth century, of course, are the almost total reversals of U.S. relations with both Germany and Japan after World War II.

However, the onset of the cold war after World War II and its sudden, dramatic collapse in the late 1980s brought two quite different patterns to the center stage of international politics. The first was a highly intense and deep-seated rivalry between two superpowers and their alliances that did not erupt in a major military confrontation in more than forty years. (John Gaddis has referred to it as the "long peace" of the cold war.)[1]

What has succeeded the cold war is much less dramatic. Over the past half-dozen years, as the varied antagonisms of the cold war have petered out, they have left behind the sticky residue of past threats, tensions, and patterns of hostile interaction. These leavings have greatly complicated the business of reversing past adversarial relations and moving toward friendlier and more productive associations.

No doubt diplomatic historians can identify similar cases from the past, but the number of cases emanating from the cold war that are of such importance in the contemporary international political system is unparalleled. This prompts the practical policy question of what the United States and others have learned about the process of reversing relations, beginning with the People's Republic of China and more recently with the Eastern European countries and the former Soviet Union. How might such lessons be applicable to ongoing cases like that of North Korea and those that may arise in the future, notably with Cuba? Indeed, the stories are far from complete even in the cases of China and Russia.

This question is not without a broader, more academic interest in terms of why states act as they do and what factors are most influential. However, whether one's interests lie at the applied, policy-oriented level or at the more conceptual-theoretical, the fact is that the reversal of relations has not to this point been systematically addressed by students of international politics. In an effort to do so, this book focuses on six major case studies as the basis for generalizations and policy guidelines.

RELEVANT CONCEPTS AND ASSUMPTIONS

We are reminded almost every day that friends and adversaries are relative terms and concepts as long as the international political system is characterized by largely autonomous state actors with interests and objectives that inevitably diverge. In even the most hostile of relationships, there are usually some continuing diplomatic contacts and other efforts at minimal communications. On the other hand, nations that have quite friendly relations overall, with many shared or overlapping interests, are likely to be highly competitive economically, particularly in the contemporary international environment.

In the past, interstate rivalries focused on the struggle for power, an enhanced ability to influence the actions of other states, which would bring rewards in terms of territory, economic gain, and an expanded role in the international political system. The ultimate arbiter was usually military power, and one way of resolving interstate rivalries, at least temporarily, was war, with its victors and its vanquished.

Politics among nations, in all of these dimensions, has been the subject of literally thousands of studies—historical, analytical, and conceptual-theoretical. The cornerstone concept, power, has probably been the most studied in all the social sciences, although the illumination provided thereby has sometimes seemed rather modest. Why wars start and why and how they end, and ways of avoiding the former and facilitating the latter, have also received substantial attention. (The Allied policy of "unconditional surrender" during World War II was based on the conclusion that the negotiated end of World War I, far from being satisfactory, had in fact helped set the stage for the war that followed.)

The adversarial relationship between the United States and the Soviet Union and their associated blocs went well beyond the traditional military and power-political avenues, although it certainly included them. It was also highly ideological in nature, as well as scientific-technological, economic, cultural, and psychological. Accordingly, this "war" was waged with an equivalent spectrum of policy instruments—from military-technological competition and standard diplomatic maneuvering to espionage and subversion, propaganda, and psychological and economic warfare.

This broad spectrum of policy instruments was inevitably reflected in the laws, rules, and regulations required to implement them. This was emphatically the case in the United States, given its traditional pattern of great specificity and detail in its legislation and in the administrative implementation thereof. Whether the issue was trade constraints or the denial of military and so-called dual-use technology to the Soviet Union and its associates, the ends were accomplished by means of elaborate legislative norms, detailed regulations, and the bureaucratic mechanisms to carry them out. (The latter now represent one major practical obstacle to the process of reversing relations.)

Although the cold war was carried out in this "total" fashion, it was nevertheless characterized by considerable variations of time, place, and circumstances. Titoist Yugoslavia's early split with Stalinist Russia quickly brought it into a very friendly relationship with the United States and the other Western powers, in spite of Yugoslavia's communist ideology. In the early 1970s, a somewhat similar change unfolded in the relations between the United States and communist China.

Even in the U.S. relationship with the Soviet Union, there were periods of détente, easing of tensions, and attempts to open up avenues of cooperation in such fields as arms control and cultural exchange. In short, even between enemies or adversaries, there are matters of degree in antagonisms. There are usually some areas of shared interest (as in the case of preventing a major thermonuclear exchange, which would damage everyone); the adversarial elements may well vary from time to time and situation to situation.

To sum up, while the question of reversing relations with former adversaries is not a new one for the Western state system, the post–cold war international environment is distinctive in terms of the absence of a major shooting war that brought the hostile relations to some definitive conclusion; in the tremendous mobilization of governmental systems and societal resources that the intense antagonism of the cold war left behind; and in the rather substantial number of nations involved in the process.

THE EMPIRICAL FOCUS

Since this book includes case studies on Iraq and Cuba, its focus on former adversaries is obviously broader than the cold war aspects. Nevertheless, the primary emphasis is on the cold war and its aftermath, and the most significant cases are former Marxist-Leninist states that are moving in different ways, at different paces, from an essentially adversarial relationship with the United States to something more amicable.[2]

In Russia, China, Nicaragua, and more recently Vietnam, there has already been considerable movement, but substantial uncertainties will probably continue to exist for quite some time to come. The former "satellite" states of Eastern or Central Europe (Poland, Hungary, the Czech and Slovak Republics of former Czechoslovakia, Rumania, and Bulgaria) are highly relevant to the topic, but their national histories and subordinate relations with the former Soviet Union make their adaptation to their new status quite different from that of Russia and China or Vietnam and Nicaragua.

North Korea (the Democratic People's Republic of Korea) has a distant potential for study as a former adversary; its complex history and rapid unfolding may well warrant inclusion in a future book. Finally, there is Cuba, which demands considerable attention because of geographical propinquity to the United States, the many American citizens of Cuban background, and the seemingly unyielding Marxism-Leninism of its leader, Fidel Castro. Cuba is the subject of study even though its movement away from adversarial status seems a distant possibility at the moment.

Turning to adversary nations that fall outside the communist camp, there are clearly bases for interstate tensions and antagonisms other than the power-political and ideological factors that fueled the cold war. Iraq is one of the Third World states where goals and ambitions run counter to U.S. interests and objectives, and it therefore views the United States as a major enemy. A number of these states, including Libya, Syria, and Khomeiniist Iran, are in the Near East or North Africa. Some of their policy instruments, such as state-supported or state-sponsored terrorism, are relatively novel and not easily subject to the usual pressures applied in interstate relations. All of these nations are, at the same time, much less powerful than the United States, although the gunboat diplomacy option of the past seems less practical in the contemporary international environment.

Regarding such states, the questions are traditional: How does the United States deter them from taking actions it opposes? On the other hand, how can it compel them to take actions favored by the United States? The questions are basic, but some of the policy instruments now being brought to bear (for example, preemptive bombing raids and economic embargoes), although familiar, are not those traditionally used.

In the case of Iraq, between 1981 and 1989 the United States tried to move the adversary nation onto a friendlier path, using a variety of inducements, most of them economic. In contrast to the communist-state examples, there was little evidence of notable change in Iraq, of either a governmental, societal, or ideological sort. But Iraq is a reminder, for the purposes of this study, that the international system includes adversary nations whose bases of enmity for the United States fall outside the Marxist-Leninist mold, and more such nations seem likely to emerge. The question in their case is what combination of inducements and threats, if any, might be successful in producing the desired policy changes.

South Africa, though not analyzed here, deserves brief mention as a more contemporary kind of case. The international community, represented by the United Nations, made a judgment that South Africa's *domestic* governmental, political, and social patterns were unacceptable, and it was prepared to force changes to be made if the South African government was unwilling or unable to do so. It was in these nontraditional terms that South Africa was defined as an adversary of the United States. This pattern is one of growing importance in the contemporary international environment. Haiti, Somalia, and Bosnia are other examples, and more are likely to emerge.

It should be recognized that this is a relatively new phenomenon in the international system. While some of the techniques for applying pressure are familiar, such as use of military force or imposition of an economic embargo, the purposes are new. The adversarial quality is established by what happens *within* the other state, rather than by actions of the state that seem to threaten American interests and objectives directly.

No doubt there are a variety of lessons to be derived from the Iraqi and South African cases and others that seem to parallel them. The two countries also share characteristics that make them quite different from the adversaries that were formerly communist states and that are significant in terms of longer-range U.S. interests and objectives in a post–cold war international environment. The former communist states represent the primary focus of this volume, though both Iraq and South Africa are interesting case studies, particularly in the use of *economic* instruments of statecraft to influence state behavior.

A Framework for Analysis

While the details of major foreign policy decisions are usually complicated, the basic framework for analyzing foreign policy is fairly straightforward. It involves a nation-state and the international environment beyond its boundaries. Every nation has needs and interests that are in some way affected by or dependent on what is taking place in that outside world. Foreign policy is the product of official governmental efforts to pursue or protect national interests in that external environment.

Most contemporary analysts of foreign policy therefore try to take both domestic and external factors into account in their studies. That is the approach in this book. The basic point of departure for U.S. foreign policy over the past fifty-five years or so has been to define the international environment as highly threatening to basic American interests, thus requiring a response. For this reason, our discussion begins with the external setting and then attempts to characterize the relevant domestic political factors.

The Impact of the External Environment

In the period before World War II, it took the Japanese attack on Pearl Harbor to overcome fundamental, traditional U.S. reluctance regarding deep involvement in the international political arena. The process was much more rapid and less painful in the transition from World War II to what became the cold war. But the driving force in both cases was the keen sense of a threat to basic national interests. From that perspective, the international environment as perceived over roughly the past half-century has been the key determinant, the independent variable, in explaining U.S. foreign policy. One critical question is how the United States has reacted when a threat seems to have changed, when an adversary nation no longer seems threatening.

It is in any event indisputable that confronting a highly adversarial international environment has been the norm for the United States over the past six decades. The threatening nation-states have ranged from Nazi Germany, Fascist Italy, and militarist Japan to the more contemporary communist states—the former Soviet Union, the People's Republic of China, and assorted lesser entities such as the East European satellites, Vietnam, and Cuba. At least one of them, Cuba, has lingered on as an adversary into the 1990s.

Understandably, then, the disappearance or notable diminution of the antagonistic actions and attitudes of formerly adversarial states will provide a stimulus for at least reflecting upon if not actually changing one or more major policy directions. If the external change is a dramatic, seemingly fundamental one, presumably it will pose the question of an equivalent change in American policy. Indeed, a broader question to be addressed is the extent to which certain external changes have the power to produce U.S. policy responses. The adversarial nations of World War II were transformed into benign international associates by the traditional route of defeat in war. Most observers would regard the processes of transformation in the cases of Germany, Japan, and Italy as quite successful.

Another pattern emerged in the cold war period and continues in what is now labeled, perhaps optimistically, the post–cold war environment. It can probably be said to have begun with President Nixon's trip to China twenty-five years ago. Essentially the pattern is one of dealing with communist states that in some ways and in varying degrees have moved from a primarily adversarial relationship with the United States to more friendly relations. The variation should be emphasized; there has been no single, standard pattern.

In no case has the change been the direct result of a war on the scale of World War II, although in several cases—China, Vietnam, perhaps Nicaragua, even Cuba—there have been direct or indirect military engagements with the United States. Of course, by far the most significant and traumatic occurred with Vietnam.

In some cases, as with the former Soviet Union and its Eastern European satellites, highly dramatic, watershed changes have taken place in their internal political systems. To a lesser extent, this may also be said of Nicaragua. In other cases—China and to a lesser extent Vietnam—the dramatic alterations have taken place in the economic systems, accompanied so far by much more limited changes in the political systems.

Iraq has been distinctive in a number of ways: noncommunist although highly authoritarian and somewhat ideological; defeated in a war; and so far unwilling or unable to make the transition from adversary to a more benign relationship in spite of vigorous U.S. efforts to encourage that process.

In all of these cases, despite the differing characteristics of the nations, the issue of changing U.S. foreign policy has arisen because of a seeming change in the internal characteristics or external behavior of a state previously viewed as an adversary. Because in none of these cases has the change been as definitive or clear-cut as total military defeat in a war, there is obviously more room, sometimes much more room, for differing views and interpretations of what has happened or is happening, the significance of the changes that have taken place, and their implications for U.S. interests and policies.

THE ROLE OF THE DOMESTIC POLITICAL AND GOVERNMENTAL ENVIRONMENT

Under these circumstances, the internal or domestic political setting for foreign policy comes into play. In all nation-states, there are governmental mechanisms through which national needs, interests, and objectives are defined; salient characteristics of the external environment are assessed; implications of the latter for the former are drawn; and courses of action are determined. In contrast to the earlier, more traditional "billiard ball" approach to the dynamics of international politics, most contemporary analysts assume that domestic political and societal characteristics do have an impact on foreign policy decision making. Although external stimuli often provide the occasion, it is domestic factors that shape and constrain the response.

However the balance between domestic and international factors may be struck in other nations, there can be no doubt that the domestic environment is quite potent in its impact on major U.S. foreign policy decisions. I would argue that domestic political factors are more significant in U.S. foreign policy making than in any other major contemporary political system.

Any explanation of major policy change that does not focus considerable attention on domestic politics would in my view be notably incomplete. This must surely be the case when a major adversary-nation is changing its role, thus requiring decisions about appropriate response. As suggested earlier, it is even more the case when the nature of the adversary's transformation and its implications for U.S. interests and objectives are far from unambiguous.

Obviously, the U.S. domestic political environment is highly complex: many government institutions; numerous, diverse citizen interests—economic, social, ethnic and ideological—that are organized and politically effective; and many avenues for the expression and communication of policy views, both directly to elected representatives and indirectly through the mass media, public opinion polls, and organized groups. If responsibility for major foreign policy decisions is usually centered on the president and the executive agencies and departments, they in turn are enmeshed in what some analysts have characterized as concentric circles of influence and constraint, beginning with the Congress and extending beyond it to the plethora of political actors and processes that characterize the U.S. political system. How might the latter be most usefully approached in analyzing cases of fading adversaries and changing policies for dealing with them?

If the executive branch usually has the responsibility for defining external situations and takes the initiative in recommending courses of action to deal with them, the first question to be asked is how well the executive branch has performed the tasks of substantive policy analysis. As indicated, this includes gathering and interpreting relevant data from the international environment, assessing its significance and its implications for U.S. interests, and recommending appropriate policy responses. Particularly relevant is the Iraq case, in which the president and the executive branch were clearly the dominant players. For a number of reasons, Iraq did not, before the Gulf war, attract strong attention from other political sectors, and the executive therefore had more room for policy maneuvering than is often the case.

If changed external circumstances require or at least suggest major policy changes, the second key question to be asked is how persuasively the case for change has been made by the executive. This second question quickly merges with a third, namely, if major policy change is being recommended, how effectively, how systematically, have the relevant factors in the domestic political environment been assessed and dealt with. The next step is to consider the domestic political environment more directly. Here it may be useful to begin with the rather simplistic observation that in the U.S. system it is much easier to block action than to move forward, particularly with new policies and initiatives.

Most Americans most of the time are relatively indifferent to foreign policy issues. Obvious exceptions are literally life-and-death matters— large-scale and even small-scale military engagements in which American lives are at risk, or major economic problems that may put U.S. jobs at risk. In recent years, short-term crises overseas, such as famine, large-scale internal violence and loss of life, and similar humanitarian concerns, have also captured urgent U.S. attention, for a short time at least. But on many foreign policy questions there is neither sustained attention nor strongly held views. In such cases, well-organized and highly motivated interest groups, even if they represent relatively small numbers of people and a relatively narrow set of concerns in terms of national interest, can have a considerable impact on policy. This is particularly true if the positions they are pushing or protecting are not seen by most Americans as harmful or inimical to U.S. interests.

And if the intention of an interest group in a particular case is to *block* a new policy or action, the available devices and institutions for doing so will make it relatively easy to have an impact.

Usually such interest groups have cultivated or otherwise developed congressional support—in terms of key senators or representatives, members of an important committee or subcommittee, or key committee staff members. The combination of well-organized and politically active interest groups and well-placed congressional support can be a potent one.

An early example in the "changing adversary" field was the strong U.S. support in the 1950s and 1960s for the Chinese Nationalist (Chiang Kai-shek) regime that had moved to Taiwan after the communist victory on the mainland in 1949. The base of support in the United States seems to have been more ideological and cultural than ethnic, and the policy had the backing of a number of active politicians, such as Senator William Knowland (R–Calif.) and Congressman Walter Judd (R–Minn.).

During the height of the cold war, one major source of opposition to any softening of U.S. policies toward the Soviet Union was the well-organized, strongly anticommunist groups of Americans of Eastern European ethnic background (such as Polish Americans), with a considerable body of supporters in the Congress. In more recent years, a powerful influence on U.S. policy toward Vietnam has been the very active and well-organized POW-MIA groups, again with strong congressional support.

Probably the best example of a powerful, ethnically oriented interest group (leaving aside Jewish Americans who offer strong support for pro-Israel policies by the U.S. government) are the Cuban Americans, based largely in the state of Florida. Their influence is a major factor in U.S. policy toward Cuba, bolstered by their very substantial presence in the politically important state of Florida. They, too, have developed strong congressional support for their policy positions.

The discussion to this point has highlighted the obstacles that usually stand in the way of proposed policy changes for dealing with fading adversaries. The basic structure of the U.S. governmental system facilitates blocking rather than taking action. If a foreign policy issue is not highly salient politically, well-organized and active interest groups, strategically supported in the Congress, can exercise policy influence and constrain policy change to a degree far out of proportion to the numbers of Americans whose views and interests they may actually represent.

The question then arises: What if a proposed change seems to promise consequences that would be beneficial both domestically and internationally? What institutional avenues and political techniques are available to the proponents of such changes? The obvious answer is that they can bring to bear the same general strategies, pressures, and techniques employed by groups with opposing views. The most recent case in point involved the People's Republic of China. The policy debate was between those favoring a very tough policy on human rights in China versus those who argued that U.S. economic interests at stake in the P.R.C. were far more important. Economic interests, they believed, should not be sacrificed to humanitarian and ideological concerns, however worthy, about Chinese domestic policies.

The specific policy issue was U.S. renewal of MFN (Most Favored Nation) status for Chinese exports to the United States. To summarize a very complex set of processes very simply, President Clinton finally made a decision in May 1994 to separate the MFN and human rights issues and make no attempt to use the former for leverage in dealing with the latter. Most assessments of this decision accord considerable weight to the well-organized and seemingly very effective campaign by U.S. business interests to underscore the great potential of the rapidly growing Chinese market for U.S. exports. A considerable number of China specialists argued that a continuation of dynamic economic growth in China was much more likely to improve political and civil rights there than would heavy-handed diplomatic and economic pressure on the Chinese government by the U.S. government.

In the end those who backed this argument politically outgunned influential members of Congress and others strongly committed to the human rights issue. A president who had made the economy his major focus was not in a position to resist a case based primarily on economic, job-creating considerations. This was undoubtedly true for many members of Congress as well. It should be noted that, as is typical of the U.S. system, this issue continues to arise each year when MFN status for China must be renewed by the Congress. So far, the economic interests have prevailed.

Presumably the same general analysis is applicable to communist Vietnam, where the leadership in recent years has been moving vigorously to open up the economy to foreign investment and free-market forces while at the same time maintaining tight political control of the country. There are, however, some key differences between the People's Republic of China and the Democratic Republic of Vietnam. An obvious one is size: China has a population estimated at more than 1 billion; Vietnam's is 60 million to 65 million. Whatever China's economic potential turns out to be, it will obviously be far greater than Vietnam's.

Equally relevant, I would argue, is that the opposing issue in the case of Vietnam has not been treatment of its own people but the treatment of some Americans—the POWs and MIAs of the Vietnam War. Despite considerable progress, such concerns had not been resolved to the satisfaction of the interested groups, particularly the POW-MIA lobby, and until the first half of 1995 the executive branch had thus moved slowly and cautiously in establishing full diplomatic relations and encouraging broader U.S. economic activity in Vietnam.

Given the increasing pressure by U.S. business interests for a share in the seemingly dynamic prospects of the Vietnamese economy, and the continuing though disputed progress with regard to the MIAs, President Clinton announced on July 11, 1995, a normalization of relations with Vietnam that has now led to the resumption of full diplomatic relations. He was provided some domestic political protection by the support of one of the best-known former POWs, Admiral (ret.) John McCain, Republican senator from Arizona. (It should be noted that while President Nixon's trip to China took place in 1972, full diplomatic recognition of China by President Carter did not take place until the end of 1978.)

In the case of Vietnam, the "jobs" argument may have finally made a difference, along with, perhaps, a growing public sense that it was finally time to put the Vietnam War behind us. In any event, the fundamental point here is that U.S. economic interests, specifically the potential for expanding U.S. exports and thus creating jobs, have become rather suddenly a factor to be considered in decisions on how to deal with former adversary-states.

So far, the economic factor has expressed itself very powerfully in the case of China, modestly vis-à-vis Vietnam, and remains for the time being largely hypothetical if not counterproductive in the case of Cuba. Economic interests are also vulnerable to changing economic circumstances and to the harsh disagreements that sometimes accompany increased economic interaction, as seen in the case of China.

The Case Studies

The major empirical focus of these comments will be the Russian, Chinese, Nicaraguan, and Vietnamese cases. Cuba at this point falls in a different category, and Iraq is in most important dimensions sui generis.

General Observations

Dealing with former adversaries represents the latest chapter in the continuing international political education of U.S. policy makers and citizens alike. We are reminded that political phenomena are complex and that underlying fundamentals of culture, values, interests, and attitudes change much more slowly than day-to-day relationships and policy issues—even more slowly than formal political and social institutions in place and presumably in control.

There have been dramatic, in some cases watershed, changes in the four countries in question, as noted. These changes have been accompanied by equally startling shifts in the relationships of the four countries with the United States. What is increasingly obvious is how many of the old problems, suspicions, and issues linger on and how quickly they have been joined by new concerns, themselves a reflection of the new relationships.

These changed relationships with former adversaries, however dramatic, represent a beginning rather than an end. While the issues that keep emerging are by no means as apocalyptic as the threat of a nuclear holocaust (a fact worth remembering and appreciating), they are certainly difficult and challenging. In short, these relationships require serious and sustained attention and cannot be taken for granted; they are subject to reversal.

The processes of political, social, and economic change in the former adversaries are inevitably complex and usually far from definitive in their consequences. Even where, as in the cases of Russia and Nicaragua, major regime changes have taken place, both individual actors and institutional processes linger on from the old regime, in some cases remaining quite powerful. Where the old political regime is still in power, as in China and Vietnam, legitimate questions can be raised as to the long-term sustainability of the economic and political changes that have been instituted.

Uncertainties about what is taking place in the former adversary-states and what will unfold over time provide a basis for continuing suspicion and even hostility toward them on the part of some elements within the United States. Some among the latter are seriously concerned about the possible reemergence of hostile communist regimes and the supporting ideology. Others less concerned still find this possibility a useful argument, in domestic political terms, with which to oppose too rapid normalization of relations.

The great difficulties faced by those communist states in trying to move toward free-market economies and democratic polities present major obstacles to those outside nations, like the United States, interested in assisting in the process. Even in the cases of the more progressive Central European states (Poland, Hungary, and the Czech and Slovak Republics), toward which the U.S. domestic political environment is generally more sympathetic and supportive, the internal roadblocks to reform are not easily overcome. In short, basic circumstances in most of the former adversary-states, combined with a constellation of U.S. domestic political forces suspicious of or downright hostile to drastically changed relationships, make such relationships difficult to achieve.

There are some factors, of course, that weigh in on the positive side.

Perhaps the most important to this point have been strategic security interests. The essential motivation for the original U.S.-Chinese rapprochement in the 1970s was the shared security interest of a common adversary, the Soviet Union. The disappearance of the latter beginning in the late 1980s no doubt helps explain the more troubled relationship of the United States and China in the early 1990s.

The continuing shared security interests of the United States with first the Soviet Union and now Russia are a core element of that relationship. The control of nuclear weapons and the maintenance of security and stability on the European continent are still critical security issues that depend on close Russian-American cooperation and collaboration. Close attention to that relationship is a requirement rather than a matter of choice. On the other hand, for that very reason those suspicious of present Russian intentions or future developments feel even freer to express their concerns and critically scrutinize U.S. policies for signs of weakness or naive overacceptance.

As noted, economic interests can provide powerful support for changing relations. That has clearly been true in the case of China and, to a much lesser extent, Vietnam. On the other hand, greatly expanded economic relations have their downside, clearly evident with China, as reflected in rapidly growing trade imbalances, blatant violations ("pirating") in the sale of such copyrighted goods as compact discs and videocassettes, and use of prison labor in manufacturing goods for export. At some future date, the repatriation of profits may well become a major issue. On their side, the Chinese push hard for U.S. support for their admission to the new World Trade Organization.

Normalization of relations also brings attention to issues that could previously be ignored, for example, compensation for the private property expropriated by the communist regimes in their heyday. The matter has already arisen in a significant way in Nicaragua. It will be an even more potent and difficult issue in the case of Cuba. In both these countries, the issue is complicated by the fact that many of those claiming compensation are now U.S. citizens.

Finally, the switch to more "normal" relations brings with it the typical differences of interest, objectives, and policy between nation-states that are not primarily adversaries. Thus, it is not surprising that the United States and Russia may differ on Bosnia and, surely, that the United States and China have underlying differences with regard to the future of Taiwan. Both China and Vietnam are likely to have long-term differences with the United States on human rights granted their citizenry.

In the end, as is usually the case in international politics, the balance of the overall relationship will be struck by the weight of the shared political, security, and economic interests as against those that sharply diverge. In the case of the former adversary-states, inherited suspicions and tensions, reflected in the U.S. domestic political environment, complicate this balancing process.

Policy Implications

As our analysis has made clear, changing the overall U.S. relationship with each of the former adversary-states is highly vulnerable to domestic political forces that for one reason or another may oppose it. As Robert Sutter makes amply clear in the concluding section of his chapter, a wide variety of obstacles stand in the way, ranging from the laws and regulations put in place in the earlier period of hostility to the continuing ideological opposition still evident, particularly in some legislative and political circles.[3]

For those who favor pursuing a changed relationship, the implication is obvious. To do so will require (has already required in some cases) working the political system as energetically and systematically as those who oppose or resist the change. Examples have already been mentioned in the cases of China and Vietnam. Business and other economic interests that see significant potential benefits in these situations can mobilize political support. By no means all Floridians share the views regarding Cuba that are held by at least the more vocal of the Cuban-American community there.

In the case of Russia, there are significant U.S. political sectors deeply concerned about the international security issues in which Russia continues to be a key player. They have been very active, for example, in developing U.S. financial support for Russian efforts to deactivate some nuclear weapons in accordance with the INF and START treaty agreements of the late 1980s.

In the case of Vietnam, President Clinton's enlisting of the support of Senator McCain for his change of policy was critical politically. So were his administration's efforts to pursue vigorously the search for MIAs and to give those efforts increased publicity and visibility.

Fundamental security interests will continue to resonate strongly with the U.S. public and key political actors. Economic interests have grown increasingly salient over the last decade, though they have a vulnerable downside. On the other hand, given the long history of cold war enmity and deep suspicion, developments in any of the former adversary-states that suggest a return to earlier regime characteristics or policy orientations are likely to be serious threats to the changed relationship.

In short, in this policy arena as in others, sustained attention and hard work in developing and maintaining broad political support are essential. Indeed, given the particular vulnerabilities that have been suggested, this must be more emphatically the case in dealing with fading adversaries.

NOTES

1. John Lewis Gaddis, "The Long Peace," *International Security* 10 (Spring 1986): 99–142.

2. It should be noted that the six case studies included in this book not only reflect distinctive situations but are also approached from quite varied perspectives. These range from standard academic, outside-observer studies to at least one with a more participant-observer orientation. Similarly, some of the case writers offer a rather judgmental view of what took place; others are inclined for the most part to let the stories speak for themselves.

What is provided by each of the *five* case studies of reversals in relations (aside from Cuba, which does not yet fall in that category) is a detailed, well-informed account of what transpired as the adversarial relationship began to fade away. There is plenty of grist for the mill of broader explanation and generalization.

3. See Robert Sutter, chapter 3 of this book.

2

Lessons from the Soviet Past

Robert Legvold

If the intent is to glean lessons about restructuring relations with former adversaries, three stages in the history of U.S.-Soviet relations might be used for making comparisons:

- Should one start with what was right and wrong with U.S. policy toward the Soviet Union at a point when the Soviet mess was deepening but leaders in Moscow seemed incapable of or unwilling to change (roughly the years of the first Reagan administration, 1980–84)?

- Or would the correct parallel be the stage after the Soviet leadership appeared to recognize the need for change, but before U.S. leaders could be sure that change would follow or, if it did, that it would be of the sort they wanted to see (roughly the first two years of Gorbachev's tenure, 1985–86)?

- Or, particularly for planning purposes, should U.S. policy makers focus more on the contribution made by U.S. policy once the Soviet change began and the possible benefits to the United States and its allies seemed evident (roughly the period after 1986)?

In at least the Soviet instance, however, the three phases cannot be separated, for one conditioned the next. However, each also represented a different challenge to U.S. policy and therefore carries different lessons. In the first case, that is, during the last years of the Brezhnev era, when the need for change had grown apparent but not so the will to undertake it, the short-term imperative was to blunt what at the time seemed to be aggressive Soviet foreign and military policies without foreclosing the perhaps remote prospect of a substantially reformed adversary. Once change became a possibility but not yet a certainty, nor the thrust of change yet clear, the task was different. U.S. leaders then needed to focus on the best way to foster change, while simultaneously guarding against false hopes, false starts, and, worse, change whose consequences might make matters worse. In the third instance, with promising change well underway, the task shifted to determining when, how, and to what degree the United States should engage itself, should come to the assistance of reform, and, most important, should deal generously with a weakened and distracted Soviet Union instead of driving the bargains it now had within its power.

While in the abstract nothing prevented U.S. policy makers from acting independently at each stage and adopting an appropriate self-contained strategy, in reality the choices made grew out of prior choices. There were at least two reasons: (1) Prior choices, as is usually the case, were based on assumptions, bureaucratic bargains back home, and sunk costs that made it hard to appreciate the need for change. (2) More important, the periods I have divided into three stages were not so clearly stages at the time. Policy makers can be excused if in the obscurity of events they did not decipher the arrival of the next phase.

Ancien Régime: Hope Dismissed

Not much of the Reagan-Bush administrations' handling of the great transition during 1987–1991 can be understood, much less evaluated, without returning to the starting point. For this purpose, that means the period six or seven years earlier, at the outset of Ronald Reagan's presidency. Of the many qualities distinguishing the Soviet Union from other cases, none stands out more than the low expectation of far-reaching Soviet change held by U.S. policy makers at the time and their nearly opposite high expectations of other changes now. The contrast, of course, owes much to the fact that what to most of us was an unimaginable transformation of the Soviet world turned out to be more than imaginable. But in the early 1980s few wasted much time on that possibility, and fewer still were ready to act on it—ready to subordinate policy to the pursuit of transformation. This failure of imagination did more than set the background for the early stage of changes in the Soviet world; it remained a critical influence through the second stage and even into the third.

In this near disbelief, however, there resided a striking irony: During the whole of the postwar era, U.S. policy toward the Soviet Union was predicated on the necessity—and therefore presumably the possibility—of a complete Soviet transformation. The "containment doctrine," as its author originally explained, rested on the assumption that, if only the United States would remain steadfast, seeking calmly but firmly to thwart Soviet designs, eventually the underlying Soviet system, not simply its external policies, would give way. "The United States has it in its power,"

George Kennan concluded the famous "X" article by saying, "to increase enormously the strains under which Soviet policy must operate, to force upon the Kremlin a far greater degree of moderation and circumspection than it has had to observe in recent years, and in this way to promote tendencies which must eventually find their outlet in either the break-up or the gradual mellowing of Soviet power."[1]

No postwar president seemed truer than Ronald Reagan to both sides of Kennan's original proposition. None believed more in increasing "enormously the strains under which Soviet policy must operate," and none seemed more convinced of the likelihood of "either the break-up or the gradual mellowing of Soviet power." Thus, as Reagan told the National Association of Evangelicals in March 1983, "I believe we shall rise to the challenge. I believe that communism is another sad, bizarre chapter in human history whose last pages even now are being written," a flourish that many at the time thought to be foolishly primitive but that looked much less so a few years later. Three years before Gorbachev came to power, when Reagan spoke of "the march of freedom and democracy which will leave Marxism-Leninism on the ash heap of history as it has left other tyrannies which stifle the freedom and muzzle the self-expression of people," he appeared genuinely to believe it.[2] The evidence, however, suggests something different. The new administration's hard line—the scathing rhetoric, the large increase in defense expenditures, the skepticism on arms control, the counteroffensive in Central America and southern Africa, and the return to economic warfare—stemmed not from faith that the Soviet Union was nearer than ever to a revolution, but from the fear that its leaders were more than ever determined to take advantage of U.S. weakness.

Eventually, having concluded that its strenuous efforts had righted matters, the administration made no attempt to hold course in order to help hasten Marxism-Leninism's dispatch to the ash heap of history. On the contrary, by mid-1983 George Shultz had persuaded the president that his point was made and that the time had come to reengage the Soviet leadership.[3] Neither man was much distracted by the prospect of a historic shift in the evolution of the Soviet Union. Instead they were refocusing on the traditional need to get on with the business of U.S.-Soviet relations. In March 1983 Shultz had passed to the White House a paper outlining the next steps intended to draw the two countries slowly but steadily into a dialogue on arms control, regional instability, human rights, and bilateral economic issues. Over the next several months members of the administration sent signals to this effect to Soviet representatives—signals of varying degrees of clarity. Then on January 16, 1984, Reagan delivered a speech

conspicuously free of "evil empire" references, accenting instead the prospect of establishing "a constructive and realistic working relationship with
the Soviet Union," to be pursued through a policy of "realism, strength,
and dialogue."[4] Not until the fall, however, on the eve of the U.S. presidential elections did these soundings produce an echo. In September, at the
close of the first Reagan administration, the president had his first meeting with a Soviet leader. Andrei Gromyko and Ronald Reagan spent the
time expressing what each thought of the other's political system and what
each feared in the other's behavior, but then stressing the need to talk.
Reagan tried out a line he would use regularly with Gorbachev: "We can't
accomplish anything talking about each other. We have to talk to each
other." And each forswore any intention of trying to do the other side in.

Coming so late in Reagan's first administration and, more to the point,
so late in the life of the Brezhnev-Andropov-Chernenko regime, the thaw
had little effect. By the time the United States had finished with the elections and inaugurated Reagan, Chernenko had a month and a half to live.
One is then left with basic historical questions. What matters? The intent
or the effect of the Reagan policy? What the president and his secretary of
state may have sought to accomplish in U.S.-Soviet relations or what they
may have (unintentionally) brought about in the evolution of the Soviet
Union? And did the policy, intentionally or not, contribute decisively to
the dramatic change that was about to overtake the Soviet Union?

These are difficult and disputed questions, for which there are not yet
clear and convincing answers. George Shultz and many other partisans of
the Reagan administration have convinced themselves that their tough-
minded approach to the Soviet Union, particularly the pressure created by
bold military programs such as the Strategic Defense Initiative, deserve
not merely a portion but the lion's share of the credit for the post-1985
turn of events. The other extreme argues that, on the contrary, Reagan's
policy added little to the grand array of long-accumulated problems and
failures facing the new Soviet leadership, and, if anything, made it more
difficult for Gorbachev and his colleagues to begin the process of change.[5]
Most likely, the truth lies somewhere in between.

From all indications Soviet leaders saw the Reagan policy not merely as
an effort to counter their actions abroad but as an assault on the regime
itself. Gromyko told George McGovern, when the latter visited him in
Yalta in July 1984, that Reagan and others around him "want to cause
trouble. They want to weaken the Soviet system. They want to bring it
down."[6] As might be expected, Soviet leaders refused to be seen as successful targets of this effort. In their speeches and public retorts they dis-

missed the folly of striving to undercut the other system. In private they spoke pessimistically about the prospects of accomplishing much with the Reagan administration, although by summer 1984 they were reconciled to the president's reelection and willing to test how solid was the basis for their pessimism. Hence, the decision to have Gromyko meet the president in September in advance of the elections.

Even if Soviet leaders were not consciously chastened—as they scarcely could be, sharing neither the administration's view of Soviet misbehavior nor its belief in the evil of the Soviet system—were they not, on a subconscious level, nonetheless yielding? Was not the administration's challenge to them, including the threat of an accelerating high-tech arms race, creating in them an inkling of the weaknesses in their system and the need to change? And even if they did not feel these effects, is the same true of those who were about to follow?

The New Regime: Hope Uncertain

Not I nor, I would guess, anyone else outside Soviet leadership circles can answer the first question. Since no member of the Brezhnev-through-Andropov politburos, to our knowledge, consulted a psychiatrist, who knows what the turnings within the deeper subconscious might have been? On occasion, such as the autumn of 1982, when Brezhnev spoke of the "food" problem (by which he meant the lamentable record of the agricultural sector) as potentially a "political" threat, the Soviet leaders appeared uneasy over the problems facing them. But nervous musings of this sort slipped out only rarely, never in the context of their country's excessive efforts abroad, and never with any suggestion that the Reagan challenge could not be met.

Gorbachev's attitude was another matter. From the testimony of close associates, from his own speeches before he took over as leader, and from a series of early actions once in power, we know that he saw his country in some trouble, that he was convinced a fateful decline in Soviet power and influence was ahead unless real changes were made, and that he recognized the role in all of this of his predecessors' foreign policy excesses.[7] We do not know, however, whether the pressures created by the Reagan administration steered or perhaps even forced Gorbachev in this direction or whether, on the contrary, they made it harder for him to act on his new convictions. Fragmentary evidence points in both directions. For our purposes, what matters more is that the Reagan administration from all appearances gave little or no thought to the prospect of a radical alteration of Soviet foreign policy, still less to changes in its domestic order. The administration therefore had no reason to contemplate whether U.S. policy should be adjusted to help bring the change about and, if so, how to do it.[8] Whatever subsequent credit the Reagan team claimed for the Gorbachev revolution, this is not what they thought they were working on in advance of the event.

Contrary to the claims of Reagan's critics at home, however, he and several other key members of the administration did view the new man in Moscow as likely to help realize their hopes for improved U.S.-Soviet relations. They also sensed very early on—in the case of George Shultz, at the funeral of Gorbachev's predecessor—that Gorbachev was likely to restore considerable dynamism to Soviet leadership. This prospect is what they set out to exploit. (Not everyone, however, shared this view. Secretary of Defense Caspar Weinberger would have none of the optimism about better U.S.-Soviet relations or the advantages of having a less infirm leader in the Kremlin, and he continued his opposition to any attempt to reach out to Moscow.)

Although the administration's task was shifting toward the real possibility of improving U.S.-Soviet relations—accompanied by the challenge of responding to a more vigorous Soviet leader—there was no shift in the administration's approach to the Soviets. Firmness had gotten the president and his advisers this far, as they saw matters, and firmness would remain the way forward. Because they conceived the realm of the possible in these relatively constricted terms, their entrenched mental framework seemed more than adequate for assessing any change the new man in the Kremlin might introduce. Doubtless the chain of cause in some measure also worked in reverse: Established ways of thinking also deadened their imaginations and blocked from view any indication of what was about to happen. But that blind spot mattered less. After all, scarcely anyone, from whatever point of departure, came close to foreseeing the scale of the change the new Soviet regime would unleash.[9] Rather, the consequences were that established outlooks determined the task at hand and shaped the reaction to change when its first shoots poked through.

At this remove it seems ironic, but when members of the Reagan administration and many others who shared their perspective on the Soviet Union first tried to size up the changes in store under Gorbachev, the overwhelming instinct was to stress the dangers they might pose for the United States and its allies. Over and over, in a dozen different contexts, the question posed most often in 1986–87, when the new Soviet leader began to prod his country out of its lethargy and decay, was whether it was in the U.S. interest for Gorbachev to succeed. To this the answer was (an answer I often tried), "That depends." It depended on how much the Soviet Union had itself changed and on whether in the process the leadership came to modify the character of its foreign policy, particularly the premises of its relationship with the United States.

That answer was not good enough. As I discovered more than once, those who posed the question about Gorbachev and U.S. interests found the qualified answer to be of little help because their frame of reference did not leave room for any qualification. The thought that a stronger Soviet Union, if changed, could be a safer and more accommodating adversary eluded them. (No one, including the experts, would have dared to answer, had anyone dreamed of it, that the whole concern was pointless because Gorbachev's efforts to revitalize the system would in short order destroy it.) Reagan's vice president provided what served as the most positive face put on the issue. After meeting Gorbachev for the first time, as Don Oberdorfer reports his reaction, George Bush offered the view that it was "'a good thing' for the Soviet Union to be coming out of its long time of troubles. 'It's up to us to meet the challenge'."[10] For others, who had no desire to see the United States further tempered, the challenge was less welcome. What mattered most, however, was that Gorbachev's coming was seen principally as a challenge, not as a historic opportunity.

As early as fall 1985, Gorbachev had begun to talk as no Soviet leader before. National security, he said, should not be thought of in narrow and self-centered terms. It must be set in the context of mutual security because any Soviet effort to improve its own security without regard for that of the United States would simply lead to a cycle diminishing the security of both. In January 1986 Gorbachev offered a blueprint for the elimination of nuclear weapons by the year 2000. A few months later at the hastily convened 27th Party Congress, to the stunned disapproval of some in his audience, he suggested that socialism's struggle with capitalism should no longer be seen as the central feature of international relations. And between these conceptual leaps, he began to offer a number of substantive concessions in the Soviet negotiating position at all of the major arms control undertakings.

The Soviet leader's flexibility on nuclear issues (notably on the question of warhead reductions under the Strategic Arms Reduction Treaty, START, and the inclusion of Soviet heavy missiles) helped to ensure a successful first meeting with President Reagan at the Geneva summit in October 1985. Reagan came away from the encounter favorably impressed with his counterpart and convinced the two countries could do business with one another. He also came away with none of his underlying assumptions altered. When he spoke to Congress on his return from Geneva, the president reminded his listeners that the "United States cannot afford illusions about the nature of the USSR. We cannot assume that their ideology and purpose will change."[11] "This implies," he continued, adding the most important of his working assumptions, "enduring competition. Our task is to assure that this competition remains peaceful."

These assumptions shaped the prism through which the administration then saw Gorbachev's slowly accelerating foreign policy innovations. Three types of reactions followed. First, any of Gorbachev's early initiatives veering from U.S. priorities were interpreted as the Soviets playing their old tricks. This was the interpretation of Gorbachev's repeated appeal for a nuclear test moratorium, notwithstanding his imposition of a unilateral halt to Soviet testing. This is how the administration regarded his April 1985 decision to terminate intermediate-range nuclear missile deployments in Europe. A similar suspicion marked the reaction to his ideas for a comprehensive denuclearization of international politics and his urgent appeals to avert a nuclear arms race in space.

Second, it was not so much a prism as a lead barrier that characterized the administration's basic assumptions in assessing Gorbachev's conceptual inventions. His wide-ranging reconsideration of the premises of past Soviet foreign policy simply went unnoticed. By 1986 he and his circle had begun to dismantle a host of traditional notions concerning the place of class struggle in international relations, the centrality of "world revolutionary process," the sacred nature of socialist alliances, the utility of military power, the "enemy image," and the nature of national security, and to substitute altogether more moderate concepts. None of this was paid much notice by the administration. Instead the watchword was, "We will judge you not by your words, but by your deeds." Doubtless at the time it seemed like good I'm-from-Missouri thinking, but it obscured a critical truth. For, in the end, a fundamental change in Soviet thinking mattered far more than any particular set of actions.

Third, because the administration's working assumptions blended a strong sense of the ultimate limits to U.S.-Soviet détente with considerable self-satisfaction over the results of prior U.S. firmness, the tendency was to "stay the course." In this context the administration allowed itself excesses that otherwise might not have seemed as unexceptionable as they apparently did. Edwin Meese, the attorney general, in Afghanistan in March 1986 excoriated the Soviets for "torture, rape and toxic gas, famine, scorched earth and genocide," all as "part of a drive to dominate the entire world."[12] In a measure taken more seriously by the Soviet side, the Pentagon in the same month ordered the penetration of Soviet coastal waters deep in the Black Sea by two intelligence-gathering naval cruisers, simply to assert a (contested) right of "innocent passage." In reports issued regularly to the

Congress on Soviet compliance with arms control agreements, serious complaints mixed with far-fetched accusations. Formal threat assessments published by the Department of Defense charged the Soviet Union with seeking military superiority in order to establish its hegemony over the world.

None of this, however, prevented U.S.-Soviet relations from advancing. By early 1987 the two countries were on the road to real progress in strategic arms control; Moscow had lifted the preconditions impeding a breakthrough on the critical INF agreement; at the Stockholm Conference on confidence-building measures in Europe, the Soviets had relented on the issue of on-site inspection, creating a crucial precedent for other arms control forums; the Soviet Union had softened its stand on human rights matters and accepted the value of a dialogue with the United States on the subject. Moreover, the decision to withdraw from Afghanistan had been taken, although not yet made public, and Reagan and Shultz were being told of it.

Behind the scenes, although the wheels of progress were turning, they were generating some friction and discomfort. Gorbachev had come to power believing that the United States, particularly during the Reagan era, intended to harm the Soviet Union as much as it safely could, and little that happened in the first two years convinced him otherwise. On an issue such as the U.S. Strategic Defense Initiative (SDI), Gorbachev's firsthand encounters with the president in Geneva in 1985 and Reykjavik in 1986 partially persuaded him that Reagan was personally deeply committed to the idea. But, symptomatically, during much of the rest of the time Gorbachev kept coming back to the notion that, in the end, the president was a prisoner of elements in the U.S. defense establishment that wanted SDI either to bring the Soviet Union to its knees or to seal its military inferiority or both.

While on one level things moved ahead, the Soviet government's official and semiofficial commentary continually harped on the administration's aggressive "neoglobalism," its stake in heating up and exploiting regional conflicts, its readiness to risk war in the pursuit of its foreign policy objectives, and its unreliability as a negotiating partner. Distorted as these impressions were, they appear to have been no less genuine than the ongoing U.S. doubts about the Soviet Union. Not only did skepticism of this sort make it harder for Gorbachev, Shevardnadze, and their allies to bring along those most deeply skeptical—primarily the Soviet military—but such doubts also apparently gave pause to the Soviet leadership itself. Raymond Garthoff recounts the far from atypical instance when Soviet observers found dark meaning, never intended, in a Reagan speech in fall 1986. The president, in making another general point, had referred to Western inaction during the 1956 Hungarian crisis, asking whether it had been "in fact in our interest to stand by, hands folded." At a time when Gorbachev was beginning to consider a different approach to Eastern Europe, Soviet officials suddenly found themselves wondering, quite inappropriately, whether the Americans meant to challenge them in their own security sphere.[13]

Thus, while the prism through which the Reagan administration viewed the opening phases of the Gorbachev era scarcely foreclosed significant steps forward, doubtless it influenced the pace of change. Eventually the Soviets did concede on key issues obstructing major arms control agreements (START and INF, in particular); eventually they announced their intention to pull out of Afghanistan; and eventually they began to show flexibility on human rights issues in their relations with the United States. But in all cases these advances appear to have been attainable at a much earlier stage had the United States been less suspicious and less determined to force these concessions from the Soviet leadership. Quite possibly, of course, had the administration been more forthcoming and pliable, early Soviet concessions would have been less generous, but even so, given the scale of change occurring on the Soviet side, the overall process would surely have moved in the same direction, only faster.

Of greater consequence, however, the prism filtered out certain opportunities altogether. One such opportunity arose when Gorbachev and other Soviet leaders in 1986–87 evoked the problem of the military standoff in Central Europe. They implied that the Soviets would be willing to consider a very different approach to the large imbalances in conventional forces, which favored them, but the administration failed to notice. So steeped in the sterile, immobile practices of the interminable MBFR negotiations were the senior Americans and so convinced that no Soviet leadership would unilaterally bargain away critical strategic superiority that they saw no reason to probe the possibility. Hence, real progress on this core issue of the cold war suffered a two-year delay, a delay that threw it into the chaos of collapsing Soviet power in Eastern Europe.

Similarly, from fall 1987 on, Gorbachev began to stress the importance of the great powers taking the initiative in shaping a post–cold war world and doing so by featuring multilateralism over unilateralism, with a concomitant effort to strengthen international institutions like the UN, ensuring that structures would be in place when needed. None of this registered on the U.S. side. The effort to think through the implications of a new international order and what it would require of the great powers was, by default, left to a later date. Unfortunately when that date arrived, the pressures and frustrations of a new world disorder made it extremely difficult for the great powers to collect themselves and recapture the initiative.

Coping with the Real Thing

When the Bush Administration came into office, it ordered a full-scale review of U.S. relations with the Soviet Union, essentially interrupting the evolution of U.S. policy during the four-month life of the study. Even at the time it seemed a strange development. By 1988, the year of Bush's election, U.S.-Soviet relations had thawed considerably. Reagan and his secretary of state had grown upbeat about the shifts occurring on the Soviet side. In May Reagan had walked arm-in-arm with his friend Mikhail around Red Square, chatted with Soviet tourists, held a small child, and told a reporter who asked about the "evil empire" that the subject belonged to another era. More important, by summer 1988, over the course of four summit conferences, the two leaderships had reached agreement in several areas of arms control, including a settlement of the INF issue, and had pushed a START agreement closer to conclusion. In February Gorbachev had formally announced the Soviet withdrawal from Afghanistan. At the United Nations in December he had outlined the "new political thinking"—his foreign policy revolution—as thoroughly and explicitly as he was ever to do, incorporating a pledge to cut unilaterally sizable numbers of tanks and men from Soviet forces deployed in Europe.

In short, 1988 was a year of gathering momentum, and one would have thought that George Bush would arrive in office already running, arm behind him ready to receive the baton. After all, Reagan was not for him the leader of the opposing party. Nor was Bush a newly elected alternative; he had been Reagan's vice president for eight years. Moreover, he brought with him into office, as secretary of state, secretary of defense, and national security adviser, seasoned officials who were a good deal more moderate than some of their predecessors.

As it turned out, however, while Bush had been critical of the hard-line confrontational approach adopted at the outset of the first Reagan administration, by 1987–88 he had scarcely more enthusiasm for what in his eyes was a premature embrace of Gorbachev. Bush saw Reagan and Gorbachev's talk of abandoning nuclear weapons at the 1986 Reykjavik summit as scandalously reckless. He believed the bonhomie of the Moscow summit in 1988 had been misleading. And Bush, together with the other members of his foreign policy team, harbored greater skepticism about Gorbachev and his promised changes than did Reagan and some of the people around him.

As a result, the ingrained caution of past policy not only continued under Bush but also gathered a brief second wind. There is not much question that by the time of the new president's inauguration, the Soviet Union had advanced far along the path of reform. Its foreign policy was already thoroughly different in both concept and action. In March 1989, two months after Bush's inauguration, when a major interagency review of U.S. policy toward the Soviet Union was just beginning, the Soviet Union held the first popular elections in its history, and Boris Yeltsin received 6 million votes as a local candidate for the Congress of People's Deputies.

When the subject of the Soviet Union had arisen during the fall campaign, Bush chose to stress that the "jury was still out," and such remained the premise of the "thorough review and analysis" undertaken in the weeks and months after his inauguration. Bush, Baker, Scowcroft, and the others felt no urgency to drive the process forward or to get on with U.S.-Soviet relations. Baker did not meet with his counterpart for a serious conversation until well into May. By then the bureaucracy, after great labor, had come forward with a series of studies that recommended not much of anything. "The report on the Soviet Union," Oberdorfer correctly notes, "said U.S. policy should not be designed either to help or to hurt Gorbachev, whom the authors credited with a better-than-even chance of surviving despite his domestic problems."[14]

As a result, throughout a period of intense ferment and change on the Soviet side, no one on the U.S. side had yet begun to think about the scale of what might be happening. Rather than indulge in a flight of imagination, Washington chose restrained hope instead, along with a prudent determination to keep the United States' powder dry. In May Richard Cheney, the secretary of defense, had predicted in a television interview that Gorbachev would "ultimately fail" in attempts at reform and would be replaced by a leader who would be "far more hostile" to the United States and its allies.

In these circumstances Bush and his advisers apparently failed even to consider far-reaching efforts to pare back and recast the United States' own defense burdens or to devise new forms of cooperation with the Soviet Union in dealing with regional conflicts. Much less did they begin to conceive a post–cold war framework for U.S.-Soviet relations. Instead, progress in the relationship continued to depend on Soviet concessions, and these came in steady succession. In START, the Soviet Union during these months yielded on a formal constraint on space-based defenses, agreed to dismantle the Krasnoyarsk large phased-array early-warning radar (which the Bush administration believed to be in violation of the ABM Treaty), and gave up on trying to limit sea-based cruise missiles. To Baker in May Gorbachev had laid out the dimensions of a massive cutback in conventional forces in Central Europe that his country was prepared to urge. (In this case Bush had answered with a proposal of his own involving 15 percent cuts in NATO and WTO armaments and 20 percent reductions in U.S. and Soviet military personnel.) On the eve of Baker's trip to Moscow, Gorbachev had privately communicated to the administration the Soviet decision taken at the end of the prior year to stop arms transfers to Nicaragua.

By fall 1989 James Baker was convinced. In Senate testimony early in October, he credited the Soviets with "an extraordinary effort at internal reform," calling the vast changes underway internally and in its foreign policy "a true revolution."[15] He repeated once more what he and the president had said before his May visit—that the United States wanted perestroika to succeed—and he added that Washington should consider ways of, at the margins, helping it to succeed. So, by fall 1989—with the Euromissile issue resolved, the Soviets out of Afghanistan, and serious progress toward a resolution of the military issue in Central Europe en train—the administration was at last prepared to accelerate the search for mutual accommodation with the Soviet Union. (Although even then Vice President Quayle continued to cast doubt on the durability and depth of the change taking place in Soviet policy; he called Gorbachev a Stalinist and suggested that it was for the Soviet Union to reform itself without U.S. sacrifice.)[16] In the end, however, the two sides were left with only a year and a half to work together to coordinate and direct the breakthroughs produced by the revolution in Soviet policy. The opportunity ceased in August 1991 when the putsch failed, signaling the beginning of the end for the Soviet Union.

Obscured in the slow, hesitant advance of U.S. policy toward a fast-changing adversary were two questions that are basic in great transitions: (1) To what degree and in what fashion should the United States engage in the processes that are transforming another country? (2) During the moment of opportunity, how much should the United States expect and demand in its dealings with the other country?

By fall 1989, Bush and Baker had decided that, in Baker's words, Gorbachev "was for real," and together they came to the conclusion that the time had arrived to do more than voice their sympathy for the success of perestroika. The United States should become actively supportive. Behind this shift Bush provided a considerable push of his own. The carefully and quietly prepared December 1989 shipboard summit in Malta offered the president the chance to prod the bureaucracy. To that point little or nothing had been done to devise forms of economic or other assistance to Gorbachev's reform effort. Indeed, almost nothing had been done to dismantle the various roadblocks to economic and technical cooperation that had been built during the days of intense cold war.

The aides told to devise a gesture of support came up with a list of twenty-odd items, which Bush then presented to Gorbachev in their first session at sea in Malta. The list included a promise to begin immediate negotiations on a trade treaty, with the aim of completing it in time for the Washington summit scheduled for June 1990; efforts to lift the Jackson-Vanik amendment barring MFN treatment in the context of Soviet policy on Jewish emigration; exploration of a U.S.-Soviet investment treaty; unspecified forms of technical assistance; possible U.S. Export-Import Bank (Eximbank) credits; and a readiness to allow the Soviet Union observer status at GATT. Bush, as noted, meant to convey to Gorbachev the United States' good-faith commitment to the success of his reform effort.

In fact, however, the start made at Malta in December 1989 never went very far. Little on the list of twenty items involved more than modest procedural adjustments. Nothing on the list promised to have a major economic impact on the course of events back in the Soviet Union. Even these procedural measures did not come easily. They ran into resistance within parts of the administration and into still more trouble in various congressional corners and sand traps. By the time Gorbachev came to Washington in June for his next-to-last bilateral summit meeting with a U.S. president, only a couple of the steps on the list had been taken. At the summit Gorbachev cajoled, importuned, and even threatened not to sign a new long-term grain purchase agreement unless the Americans became serious about signing a trade agreement. Bush found it hard to satisfy Gorbachev on this score, and he faced many key members of Congress who were reluctant to go along. Only in an eleventh-hour decision during the summit did he decide to reverse himself and sign such an agreement, illustrating in the process the extreme timidity with which the United States viewed its role in perestroika.

The reasons for this hesitation are several, each of them instructive. First, the course of U.S.-Soviet relations depended not only on the progress made on issues central to the bilateral relationship. Every ripple in other areas of Soviet policy echoed back through the U.S.-Soviet relations. Thus, for example, when in fall 1990 Gorbachev took a more conservative tack toward reform and the domestic crises brewing in his country, eyebrows in Washington began to rise. When Soviet tanks crushed Lithuanian demonstrators in January 1991, the raised eyebrows understandably gave way to cold feet. It was predictable that the Soviet Union could not undergo wholesale change without sparking troubles. It was equally predictable that official Soviet responses would often be inept or worse. And, to complete the chain, given the years of hostility and suspicion, it was still more predictable that these responses would instantly trigger second thoughts in Washington or, at a minimum, a desire on the part of the administration not to seem soft on the reformers.

Second, in fluid environments such as the one that emerged in U.S.-Soviet relations after fall 1989, the advantage does not go to those U.S. politicians arguing for a bold exploitation of opportunity. (There are, in any event, few such politicians.) Rather, circumstances invariably favor those who prefer to wait and see. One could scarcely have had a more graphic demonstration than when Gorbachev came to Washington for the last time in June 1990. On his second morning in the city, he had breakfast with the leading lights of the House and Senate. Before a somewhat starstruck audience and in front of CNN cameras, which neither side knew were filming the occasion, Gorbachev came as close as a public figure can to baring his soul. He confessed that the process of reform was far more difficult and painful than anyone could have imagined, that the old system had been dismantled but the new had hardly begun to take shape, and that neither he nor the others knew quite how to proceed. His guests—for the meeting was at the Soviet Embassy—left still in the glow of a fascinating and celebrated global leader, but none, with the exception of Congressman Richard Gephardt, ventured the slightest interest in putting the U.S. shoulder to the wheel of perestroika.

Finally, the core problem was within the administration itself. For Bush and his people, perestroika, in both its political and economic forms, had always been basically a pig in a poke, and they were not buying it. That is, while coming to admire Gorbachev for undertaking change and genuinely wanting him to succeed, they were not prepared to make more than token contributions until he had proved himself by succeeding. Policy remained based on the notion that the West should enter the picture after the processes of democratization and market reform were safely and definitively underway, not beforehand in order to bring them about.

It would be unfair to President Bush and his colleagues to dismiss the assistance they did provide the Soviet Union. There were a considerable number of small steps taken, all of them intended as gestures of good will. Therein was the problem: Gestures are what they were, not a sizable and substantive investment in the process of change. Thus, for example, in the months before Gorbachev came to Washington in summer 1990, the ad-

ministration, following the Europeans' lead, began the process of liberaliz-
ing Coordinating Committee of Multilateral Export Controls (COCOM)
restrictions on technology transfer to the former Soviet bloc. But the real
impulse behind this action was the need to fashion a different policy toward a newly liberated Eastern Europe. Not much was done to alter the
terms as applied to the Soviet Union, nor, despite Gorbachev's pleading
then and a year later in his last meetings with Bush, would much be done
until the Soviet Union no longer existed.

Similarly, in the waning moments of the Gorbachev era, the administration rallied behind a modest G-7 aid package to the Soviet Union, but
even this was intended as something of a preemptive offering, meant to
fend off those who wanted to do a great deal more. By now there were
others urging a "Grand Bargain," by which the West would commit itself
to large-scale economic assistance in return for radical market reform.[17]
Bush, Baker, Scowcroft, and the others thought this a bad idea and quickly
scuttled it. In their defense, it is true they feared that any funds transferred to the Soviet Union in its state of confusion and disarray would
simply be money down a rat hole, a far from groundless fear. But this fails
to tell the whole story. The broader mentality of which it was a part was
also responsible for the administration's veto of Soviet participation in the
newly created European Bank for Reconstruction and Development, expressly designed to promote reform in the East, and its coolness to Soviet
observer status at the IMF. The administration's good intentions, real as
they were, were not conceived in terms of a serious direct U.S. engagement in the reform effort.

All this does not mean that the Bush administration's policy was without merit, as I will discuss later. Here, however, what deserves noting is the
link to the prior two stages of U.S.-Soviet relations. Because of what had
gone before, Bush and his team inevitably operated with a constricted outlook and psychology. Even when persuaded that the changes introduced
by the Gorbachev regime were large and important, nothing impelled them
to weigh different U.S. alternatives. Having shared the original preoccupation with the threat posed by the old Soviet Union and the cautious, tough-
minded reaction to Gorbachev when he first appeared on the scene, they
saw no reason to abandon that policy for a more adventurous approach.

The same quality governed the Bush administration's answer to the
second basic question: What kind of bargain should they seek with a willing Soviet leadership? For the most part, the answer was that any significant issue would be resolved largely on U.S. terms, that is, on terms that
reflected the balance of power between the two countries. Bush, Baker, and
the others were not ungracious to their counterparts nor preemptory in

their dealings with them. But the accords reached on the important issues—START, conventional arms control in Europe, German reunification, and a reunified Germany's membership in NATO—bowed very little to Soviet concerns.

On the road to a strategic arms limitation agreement, the Soviet Union in 1989 had made the major concessions allowing the process to go forward. Still, even after Bush and Baker had crossed the threshold and come to believe in Gorbachev in fall 1989, the U.S. government insisted on proving its negotiating toughness, sometimes concerning the least significant detail. Garthoff recounts how, after the Soviet side had conceded a limit for sea-based cruise missiles equal to the number the Americans planned to build, the U.S. side demanded a number closer to their maximum position, which was 40 percent more than their plans called for and 60 percent more than the U.S. Congress had funded.[18] In the same manner, they would not hear of excluding a particular model of nonnuclear missile under the air-launched cruise missile limitation. In these and a number of other cases, the substance of any single concession mattered less than the steady insistence on one after another of them. With each additional concession a disgruntled Soviet military grew more deeply convinced that the Americans were not interested in an equitable agreement but simply in forcing the hand of a weakening Soviet leadership. The same could be said of the U.S. approach to the ultimate details of an agreement on conventional forces in Europe (CFE). In this case the administration compelled Gorbachev and Shevardnadze to cave in on points of waning military significance—what with the Warsaw Pact collapsing—in what seemed to many Soviets to be a passion for wringing from Gorbachev every last concession. In the case of German reunification and a new Germany's role in NATO, the administration only in the last stages sought to soften the impact of this vast reversal in history. Eventually the Germans, with U.S. urging, did agree to an overall limit on their military forces, to stationing constraints on nuclear weapons in the former East Germany, to compensation for withdrawing Soviet forces, and to half a dozen additional gestures. But little was done to ease Soviet agony in the face of the more or less inevitable German outcome by making it a part of a serious discussion on revamping and upgrading Europe's other institutions, such as the Conference on Security and Cooperation in Europe, as Soviet leaders desperately wished.

CONCLUSIONS

There are several ways to think about U.S. policy during the last fateful years of the Soviet Union. First, it is entirely plausible to argue, as would members and partisans of the Bush administration, that they handled a historic transition as well as could be done. By maintaining a steady, firm, cautious approach, they safely guided East-West relations through the collapse of Soviet power in Eastern Europe, the reunification of Germany, and ultimately the demise of the Soviet Union itself. A steady, firm hand, moreover, had from the beginning kept Gorbachev on the path of ever more substantial foreign policy concessions. Small things might have been done differently (for example, it might have been better had Bush never delivered his appeal for Ukrainian moderation while in Kiev in summer 1991), but on balance no better outcome could have been expected, and for that the administration deserves much credit.

An alternative view might argue that policy during the Bush years was less than optimal but that in the end it does not much matter. Even if one believes the post–cold war world would have turned out better had the Soviet Union not collapsed so soon and so decisively, or had German reunification occurred in the context of a new architecture for European security, or had U.S.-Soviet collaboration flourished and formed the basis for the new order, none of these possibilities was within the reach of U.S. policy. Thus, while it may be true that the Bush administration lacked vision and imagination in dealing with Gorbachev's Soviet Union, no amount of imagination and vision could have yielded the preferred outcomes. Even the inherent conservatism and inflexibility of U.S. policy described here had no large or lasting impact. Perhaps U.S. policy made Gorbachev's task more difficult by stirring domestic opposition to his foreign policy or by depriving him of marginally useful material aid, but in the grander course of history these deficiencies or costs have scarcely any meaning.

There is, however, a third perspective, one suggesting a greater range of possibilities and, therefore, of missed opportunities. Had the West—for the United States could not have accomplished this alone—committed itself early and generously to the success of perestroika, conceivably the process might have turned out differently. More than substantial economic assistance would have been required to enable an alternative outcome of this magnitude. From the start, the industrialized democracies would have had to invest themselves in promoting the change, encouraging Gorbachev and his colleagues to take greater risks on behalf of reform than the Soviet leadership was otherwise prepared to run, as well as anticipating sooner than they (or Gorbachev) did the changes required were the country itself to remain intact. So, too, would they have had to craft a swifter and far more extensive transformation of the international setting in which a reformed Soviet Union might find a new and constructive role to play.

Nations do not easily act decisively faced with challenges of this magnitude, and merely to recite what would have been required comes close to

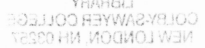

offering its own refutation. It takes little creativity to point out the many factors obstructing bold choices. Without powerful U.S. leadership, others would not have done their share, and the obstacles to strong U.S. leadership were formidable. Still, this alternative scenario, while improbable, is not intellectually illogical. Hence, it reminds us of how much greater the stakes may be at such moments than minds attuned to the normalcy of politics naturally assume.

More to the point, there is another version of the same perspective that is much less far-fetched, although not greatly less dramatic. Accordingly, it is perfectly thinkable that a bolder U.S.-Western initiative, although unable to save the Soviet Union from its eventual doom, might have prepared a safer and more promising post-Soviet environment. Not only could more have been done with Gorbachev and his colleagues to build institutions and relationships that would have been more serviceable in the international setting that we now have, but a more generous treatment of a fading Soviet leadership would also have lessened the nationalist backlash in a post-Soviet Russia. Much of the current problem with Russia owes not simply to the death of empire but to the nature of its passing.

THE RUSSIAN POSTSCRIPT

On the second weekend in December 1991, Boris Yeltsin, the Ukrainian leader, Leonid Kravchuk, and their counterpart from Belarussia, Stanislau Shushkevich, met in a Belarussian town and decided to undo the Soviet Union. Three weeks later the Soviet Union crumbled into fifteen newly sovereign states, each faced with a passage more formidable than any country—new or old—had ever confronted. Before them stood not only the challenge of turning an authoritarian political system into a modern democratic one but also the task of building a market-based economy out of the ruins of a physically planned one. The combination of these difficulties made the magnitude of the transitions greater than any attempted by the states of Latin America, southern Europe, or East Asia over the prior quarter of a century. But that is not all. What truly distinguishes the challenge faced by these states is a series of further revolutions: One, of decolonization; another, of state formation; a third, the very process of nation building to create functioning states where none has existed, or not for centuries, which is separate from the challenge of welding peoples' loyalties to nations, and both are formidable.

For other reasons, a comparison with Cuba, Iran, Nicaragua, or other cases breaks down after the collapse of the Soviet Union. The disintegration of the Soviet Union turned a state into a region and in the process produced a fundamental foreign policy challenge for the major powers on the outside, including the United States. Henceforth, every aspect of U.S. policy toward any of the new states, including Russia, would be affected by their struggle to work out their mutual relationships and, in particular, Russia's relationships with new neighbors that were but a moment ago integral to its now lost empire. Every issue—nuclear weapons, building democracy, decrepit nuclear power facilities, macroeconomic stabilization, minority rights, or ethnic conflict—was sooner or later affected by the new and sometimes turbulent relations among the post-Soviet states. Because Russia's democratic transition and struggle toward economic reform depended so fundamentally on Russia's uneasy effort to work out its role and responsibilities in the region, the course of U.S. efforts to aid Russia's internal transition was also hostage to developments in this other realm.

Still, granted these fundamental underlying differences from the other cases, there are useful lessons in the subsequent evolution of U.S. policy toward Russia. Frequently these lessons turn out to be the opposite of those identified for earlier periods.

From the moment of Russian independence—indeed, even before—Yeltsin and those around him made evident their determination to break with everything Soviet: with the old foreign policy, the old political system and Gorbachev's cautious attempts at reforming it, the old economic order, now in half ruins, and especially the old ideology. Thus, for the United States the collapse of the Soviet Union had two great consequences: First, it brought to power in Russia leaders whose far-reaching economic and political measures left no doubt of their intention to transform their country in a most fundamental fashion, and thus at last offered the Bush administration the convincing evidence it had long demanded before anteing up real material support. Second, the demise terminated the Soviet threat, removing the great preoccupation of postwar U.S. foreign policy. As fortune would have it, the two consequences worked at cross-purposes.

Despite Bush's rather jaundiced view of Yeltsin after their 1989 encounter, when the Russian leader mounted the barricades in August 1991 the president rallied quickly and firmly to his side. From then on, notwithstanding the administration's ambivalence toward the abrupt disintegration of the Soviet Union, Yeltsin, Andrei Kozyrev, and eventually Egor Gaidar became objects of its admiration and confidence. Still, however, U.S. economic aid did not flow. The year of Russian independence, 1992, was a presidential election year in the United States, and the electorate was turning sharply inward in its preoccupations. Bush thus found it hard to make the case for a large and elaborate U.S. involvement in Russia's struggle. As he said in March, when stung by sharp criticism from Richard Nixon for doing too little, "We're living in a time of constrained resources. There isn't a lot of money around. We are spending too much as it already is. So to do the things I would really like to do, I don't have a blank check for all that."[19]

Nixon had accused the administration of providing "pathetically" insufficient assistance to Russia and then added, "The hot-button issue in the 1950s was 'Who lost China?' If Yeltsin goes down, the question 'Who lost Russia?' will be an infinitely more devastating issue in the 1990s."[20] Nixon, who was something of an expert on the political consequences of "who-lost-country" arguments, struck a nerve. In the spring of 1992, in the turmoil of the Gaidar reforms, it was fashionable in Moscow and Washington to worry about reactionary, antireform forces, perhaps led by the military, plotting to oust Yeltsin. When combined with the confused but apparently critical comments of Democratic presidential candidates, such as Bill Clinton and Paul Tsongas, this concern was enough to galvanize the Bush administration into assembling as many small, discrete pieces of aid as possible into something made to sound rather grand under the title of the Freedom Support Act. Announced by the president on April 1, the package was, as Robert Kasten, a Republican Congressman from Wisconsin, admitted, "mirrors, paper clips and smoke."[21]

Bush's first instincts turned out to have been correct. Although the program he eventually put to the U.S. Congress remained modest—far more so than the imposing sums advertised by spokesmen for the administration—even it was coldly received. With the Soviet threat gone, the legislators, like their constituents, could not be easily convinced that any foreign policy issue, including Russia's fate, deserved money they meant to apply to domestic need.[22] According to administration claims, Russia was to receive in 1992 $24 billion in international assistance, $4.5 billion of it from the United States. Most of the U.S. share, however, represented sums long committed to the IMF and World Bank. Of the remainder, the lion's share, $2.1 billion, was in agricultural export credits. Hence, in good conscience the president could assure the Congress that little in the Freedom Support Act would require new authorizations. Even so, without considerable lobbying on the administration's part and an emotionally charged appearance before the Congress by Yeltsin during the June 1992 summit, the bill would not have passed. Its troubled course was not only a sign of the times but of what was to come—and keep coming.

To be sure, U.S. policy toward Russia had been profoundly altered. From the moment the Soviet Union collapsed, the Bush administration reversed its position on a host of issues. Having long fought the notion of bringing the Soviet Union into the IMF and World Bank, it now took the lead in welcoming Russia into these organizations. It not only lifted COCOM restrictions on technology trade with Russia but also proposed Russian membership in a special COCOM Cooperation Forum on Export Controls. And, although it took months and the Nixon criticism to prompt concrete action, key members of the administration, including Secretary of Treasury Nicholas Brady, had accepted the need to provide some kind of economic assistance to Russian reform. By the close of the June 1992 summit, the United States had reached dozens of new agreements with Russia, including cooperation on defense conversion, fuels and energy development, nuclear reactor safety, an investment treaty, an OPIC accord, and, in particular, a decision to cut strategic warheads by the year 2003 substantially beyond the totals envisaged in the START II treaty. All of this reflected the fundamentally different spirit with which the two countries now regarded one another. At the same time, the tortured history of the Freedom Support Act demonstrated how little the U.S. body politic was prepared to pay for the new relationship.

Candidate Clinton during the election campaign had criticized Bush for timidity in addressing the challenge of Russia and the other post-Soviet states, and he implied that as president he would seek a more ambitious level of assistance. In fact, when Clinton was confronted early in his administration with basic choices concerning Russia, he did decide on the bolder course. Scarcely two months into the new administration, Yeltsin, deeply embroiled in a deepening confrontation with the Russian Supreme Soviet, announced that he was declaring a state of emergency (the term used was "special rule") and would govern without the parliament. In the confused days that followed, the Russian Supreme Court ruled Yeltsin's rumored proclamation unconstitutional, although its chief judge acted without actually seeing the document, and Yeltsin at no point submitted anything to the parliament or the court. Instead he announced that in mid-April he was calling a national referendum on his reform program and his stewardship as president.

Before Yeltsin's bluff emerged as only that, however, President Clinton rallied instantly behind his action. It was the first and decisive step by which the administration aligned itself vigorously, indeed, for the most part, unconditionally with Yeltsin. Clinton's decision depended on a number of assumptions: (1) that Yeltsin represented the best hope for reform, (2) that his opponents, particularly in the parliament, were reactionary and potentially dangerous to U.S. interests, (3) that Yeltsin could lose to them, and (4) that U.S. assistance could make a difference, perhaps *the* difference. As Thomas Friedman wrote in the *New York Times* early in March, Clinton had concluded "that President Yeltsin is in an increasingly perilous political state and that both he and the Russian reformers allied to him need a commitment of assistance that will be visible and whose impact will be felt reasonably quickly."[23]

With this intensified sense of the stakes, Clinton set about to mobilize support for Yeltsin's regime, not simply U.S. support but that of the other Western powers. On April 1 in Annapolis, he delivered the single most comprehensive and compelling statement that a Western leader had made on the importance to the West of Russia's successful adoption of democracy and a market-based economy. Annapolis was a stop on the way to Vancouver and Clinton's first summit with Yeltsin, and he used both occasions to sharpen the impression of urgency in coming to the aid of an embattled Yeltsin. In Vancouver he announced a number of new measures designed to ease Russia's economic burdens. Subsequently, however, his team's real energy went into motivating the international community, first, by pressuring the IMF and World Bank to relax the preconditions of their assistance and, second, by persuading the other G-7 nations to add to prior commitments. Much of this work was done before the scheduled April 15 referendum in Russia, expressly to enhance Yeltsin's chances of carrying the day.

There is no reason to doubt the sincerity of the president's concern nor the genuineness of his determination to prod a much greater effort from Japan and the West European nations. At the Tokyo G-7 meeting in summer 1993, Clinton emerged as a dominating figure, a status that owed much to his energetic orchestration of a $43 billion composite multilateral program of aid to Russia. As with the $24 billion program a year earlier, however, most of the burden for meeting these targets fell to the international financial institutions, and the U.S. share involved comparatively modest increments to initiatives already launched by the Bush administration. Indeed, much of the Clinton program amounted to making good on the unmet undertakings promised by the prior administration. For all the passion in the president's commitment, he had discovered what Bush already knew: Neither the public nor the Congress wished to fund the responsibility Clinton urged. "We have come so far," Warren Christopher, secretary of state, said in a speech in Minneapolis in May. "We have spent so much. We have earned the promise of a safer, freer and better world. To retreat now would be to walk away from nearly a half century of American leadership, sacrifice and commitment."[24] But walk away is what the country meant to do.

In Clinton's case, however, the gap between his sense of the need and what he could deliver had more serious consequences. The problem arose from the destructive effects of mutual false expectations. On the Russian side, Yeltsin and his advisers not only misled themselves into believing the United States and its Western allies would contribute much more than they did, and, in the process, encouraged false hopes in their supporters and the public at large. They also misconceived the payoff from Western aid. Yeltsin's misconception shone with special luminescence during his June 1992 summit with Bush. After grittily repeating that Russia did not need or expect anyone's charity, simply a willingness to do business, Yeltsin went on to say that IMF credits were not so important in themselves. "The most important thing is that once the IMF decides this issue, this will open the door for a powerful stream of private capital . . . not credits . . . but direct investment . . . and that will be a matter of hundreds of billions of dollars."[25] Under Clinton, the effects of this wildly distorted idea paralleled the administration's own false expectations. Clinton's Russian policy rested on the assumption that Yeltsin and his team were the most reliable protagonists of a democratic transition, fiscal restraint, and market reform, indeed the only practical choice for the administration. Policy was geared principally to doing all within U.S. power to strengthen them against their opposition.

Fear of the consequences should the "democrats" fail and the reactionaries, the authoritarians, or the crude nationalists triumph, of course, was a perfectly natural inspiration for policy. The trouble is that in the vast and complex transitions through which the post-Soviet states were passing, outcomes rarely turned out so black and white. Instead it was Yeltsin who, when the confrontation with parliament reached a crisis, first began to behave with a ruthlessness unbecoming a purer democrat, and soon there followed the Zhirinovsky surprise triumph in the December 1993 elections. Clinton, having hitched his policy to Yeltsin's star back in March, a choice that Yeltsin's victory in the April 1993 referendum seemed to vindicate, suddenly found himself with his options awkwardly constrained.

Moreover, as Yeltsin's popularity waned, U.S. policy began to suffer the scorn of politicians and segments of the public who resented the administration's seemingly unwavering and uncritical identification with the Russian leader. In his Minneapolis speech in May, Christopher, still in the glow of the Vancouver summit and Yeltsin's referendum victory, had spoken headily of what the United States meant to do for the Russians: "We want to deliver quick and tangible benefits to the Russian people. If the faith demonstrated in last month's referendum is to be sustained, they must see that they are the beneficiaries of reform and not its unintentional victims."[26] That was a sound proposition, but when the administration could do little to help produce those "quick and tangible benefits," not only the good name of reform but the credibility of U.S. policy declined. Clinton's alignment with Yeltsin frustrated many Russians, not least because this interference, as they saw it, came without any offsetting material advantage. The United States was quick to offer advice and to take sides, but not to sacrifice for the ends that its leaders claimed to have.

In fairness to the Clinton administration, an alternative approach was easier urged than executed. Critics in both countries faulted the administration for having tied itself too closely to a particular leader instead of committing itself to a process or to the principles of democracy and economic reform. Both, however, are no more than abstractions, and, as the president might have responded, no process and no principles could be pursued without choosing among the political contenders on whose actions their advance depended. Who, if not Yeltsin, should the administration have supported? He was the legitimately elected president of the country and a plausible proponent of reform. And, having embraced him, how was the administration to distance itself, when some of his actions displeased, without undermining him?

The not altogether satisfactory answer is, with infinite care. The political differentiations called for are subtle and difficult, but the lesson of this period is that the vagaries of events and the convolutions of the political actors will be great, and policy must protect itself against both. That can only be done by disentangling policy from allegiance to any one political figure or faction, no matter how appealing, and by attaching policy to standards of democratic action and progressive economic change. Placing these standards at the center should not preclude support for a given leader but will rule out offering him or her a blank check.

The United States, in fact, has two fundamental interests in societies evolving out of their authoritarian Marxist-Leninist past, and they do not necessarily unfold in tandem. One is movement toward modern democratic polities and vibrant, presumably market-oriented economies. The second, often neglected by U.S. policy makers at the outset, is a stable process of change, free of the domestic and international turmoil capable of threatening the outside world's tranquility and welfare. The actions of political leaders in a country like Russia ought to be judged against both objectives by those guiding U.S. foreign policy. U.S. political support should be granted and withheld accordingly. But, in the end, the ultimate lesson of both the Bush and Clinton administrations, before and after the collapse of the Soviet Union, is that U.S. influence in these grand processes cannot be substantial if it is only a matter of political advice and favor, unsustained by sizable material resources. Alas, the course of politics in the United States over this period—one that appears to be intensifying—suggests that this ultimate lesson will continue to go unlearned.

NOTES

1. George F. Kennan ("X"), "The Sources of Soviet Conduct," *Foreign Affairs* (July 1947), reprinted in Hamilton Fish Armstrong, ed., *Fifty Years of Foreign Affairs* (New York: Praeger, 1972), p. 205.

2. This in his address to members of the British Parliament, June 8, 1982.

3. A good description of Shultz's efforts during February to May 1983 can be found in Don Oberdorfer, *The Turn: From the Cold War to the New Era* (New York: Poseidon Press, 1991), pp. 15–36.

4. "Soviet-American Relations," January 16, 1984, *Weekly Compilation of Presidential Documents* 20 (January 23, 1984), p. 41.

5. Raymond L. Garthoff argues this case in *The Great Transition: American-Soviet Relations and the End of the Cold War* (Washington, D.C.: Brookings Institution, 1994).

6. Quoted in Oberdorfer, p. 89.

7. Eduard Shevardnadze describes early conversations he had with Gorbachev on these themes. (See his *Future Belongs to Freedom* [New York: Free Press, 1991], pp. 23–26.) The most dramatic Gorbachev speech along these lines (not published at the time) was his address to a special Communist Party conference, December 10, 1984. (See M. S. Gorbachev, *Izbrannye rechi and statyi*, vol. 2 [Moscow: Politizdat, 1987], pp. 75–107.)

8. To a degree, George Shultz may have been an exception, albeit only partially, and that possibility explains my slightly qualified phrase, "little or no thought." I will come back to the point in a different context.

9. For a good illustration of how unprescient most folks were, one might consult a report of a conference of most of the country's leading specialists on Soviet politics, economics, and foreign policy held at Arden House in April 1986, a few months after the 27th CPSU Congress.

10. Oberdorfer, p. 111.

11. For the speech, see the State Department *Bulletin* 86 (January 1986), pp. 13–14.

12. Quoted in Garthoff, p. 272.

13. Garthoff, p. 295.

14. Oberdorfer, p. 333.

15. See Department of State *Bulletin* 89 (December 1989), p. 20.

16. See Garthoff, pp. 387–88. Although by then President Bush appears to have had quite another view, he made no effort to rein Quayle in or to indicate a disagreement with him, leading to some public uncertainty over where Bush actually stood.

17. The most concrete expression of the idea was a joint invention of a group of scholars at Harvard's Kennedy School and a team working with the Soviet economist

Gregory Yavlinsky. Among some of the Western European governments, particularly the Germans, there was also an openness to a more ambitious Western involvement in economic reform than Bush and his people favored.

18. Garthoff, pp. 423–24.

19. *New York Times,* March 12, 1992, p. 1.

20. Nixon's memorandum as reported in the *New York Times,* March 11, 1992, p. 5.

21. *New York Times,* May 7, 1992, p. 14.

22. At the time House Democrats, led by David Bonior, their whip, circulated a letter that read: "Dear Mr. President: Last week you announced that the time has come for the United States to provide billions in aid to the former Soviet republics. Today we are writing you with a very simple message: jobs for Americans must come first." *New York Times,* May 1, 1992, p. 3.

23. *New York Times,* March 6, 1992, p. 1.

24. "U.S. Support for Russian Reform: An Investment in America's Security," U.S. Department of State, *Dispatch* 4, no. 22 (May 27, 1993), p. 4.

25. White House press release, "A New U.S.-Russian Partnership," Yeltsin-Bush Press Conference, June 17, 1992, p. 7.

26. "U.S. Support for Russian Reform," p. 3.

3

Normalization with China

ROBERT G. SUTTER

Policy toward China became a bone of contention in American foreign policy after World War II. Some of those in Congress and the postwar administrations supported the views of what came to be known as the China lobby in U.S. politics. The lobby was made up of loosely organized groups of pro–Nationalist China legislators, lobbyists, publicists, and others. Taking advantage of the anticommunist atmosphere that prevailed in the U.S. during the later 1940s and early 1950s and of the harshly anti-American policies of the People's Republic of China (P.R.C.), the China lobby persuaded government leaders to establish a strong U.S. policy of containment and isolation of mainland China. They successfully discredited officials on the other side of the debate, who favored moderation in U.S. policy toward Beijing or reductions in U.S. support for Taiwan. Indeed, the lobby's strength seemed so formidable that U.S. officials were reluctant to incur its members' disfavor by taking initiatives in China policy that could be seen as moderating the United States' hard line.[1]

By the late 1960s, however, influenced by the relative decline in U.S. power in world affairs and by the more discriminating U.S. attitudes toward communist countries after almost two decades of cold war, U.S. policy makers began showing more openness toward improved relations with the P.R.C. The frustration of U.S. military involvement in Vietnam, the emergence of a wide Sino-Soviet rift, and the perceived need for U.S. communication with the world's most populous nation, also a major nuclear power— all were cited as reasons compelling the United States to begin the process of seeking more normal interchange with Beijing. Surveys of public opinion supported this trend. In one major study of American attitudes toward the P.R.C., undertaken by the University of Michigan's Survey Research Center in the mid-1960s, 51 percent favored "exchanging ambassadors with communist China the way we do with other countries." Only 34 percent opposed this step.[2]

The Senate Foreign Relations Committee took one of the most important initial steps in 1966 by holding a series of hearings devoted to U.S. policy toward China. The majority of witnesses proposed three basic changes in U.S. policy: official recognition of communist China by the United States, development of trade relations with the P.R.C., and an end to the United States' prevention of its admission to the United Nations. In May 1966 the House Foreign Affairs Subcommittee on Far Eastern and Pacific Affairs released a report on its own hearings, held earlier in the year, which recommended that the United States seek peaceful contacts with China while also blocking aggressive Chinese expansion.[3]

NIXON ADMINISTRATION

President Nixon's early initiatives toward China and action by Congress during the first two years of the Nixon administration demonstrated a further erosion of anti-P.R.C. feelings among U.S. leaders. The administration's calls for improved trade and other interchange with China were complemented by similar appeals by many prominent legislators. In the fall of 1970, the House Foreign Affairs Subcommittee on Asian and Pacific Affairs held its first hearings on China policy since 1966. Most of the experts on China and the Soviet Union urged a normalization of relations with mainland China. Many of the same witnesses later testified in June 1971 before the Senate Foreign Relations Committee, again recommending improved relations with Beijing.[4]

President Nixon's announcement in July 1971 that he would travel to Beijing was greeted with general support in Congress, even by some conservatives. In 1969 and 1970, the Nixon administration had made several cautious moves toward increasing U.S. contacts with the P.R.C. by lifting certain travel and trade restrictions. In 1971 the State Department announced it had terminated all restrictions on travel to China. The administration announced on June 10 that the United States would end its trade embargo against the P.R.C. On August 2, 1971, it also disclosed that the United States would no longer oppose the admission of the P.R.C. into the United Nations but would continue to fight efforts to expel Taiwan from the world body. The UN issue was a sensitive one for Congress since its members had voted in each of the past twenty years to oppose communist China's admission to the United Nations. They were particularly concerned that the P.R.C. would exert undue influence as one of the five members of the UN Security Council. Nonetheless, 1971 marked the first year since the Korean War that Congress did not pass such a resolution. In pressuring the United Nations during its vote on Chinese representation, members of Congress supported the Nixon administration's efforts to preserve

Taiwan's seat; they reacted angrily to the October 25 vote expelling the Chinese Nationalists, but no formal congressional action was taken.[5]

On February 14, 1972—the week before his departure for the P.R.C.— President Nixon ordered the reassignment of China from country Group Z to country Group Y with respect to U.S. export control policy. In effect, this move placed China on the same level of U.S. trade restrictions as the Soviet Union and the Warsaw Pact countries. Furthermore, President Nixon directed the Treasury Department to remove the requirement that U.S.-controlled firms abroad obtain Treasury approval for the export of strategic goods and foreign technology to the P.R.C.

President Nixon returned from Beijing to bipartisan praise. Although some congressional leaders criticized parts of the communiqué governing U.S.-P.R.C. relations that was released in Shanghai at the end of Nixon's visit, most echoed the favorable comments voiced by such disparate spokesmen as Senators George McGovern, Edward Kennedy, and Barry Goldwater.

The signing of the Shanghai Communiqué marked the end of twenty years of U.S. efforts to block the spread of Chinese communist influence in Asia and signaled the formal beginning of U.S.-P.R.C. normalization. The communiqué had two major features: On the one hand, it noted that the two countries had reached general agreement about the international order in East Asia. In particular, they pledged to cooperate to ensure that the region would not become subject to international "hegemony"—code word used by the P.R.C. to denote Soviet expansion. On the other hand, the communiqué affirmed that the Taiwan issue represented a major stumbling block in the normalization of Sino-American relations. The P.R.C. claimed that Taiwan was a province of China, that its "liberation" was China's internal affair, and that all U.S. military forces had to be withdrawn from Taiwan. For its part, the United States acknowledged "that all Chinese on either side of the Taiwan Strait maintain there is but one China and Taiwan is part of China." The United States did not challenge that position and reaffirmed its interest in a "peaceful settlement of the Taiwan question by the Chinese themselves." With this in mind, the United States declared that its ultimate objective was to withdraw all U.S. forces and military installations from Taiwan. Both sides pledged to continue negotiations on the normalization of relations.

The Shanghai Communiqué showed that the United States and the P.R.C. were willing at that time to defer problems of diplomatic relations in order to work together on the basis of their common strategic interests in East Asia. Prospects for such cooperation were enhanced during the Nixon administration by the reduction of the U.S. military role in Vietnam and along the P.R.C.'s periphery in East Asia. Facing heavy Soviet military pressure in the wake of the Sino-Soviet border clashes of 1969, the Chinese viewed the Soviet Union as their major adversary and now saw the United States as a source of useful leverage against the Soviet "threat."

The Developing U.S.-P.R.C. Reconciliation

Over the next five years, the Nixon and Ford administrations emphasized common U.S.-P.R.C. strategic interests against international "hegemony" and encouraged closer U.S. contacts with the P.R.C., but they did not significantly alter formal U.S. diplomatic and defense ties with Taiwan. As promised in the Shanghai Communiqué, the United States gradually reduced its military forces in Taiwan to fewer than one thousand by the end of the Ford administration, down from around ten thousand at the height of the Vietnam War.

This policy seemed acceptable to the P.R.C., and relations gradually improved. In particular, Beijing saw the withdrawal of U.S. forces from East Asia, under the Nixon Doctrine, as conducive to a slow expansion of Chinese influence in the region. Beijing probably expected the United States to avoid a precipitous pullback and to maintain sufficient forces in the area—especially naval and air forces—to help the P.R.C. offset possible Soviet expansion in Asia. At the same time, Beijing assumed that the United States would continue vigilantly to check Soviet moves in Europe and the Middle East, thereby compelling the USSR to focus its strategic attention westward, away from China.[6]

The P.R.C. and the United States veered from their collision course, toned down their ideological rhetoric, and began to explore cooperation rather than conflict. Sino-American understanding rested on several parallel strategic interests: (1) opposing Soviet expansionism, especially in Asia and the Pacific; (2) withdrawing U.S. military personnel from Vietnam and some other parts of Asia; (3) maintaining a strong U.S. naval and air presence in the Pacific to counteract possible Soviet expansion; (4) encouraging stability on the Korean peninsula to avoid the possibility of a war involving the United States, the P.R.C., and the USSR; and (5) dealing with the Taiwan issue in a way that would not provoke Taiwan to pursue independence, to develop a strong nuclear arms capability, or to seek alliance with the Soviet Union.[7]

Discovery and pursuit of these parallel goals helped bring greater stability to Asian affairs in the early 1970s, with considerable progress being made in several areas. However, many of the goals hinged on common P.R.C. and U.S. tensions with the Soviet Union and thus were subject to the uncertainties of triangular politics. Although concern about Soviet expansion remained a key element in the foreign policy calculations of both Washington and Beijing, it did not provide an enduring foundation for cordial, cooperative Sino-American relations. President Nixon and Secretary of State Henry Kissinger opened the door to reconciliation, but they failed to leave behind a clearly defined, long-term agenda for bilateral and multilateral relations in Asian and global affairs.

Sino-American relations in the areas of diplomacy, trade, and cultural and scientific exchange showed a pattern similar to that of strategic relations between the two nations—a peak of action from 1972 to 1974, followed by a plateau and some uncertainty from 1975 to 1977. In the early 1970s, Sino-American détente was a powerful new ingredient in world affairs, its chief engineers were still in power in Washington and Beijing, and both sides assumed that diplomatic recognition would be forthcoming relatively soon. Then in the mid-1970s both nations became absorbed with the politics of domestic leadership succession, and Sino-American rapprochement lost some of its momentum.

Washington and Beijing moved quickly from 1972 to 1974 to fulfill the content and spirit of the Shanghai Communiqué. In 1973 liaison offices, headed by senior diplomats, were established in Beijing and Washington to perform most of the functions of full-scale embassies. In April 1973 Congress approved a bill (PL 93–22) that extended diplomatic immunities and privileges to the staff of the liaison office of the P.R.C. when it opened the following month.

Some U.S. observers saw Beijing's approval of liaison offices as a major P.R.C. concession, made in the expectation that normalized relations soon would follow. Secretary Kissinger started including Beijing as a frequent stop in his various global missions. Bipartisan congressional delegations began to travel to the P.R.C., publishing lengthy reports of their impressions of the "New China."

Sino-American trade grew from $5 million in 1971 to $930 million by 1974. Exports from the United States to the P.R.C. constituted over four-fifths of the trade, with agricultural goods composing half of the U.S. exports. Other exports included such high-technology items as Boeing 707 aircraft, Pratt and Whitney jet engines, and RCA satellite systems. Exchanges also grew apace. By 1975 several hundred Chinese had visited the United States and roughly ten thousand Americans had traveled to the P.R.C. Some exchanges made a spectacular public relations splash, as did the Chinese archaeological exhibit sent to the United States in 1975 and the tour of the Philadelphia Orchestra in the P.R.C. in 1973. In terms of popular interest, the United States seemed particularly enamored with the P.R.C. in the early 1970s.

Beginning in 1975, however, the Sino-American relationship started to level off, and uncertainties and anxieties cropped up to complicate bilateral relations. Although the number of travelers continued to increase (in total, about one thousand mainland Chinese came to the United States and fifteen thousand Americans went to the P.R.C. between 1971 and 1977), problems arose in cultural exchanges. In 1975 a visit of performing artists from the P.R.C. was canceled because of the last-minute inclusion of a song about "liberating Taiwan." Similarly, a visit of American mayors to China was canceled because the Chinese objected to the inclusion of the mayor of San Juan, a gesture in keeping with their view of Puerto Rico as a U.S. colony chafing for independence. In 1976 Sino-American trade fell sharply, to $336 million. Some of the drop reflected improved harvests in the P.R.C. and a resulting decline in Chinese need for U.S. agricultural products. The P.R.C. leaders' desire for a balance in trade with the United States also contributed to the reduction, and China ran a small surplus in trade with the United States in 1976.

Behind the surface tensions in the mid-1970s were problems centering on Taiwan and on leadership issues in both Beijing and Washington. The Taiwan problem remained the litmus test in relations between the two powers. The Shanghai Communiqué vividly demonstrated the gap between U.S. and P.R.C. views on the issue, but it also seemed to imply that there was room for maneuver and negotiation in the interest of normalizing relations. The United States duly reduced its troop strength in Taiwan, though U.S. diplomatic recognition and security ties with Taipei remained intact. U.S. trade with Taiwan increased considerably, reaching $4.8 billion in 1976, more than ten times the level of U.S.-P.R.C. trade, and several new Taiwan consulates were opened in the United States.

Leadership problems in the United States exacerbated difficulties over Taiwan and other bilateral issues. President Nixon had appeared ready to establish diplomatic relations with the P.R.C. during his second term. But, because of frequently strong opposition from the right wing of his own party, Gerald Ford was unable to exert strong leadership on China policy and had to be content with endorsing Nixon's policy while avoiding new initiatives toward Beijing.

CARTER ADMINISTRATION POLICIES

Following the election of President Jimmy Carter, the death of Mao, and the arrest of the Gang of Four in China in 1976, the new leaders in both capitals took steps to restore momentum to the stalled normalization process. P.R.C. leaders reaffirmed their desire to maintain a good political relationship with the United States, showing more interest in developing closer economic and technical ties with the United States and other capitalist countries. In early 1977 Beijing discussed with the Carter administration a settlement of the issue of Chinese assets frozen in the United States during the Korean War—a step that would facilitate Sino-American trade.[8] Beijing also began sending delegations abroad to discuss purchases of advanced technology from the West, moved fairly rapidly away from the autarkic economic policies that had characterized the P.R.C.'s past development, and favored closer economic ties with the developed world.

The Carter administration reaffirmed its intention to work for the full normalization of U.S.-P.R.C. relations, although it remained concerned about the security of Taiwan and sidestepped comment on a timetable for normalization.[9] Secretary of State Cyrus Vance's trip to Beijing on August 22–26, 1977, was marked by more than a dozen hours of talks with Chinese leaders. Vance repeatedly emphasized that his visit—the first by a high-level Carter administration official to China—was "exploratory" in nature, designed to give U.S. leaders a firsthand look at the P.R.C.'s post-Mao leaders and to familiarize them with U.S. policies on a broad range of international issues, including Sino-American relations.

Although P.R.C. media described the visit positively, neither side offered any indication that there had been significant forward movement on the key question of Taiwan. President Carter said in welcoming Secretary Vance back to Washington on August 27 that the P.R.C. leaders had sent him word that the talks with Vance had been very fruitful from their point of view, and he added that the visit represented "a major step forward" in normalizing U.S.-P.R.C. relations.[10] Ten days later, Deng Xiaoping indirectly contradicted the president when he told visiting U.S. journalists that reports of progress on the normalization issue during Vance's visit were wrong.[11]

The Carter administration resumed deliberations over China policy in preparation for Zbigniew Brzezinski's visit to Beijing in May 1978—a visit that initiated the negotiations leading to the announcement of the normalization agreement between Washington and Beijing in December of that year. Although the deliberations leading to the agreement were held in secret and their importance was apparent only after President Carter's surprise announcement on December 15, 1978, of the establishment of U.S.-P.R.C. diplomatic relations, Congress took several steps to clarify the state of play in the continuing discussion of China policy in the United States. Most notably, the House International Relations Subcommittee on

Asian and Pacific Affairs held a major set of unusually comprehensive hearings in late 1977 dealing with the implications for the United States of U.S.-P.R.C. normalization.[12] The testimony of twenty-two witnesses—including several members of Congress and other prominent Americans—underscored recent signs in the press, opinion polls, and elsewhere demonstrating that U.S. leaders had agreed on several important questions regarding U.S.-P.R.C. relations, although U.S. officials remained strongly divided over some issues—notably Taiwan—that continued to block progress toward normalization with the P.R.C.[13]

In particular, a number of experts within and outside government argued that rapid movement toward the establishment of formal U.S. diplomatic relations with the P.R.C. was needed to maintain and enhance cordial Sino-American relations. That would necessitate a break in U.S. diplomatic and defense ties with the Republic of China on Taiwan and a withdrawal of U.S. forces from the island. Other experts opposed any rapid policy changes, arguing that Beijing would be patient about the development of U.S.-P.R.C. diplomatic relations. They claimed that Beijing's primary concern was that the United States remain strategically strong vis-à-vis the Soviet Union so as to offset what Beijing perceived as heavy Soviet pressure against the P.R.C. Many experts of this persuasion maintained that the current state of relations between the United States and the P.R.C. would suffice until the advantages and costs to the United States of improved relations became more satisfactorily balanced.

Legal Implications of Normalization

U.S. leaders in the Carter administration and Congress also devoted considerable attention to the possible implications of U.S.-P.R.C. normalization for U.S. laws and regulations, especially laws governing relations with Taiwan and the P.R.C.[14] It seemed obvious that if the United States broke ties with Taiwan to establish full diplomatic relations with the P.R.C., it would no longer be extending de jure recognition to the government in Taipei. This posed problems in terms of general U.S. laws and specific U.S. treaties with the Taipei administration.

There were a number of important statutory schemes involving economic and military relations and aid that the United States applied to so-called friendly countries—a category that in the past had included Taiwan. These programs included military sales and assistance, Overseas Private Investment Corporation (OPIC), sales of U.S. agricultural surplus on credit terms or for foreign currency by the Commodity Credit Corporation, loans to small farmers of predominantly rural countries, and expenditures of funds pursuant to the Agricultural Trade Development and Assistance Act of 1954. Although nowhere in these statutes was the term *friendly* defined, withdrawal of recognition was seen as possibly being interpreted as a loss of friendliness, which in turn might have precluded the application of programs under these statutes to the Taipei government.

Also, several laws imposed sanctions upon countries with which the United States had severed diplomatic relations. The Foreign Assistance Act, which affected both economic and military aid, included a blanket provision to this effect, and some laws placed restrictions on dealings with "communist countries." If Taiwan were considered part of a communist country after normalization, then the Eximbank, the generalized system of preferences (GSP), and tariff rates might be affected to the detriment of U.S.-Taiwan ties.

It was suggested that these difficulties could be overcome and obstacles to maintaining existing economic, cultural, and other ties with Taiwan could be removed by legislation that would acknowledge the Taiwan authorities de facto control of their territory and "friendly" status, and would remove possible restrictions on dealings with "communist countries" or countries with whom diplomatic relations were severed. (It was this kind of planning that laid the foundation for U.S. determination to pass the Taiwan Relations Act, which would govern U.S. interchange with Taiwan after the establishment of U.S.-P.R.C. diplomatic relations.)

A second area of concern involved important U.S. treaties with Taipei, treaties governing mutual defense, trade and navigation, air transport, and civilian uses of atomic energy, as well as agreements on quotas for Taiwan's exports of certain commodities, such as textiles, to the United States. Some experts felt that these treaties would lapse after the United States recognized the P.R.C., thus calling for new mechanisms for unofficial U.S. relations with Taiwan. Other experts maintained that the legal effect of withdrawing recognition in such circumstances was unclear and that the United States had the choice of either formally terminating or continuing the treaties after normalization. (This interpretation became the official U.S. view following diplomatic normalization with the P.R.C.)

Many U.S. officials judged that after diplomatic relations were established with the P.R.C., Beijing probably would step up its demands for MFN nondiscriminatory tariff treatment by the United States. In the Trade Expansion Act of 1962, as amended, section 231 provided for mandatory continuation of the prohibition against MFN tariff treatment for countries under communist rule. This provision was still in effect through the Trade Act of 1974, though that law also provided a mechanism by which MFN tariff treatment for China might eventually be restored. However, under terms of the Jackson-Vanik amendment, MFN status was not to be extended to any non-market-economy nation that denied its citizens the right or opportunity to emigrate or that imposed more than nominal exit fees or taxes on documents or individuals—provisions that seemed to apply directly to the P.R.C.

Settlement of the issues of P.R.C. assets blocked in the United States and U.S. private claims against the P.R.C. was seen as required before certain steps in commercial relations between the two could be taken. The United States had blocked P.R.C. dollar-denominated accounts and other assets on December 17, 1950, after P.R.C. military forces entered North Korea; soon afterward, on December 29, 1950, a Beijing decree announced the seizure of U.S. public and private property in the P.R.C. In 1978 claims by private U.S. citizens and corporations totaled about $197 million, while the value of P.R.C. assets held by the United States was put at $76.5 million. In addition to the private claims of U.S. nationals, there was the potential for public claims arising from Eximbank loans, from large Lend-Lease loans of money and equipment during the Sino-Japanese War, and from other obligations of previous Chinese governments.

In the wake of normalized U.S.-P.R.C. diplomatic relations, legislation would be needed to ease restrictions on U.S. aid and credits to the P.R.C. For instance, the assistance provided under Public Law 480 was specifically prohibited in the case of communist countries. Similarly, the Foreign Assistance Act of 1961 limited itself to providing aid to "friendly countries." Although the act did not explicitly define that term, it specifically banned aid covered by the act to a communist country unless the president issued a very narrowly defined waiver. Also exempt, upon presidential waiver in the national interest, were programs administered by OPIC, which provided investment guarantees to U.S. firms investing abroad. Similarly, the Export-Import Bank Act of 1945 as amended prohibited the bank from entering into any credit transaction directly or indirectly involving a communist country, unless the president determined that such a transaction was in the national interest.

CARTER'S INITIATIVE AND U.S. REACTIONS

President Carter attempted to cut boldly through the maze of the various arguments and legal and other complications that hindered the forging of a new, closer U.S. relationship with the P.R.C. In broad terms, his administration's goals were consistent with those of the two previous administrations:

1. to position itself favorably in the U.S.-Soviet-P.R.C. triangular relationship;

2. to use improved relations with Beijing to help stabilize Asian affairs, secure a balance of forces in the region favorable to the United
   States and China, and foster a peaceful, prosperous future for Taiwan;

3. to build mutually beneficial economic, cultural, and other ties with
   the P.R.C.; and

4. to work more closely with the P.R.C. on international issues such
   as world food supply, population control, and arms limitation.

As the Carter administration moved toward a decidedly more anti-Soviet
position in its foreign policy, it increasingly viewed the P.R.C. as an important global and regional power in the Third World. The president and his
advisers thought that China could work closely with the United States and
its allies in the developed world and help counter what they came to see as
the major U.S. strategic problem over the next decade—the containment
of expanding Soviet military power and influence in world affairs.

In October 1978 President Carter signed the Agricultural Trade Act of
1978 (PL 95–501), part of which allowed the Commodity Credit Corporation to extend short-term credit (up to three years) to the P.R.C. The P.R.C.
had been ineligible for such credit under the Jackson-Vanik amendment to
the 1974 Trade Act.

On December 15, 1978, President Carter announced that beginning on
January 1, 1979, the United States and the P.R.C. would establish diplomatic
relations, and the United States would discontinue official relations with
Taiwan. The exchange of ambassadors would take place in March 1979. The
terms of the agreement called on the United States to: (1) recognize the P.R.C.
as the sole legitimate government of China, (2) acknowledge that Taiwan
was part of China, and (3) end all official governmental relations with Taiwan and withdraw its troops from the island within four months. At the
same time, the United States could maintain and develop its existing nongovernmental relations with Taiwan on a "people to people" basis.

The final agreement involved concessions by both sides. The agreement
allowed the United States to end its Mutual Defense Treaty with Taiwan
one year following either side's notification of intent to end the treaty,
which was stipulated in the original treaty. Second, Beijing did not contra-
dict the unilateral statement by Washington that the United States "ex-
pects" the Taiwan issue to be resolved peacefully. Third, Beijing proceeded
with normalization despite the announced intentions of the United States
to continue to supply Taiwan with "defensive" weapons. For its part, Washington accepted the terms for normalization without any formal assurance by Beijing that it would not use force to take Taiwan.

Close on the heels of Carter's December 1978 announcement, Chinese Vice Premier Deng Xiaoping made a widely publicized tour of the United States in January 1979. The administration followed up with a series of major initiatives as high-level U.S. officials visited China during the next two years. It also worked hard to build a consensus behind those initiatives within the executive branch, in Congress, and among the public at large. Thus, scores of officials in State, Commerce, and other departments were mobilized to lobby on Capitol Hill and throughout the country for the new policy.

During his visit early in 1979, Deng Xiaoping signed a series of agreements that (1) provided for the establishment of consulates in both countries, (2) established an overall science and technology agreement, (3) authorized U.S. aid for building a nuclear accelerator in China, (4) entitled the P.R.C. to launch a communications satellite through NASA, (5) established a cultural exchange agreement, and (6) provided for student exchanges. In March 1979 the U.S. Treasury negotiated an agreement with the Chinese Finance Ministry under which claims by U.S. citizens would be settled at 41 cents on the dollar. China would thus pay $80 million to the U.S. Treasury in settlement of U.S. claims totaling $197 million. The United States agreed to release, in October 1979, $80 million of Chinese assets that had been frozen during the Korean War. The agreement allowed Chinese trade with the United States to proceed without fear of seizure of goods. In short, the administration was remarkably successful in moving U.S.-P.R.C. relations forward, but it was less successful at consensus building. The new approaches to Beijing aroused strong opposition, especially in Congress.[15]

Heavily influencing that congressional opposition was the Carter administration's shift from a cautious approach toward the P.R.C. (seen in Secretary Vance's visit to Beijing in August 1977) to the bold approach of 1978–80 without major pressure from U.S. constituencies, China, or other international forces. There had been no domestic consensus demanding that the administration move ahead on Beijing's terms, as demonstrated by the continued debate in the United States over normalization. Indeed, U.S. public opinion remained particularly opposed to the total official break with Taipei that Beijing required as a condition for improved U.S.-P.R.C. diplomatic relations. Meanwhile, China continued to show its interest in maintaining good relations with the United States despite the absence of formal diplomatic recognition. (Those U.S. experts who warned that Sino-American relations might seriously retrogress if the United States refused to meet Beijing's terms for normalization could point to few signs of current impatience in the P.R.C. over the U.S. delay.)

According to senior Carter administration officials, pressure for a change in China policy came almost exclusively from within the administration. Two factors were said to be uppermost in the minds of the president and his advisers as they decided to push ahead with improved relations with the P.R.C. The first was the administration's commitment, made in private policy meetings after the 1976 election, to seek normal relations with Beijing. Achieving that goal had been delayed when Secretary Vance visited China, partly because the administration had to devote its major efforts to the Panama Canal treaties if it hoped to secure their passage by Congress. The ratification of the treaties in spring 1978 opened the way for new efforts to normalize diplomatic relations with China.

The second factor was a shift in the administration's attitudes and policy toward the Soviet Union. Until early 1978, President Carter remained generally committed to the view—associated with Secretary Vance—that relations with China should not be allowed to complicate seriously U.S. efforts to reach an understanding with the Soviet Union over strategic arms limitation. Continued Soviet expansion in the Third World, a growing American perception of reduced U.S. ability to halt such expansion, and a perceived decline in U.S. strength vis-à-vis Moscow's growing strategic and conventional military might combined to shift the administration gradually away from Secretary Vance's approach. Instead, the leaders in the administration increasingly favored a policy associated with Brzezinski: attempting to develop relations with a wide range of countries that could cooperate in a global effort to confront Soviet expansionism. With its stridently anti-Soviet foreign policy and its strategic position along the long, hard-to-defend Soviet Asian frontier, China became an important element in that newly perceived strategic equation. In addition, after the P.R.C. was formally recognized, China's importance increased as a result of both international and domestic events—notably, the Soviet-backed Vietnamese invasion of Cambodia in December 1978, the holding of U.S. hostages in Iran from November 1979 to January 1981 (with the perception of U.S. weakness that followed), the congressional debate over U.S. military preparedness during deliberations on the SALT II treaty in 1979, and the Soviet invasion of Afghanistan in December 1979. These events solidified further the consensus within the administration behind those officials who would use relations with the P.R.C. to help the United States contend with Soviet global power.

Because the new approach to the P.R.C. was formulated in great secrecy, the president's announcement of a normalization of relations surprised all but a handful of U.S. leaders. Congressional officials with high standing in foreign affairs reported that they had been kept in the dark about the administration's plans until a few hours before the decision was announced. Although it marked the start of a dramatic new era in U.S.-China policy, the recognition of the P.R.C. also began one of the most contentious periods in congressional-executive relations concerning that policy.

Several implications of the change in China policy concerned members of Congress and many of their constituents; yet, according to both congressional and administration sources, the president and his aides never offered any real consultations on the shift in policy. Thus, congressional officials were unclear how the new policy would fit in with U.S.-Soviet relations and with U.S. interests in Taiwan and the rest of Asia. They were also uncertain of the new policy's possible political repercussions inside the United States. They judged that the president's action was a serious encroachment on their prerogatives in forming U.S. policy in this important area, especially since they had gone on record earlier in the year about their interest in being consulted before any major changes were made in relations with the P.R.C. and Taiwan.

Administration officials acknowledged that the tight secrecy compounded their problems in dealing with Congress after the normalization agreement was announced, but they insisted that there were several good reasons for keeping Congress in the dark. Few in the administration were prepared to answer the deluge of congressional and other queries about the new approach, and some misinformation was passed to Congress by administration briefers who were unaware of the full details of the new policy. Because of the secrecy, the administration was unable to formulate promptly the legislation needed to protect future U.S.-Taiwan relations, and that caused Congress to feel under excessive pressure to pass such legislation before official U.S. ties with Taiwan lapsed.

The passage of the Taiwan Relations Act in April 1979 temporarily eased congressional-executive friction over China policy. Later in the year, however, new disputes arose over the administration's handling of U.S. agreements with the Taipei government, over the transfer of U.S. arms to Taiwan, and over suspected efforts by the administration to use improved relations with the P.R.C. as a source of leverage against the USSR. Many congressional officials thought they had been misled by the administration into thinking that all U.S. agreements with Taiwan except for the defense agreement would remain in effect after normalization. In fact, the administration planned to phase out many of those official accords—an intention that did not become widely known until August 1979.

In July 1979 the United States and the P.R.C. signed a three-year self-renewable trade agreement that established the framework for normal commercial relations between the two countries and paved the way for the

United States to grant the P.R.C. most-favored-nation (MFN) status, within the requirements of the freedom of emigration (Jackson-Vanik) amendment of the Trade Act of 1974. The trade agreement was signed, however, only after the United States imposed unilateral quotas on textile imports from China. The agreement entered into force on February 1, 1980, after the president, on October 23, 1979, granted a Jackson-Vanik waiver and the Congress, on January 24, 1980, approved the agreement. The textile trade agreement was signed after prolonged negotiations on September 17, 1980, retroactive to January 1, 1980, and was subsequently extended several times.

The presidential waiver removed the Jackson-Vanik amendment's roadblock to the full range of U.S. government export credits for China. In addition, the specific ban on extending Export-Import Bank credits to communist countries in section 2(b)(2) of the Export-Import Bank Act was rescinded by a presidential determination of national interest (45 FR 26017, April 17, 1980).

The waiver removed one obstacle to China's access to the facilities of the Overseas Private Investment Corporation. The other obstacle was the general prohibition of foreign aid to communist countries in section 620(f) of the Foreign Assistance Act of 1961 (22 USC 2370[f]), which could be waived in the national interest only under very restrictive conditions. China was unlikely to qualify for the waiver. For this reason an existing statute was amended (PL 96–327; 94 Stat. 1026; August 8, 1980) to authorize OPIC operations in China if the president determined it to be important to the national interest (22 USC 2199[f]). Such a determination (no. 80–25, 45 FR 54299) was made on August 8, 1980, and an investment guaranty agreement was signed with China effective October 30, 1980.

In 1980 congressional members complained that the administration had misled them about U.S. policy on military ties with China. Although Carter officials repeatedly denied that they had any interest in playing the Chinese card, many congressional leaders judged that the administration was being more vigorous than any previous U.S. government in its pursuit of closer strategic cooperation with China against the USSR. By mid-1980 congressional members and staff most closely associated with Asian affairs were among the most suspicious and critical of the president's policy, reflecting the serious mutual misunderstanding and disrespect that had emerged between some administration officers and some members of Congress. Officials on each side were increasingly defensive of their prerogatives in foreign affairs in the face of what they saw as repeated challenges from the other side.

Toward a U.S. Consensus in the Reagan Years

After the election of Ronald Reagan, the new administration followed policies that reassured conservatives of the president's leanings in favor of Taiwan while avoiding precipitous actions to upgrade U.S. relations in ways that would alienate Beijing.[16] The Chinese government pressed the administration for greater concessions on Taiwan and got them, in a communiqué on August 17, 1982, that restricted U.S. arms sales to the island. But U.S. willingness to cater to Beijing over Taiwan and other issues had reached a high point and was in decline. Under a new foreign policy team led by Secretary of State George Shultz, the Reagan administration downgraded the strategic importance of China to the United States and in the process succeeded in fostering a consensus in U.S. opinion on China policy greater than any that had prevailed since Nixon's opening to Beijing. Chinese leaders did not like the loss of influence that came from the U.S. reassessment but judged that their interests were best served by working with the Reagan administration.

The change in U.S.-China policy occurred after the 1982 resignation of Secretary of State Alexander Haig, a high-level advocate in the Reagan administration of sustaining good relations with China as an important strategic means to counter the USSR. Secretary of State George Shultz and his new assistant secretary for East Asian affairs, Paul Wolfowitz, were less identified with this approach. Shultz held a series of meetings with government and nongovernment Asian specialists in Washington in early 1983, in order to review Asian policy in general and policy toward China in particular.[17] The results of this reassessment—implicitly but clearly downgrading China's importance to the United States—were reflected in speeches by Shultz and Wolfowitz later in the year.[18]

U.S. planners at that time appeared to judge that efforts to improve relations with China were less important than in the recent past for several reasons:

· China seemed unlikely to cooperate further with the United States (through military sales or security consultations, for instance against the Soviet Union) at a time when the P.R.C. had publicly distanced itself from the United States and had reopened talks on normalization of relations with the USSR.

· At the same time, China's continued preoccupation with pragmatic economic modernization and internal development made it appear unlikely that the P.R.C. would revert to a highly disruptive position in East Asia that would adversely affect U.S. interest in the stability of the region.

· China's demands on Taiwan and other bilateral disputes, accompanied by threats to downgrade U.S.-Chinese relations if its demands were not met, appeared open-ended and excessive.

· The U.S. ability to deal militarily and politically with the USSR had improved, particularly because of the Reagan administration's large-scale military budget increases and the perceptions of serious internal and international difficulties of the USSR.

· U.S. allies, for the first time in years, were working more closely with Washington in dealing with the Soviet military threat. This was notably true in Asia, where Prime Minister Nakasone took positions and initiatives underlining common Japanese-U.S. concerns against the Soviet danger.

· Japan and U.S. allies and friends in Southeast Asia—such as China—appeared to be more immediately important to the United States in protecting against what was seen as the primary U.S. strategic concern in the region—safeguarding air and sea access to East Asia, the Indian Ocean, and the Persian Gulf against Soviet attack.[19] China appeared less important in dealing with this perceived Soviet danger.

Western press reports[20] quoting authoritative sources in Washington alerted China to the implications of this shift in the U.S. approach. In effect, the shift meant a sharp reduction in China's ability to exploit the U.S. interest in strategic relations by making demands about Taiwan and other questions. Underlining the change was the U.S. resistance during this period to high-level pressure from the P.R.C. over Taiwan, the asylum case of Hu Na, the Chinese representation issue in the Asian Development Bank, and other questions. The Reagan administration publicly stated that U.S. policy on these questions would remain constant whether or not Beijing decided to retaliate or threatened to downgrade relations by withdrawing its ambassador from Washington, or took some other action.

Moreover, Beijing saw that its perceived political leverage in the United States was small. The Chinese press reported the strong revival in the U.S. economy in 1983 and the positive political implications this had for President Reagan's re-election campaign.[21] China also must have been aware, through contacts with leading Democrats, notably Speaker of the House Tip O'Neill, that Beijing could expect little change in U.S. policy toward Taiwan under a Democratic administration.[22] As 1983 wore on, the Chinese saw an alarming rise in the influence of U.S. advocates of self-determination for Taiwan among liberal Democrats. In particular Senator Claiborne Pell took the lead in gaining passage of a controversial resolution in the Senate Foreign Relations Committee that endorsed, among other things, the principle of self-determination for Taiwan—an anathema to Beijing.[23]

Meanwhile, although Sino-Soviet trade, cultural, and technical contacts were increasing, Beijing saw little sign of Soviet willingness to compromise on basic political and security issues during the ministerial talks that began in October 1982. And the Soviet military buildup in Asia continued—including the deployment of highly accurate SS-20 intermediate-range missiles.

In short, Beijing faced the prospect of a period of prolonged decline in Sino-American relations—possibly lasting until the end of Reagan's second presidential term—if China continued to follow the hard line of the previous two years in relations with the United States. This decline brought the risk of cutting off the implicit but vitally important Chinese strategic understanding with the United States in the face of a prolonged danger posed by the USSR.

The Chinese also recognized that a substantial decline in relations with the United States would have undercut their already limited leverage with Moscow; the decline would likely have reduced substantially any possible Soviet interest in accommodating China in order to preclude closer U.S.-Chinese security ties or collaboration against the USSR. The decline also would have run the risk of upsetting China's ability to gain greater access not only to U.S. markets and financial and technical assistance and expertise but also to those of other important capitalist countries.

China had to calculate as well that a serious decline in U.S.-Chinese relations would likely result in a concurrent increase in U.S.-Taiwanese ties. That would be a serious setback for Beijing's chances of using Taiwan's isolation to prompt Taipei to move toward reunification in accord with P.R.C. interests.

The United States continued the process of forward movement in several areas of U.S.-Chinese exchanges. The U.S. government eased further technology transfer restrictions, began military sales to China, and changed the Foreign Assistance Act to make it easier for the president to grant a waiver to give aid to communist countries such as China.

A review of export control policies by the United States and the Coordinating Committee on Multilateral Export Controls (COCOM) suggested the appropriateness of a continuing relaxation of U.S. policy on exports that required COCOM approval to China. This widened the gap between more liberal treatment of China and continued strict treatment of the Warsaw Pact countries. Because of this differentiation, China had been reassigned in April 1980 to a unique country group (Group P). The policy of approving licenses for export to China of dual-use (economic and military) commodities, with specified exceptions, was instituted. In the following year, the United States changed its policy on exports to general approval of dual-use items to China to the technological level—approximately to twice the threshold requiring COCOM approval. In November 1983, China was reassigned to country Group V—containing the majority of U.S. trading partners outside the Western Hemisphere—although exports to China of certain sensitive strategic dual-use commodities that would normally be licensed for export to Group V might require extended review or denial.

As to its multilateral economic relations, the P.R.C. had become a member of the International Monetary Fund and the World Bank in 1980, replacing therein the Republic of China (Taiwan). The P.R.C. had also acceded to the Multifiber Arrangement on January 18, 1984, had become an observer in the GATT in 1982, and was being examined for GATT membership, having filed an application in 1986 to resume the GATT seat that had been abandoned in 1950 by Taipei.

In short, the Sino-American relationship had become multifaceted and normal in many respects by the end of the Reagan administration. This normalcy proved short-lived. The Chinese crackdown on internal dissent following the Tiananmen demonstration in 1989 coincided with a major U.S. reassessment of China's strategic importance following the collapse of communism in Europe and eventually the collapse of the USSR. U.S. sanctions and other restrictions were imposed that are only slowly being removed in the 1990s.

CONCLUSIONS

The record of U.S.-China normalization leads to several conclusions that are at least partly relevant to considerations of reversing relations with other adversaries.

· The Chinese normalization was grounded in the primary concern of U.S. foreign policy: containment of Soviet expansionism and power. China shared this strategic concern.

· Even with a strong strategic imperative, the administrations of the presidents concerned, especially that of President Carter, met serious resistance in Congress and elsewhere when they tried to push the relationship forward rapidly in ways or in policy areas unacceptable to powerful U.S. constituencies. Exploiting areas of forward movement that were not of central concern to U.S. domestic constituencies was an easier and more effective way to promote normalization.

· U.S. laws and regulations from the cold war provided a thicket of potential obstacles to normalization. They are hard to deal with comprehensively unless there is a clear U.S. political consensus in favor of wholesale normalization. A piecemeal approach moves logically along several tracks (such as diplomatic relations, commercial relations, foreign assistance, military relations). U.S. policy makers are free to focus on one or more of these tracks, recognizing that U.S. political opponents of normalization can use existing laws and regulations to block or delay the normalization process in each track.

· In addition to using the strategic anti-Soviet imperative, the administrations concerned, especially that of President Carter, were able to push forward the normalization process by engaging a wide spectrum of the bureaucracy and the Congress in the process, especially through visits to China. Such "visit diplomacy" resulted in repeated steps forward in U.S. commitments to normalization with China in the 1970s and 1980s.

· U.S. policy toward China was basically compatible with that of major multinational organizations, including the major international financial institutions. This reinforced the U.S. push toward normalization.

· The U.S. domestic consensus in favor of normalization with China— achieved in the mid-1980s after great difficulty—broke down with the collapse of the Soviet bloc and China's internal crackdown on dissent. So long as the United States and its adversaries remain at odds over ideological, foreign, and domestic issues, it seems likely that whatever U.S. consensus that can be built in favor of normalization will remain fragile and subject to reverses, as in the case of China.

NOTES

1. Some observers in the United States and the P.R.C. insist that the China lobby remains a strong influence on U.S. politics, particularly in the Congress, and they blame the lobby for some of the dilemmas in contemporary U.S. policy toward China. They have alleged, for example, that the work of the lobby is reflected in large measure in Congress's protection of U.S. ties with Taiwan by such means as controversial amendments to the Taiwan Relations Act in 1979 and the sale of U.S. fighter aircraft to Taiwan. In fact, the record shows that the lobby's importance in formulating U.S. policy on

China has been on the wane since the late 1960s. The record demonstrates as well that congressional attitudes have come to be based far more on an increasingly sophisticated view of the P.R.C., Taiwan, and U.S. relations with them than on the influence of any lobby group.

2. Cited in William Watts et al., *Japan, Korea and China: American Perceptions and Policies* (Lexington, Mass.: D. C. Heath, 1979), p. 128.

3. The hearings are reviewed in *China: U.S. Policy since 1945* (Washington, D.C.: Congressional Quarterly, 1980), p. 33.

4. *China: U.S. Policy since 1945*, p. 36.

5. For a good wrap-up of congressional reaction to Nixon's policy and the UN vote, see *China: U.S. Policy since 1945*, pp. 36–39.

6. For background on U.S.-P.R.C. relations during the Nixon and Ford administrations, see Harry Harding, *A Fragile Relationship* (Washington, D.C.: Brookings Institution, 1992); A. Doak Barnett, *China and the Major Powers in East Asia* (Washington, D.C.: Brookings Institution, 1987); Michael Oksenberg and Robert B. Oxnam, *Dragon and Eagle* (New York: Basic Books, 1978); Robert G. Sutter, *China Watch: Toward Sino-American Reconciliation* (Baltimore: Johns Hopkins University Press, 1978); and U.S. Library of Congress, Congressional Research Service, *China-U.S. Relations,* Issue Brief no. 76053, December 13, 1978 (Washington, D.C.: Congressional Research Service), pp. 1–4.

7. See Barnett; Oksenberg and Oxnam; Sutter; and Watts et al, pp. 103–23.

8. See Secretary of State Cyrus Vance's remarks on this issue in the *New York Times,* February 10, 1977, p. 1.

9. See Secretary Vance's remarks to reporters after he met with the head of the P.R.C. Liaison Office, *New York Times,* January 12, 1977, p. 10.

10. *New York Times,* August 28, 1977, p. 1.

11. *Washington Post,* September 7, 1977, p. 10.

12. U.S. Congress, House Committee on International Relations, Subcommittee on Asian and Pacific Affairs, *Normalization of Relations with the People's Republic of China: Practical Implications* (Washington, D.C.: U.S. Government Printing Office, 1977).

13. Watts, pp. 125–38.

14. This section is based on testimony given by Jerome Cohen, Victor Li, Eugene Theroux, and former Secretary of the U.S. Senate Francis Valeo, U.S. Congress, *Normalization of Relations with the People's Republic of China,* pp. 80–136. It also draws heavily on studies of the subject, including William Clarke and Martha Avery, "The Sino-American Commercial Relationship," and Eugene Theroux, "Legal and Practical Problems in the China Trade," in U.S. Congress, Joint Economic Committee, *China: A Reassessment of the Economy* (Washington, D.C.: U.S. Government Printing Office, 1975). Another study of particular use is Victor Li, *Derecognizing Taiwan: The Legal Problems* (Washington, D.C.: Carnegie Endowment for International Peace, 1977).

15. For a wrap-up of congressional and administration views on this issue, see U.S. Congress, House Committee on Foreign Affairs, *Executive-Legislative Consultations on China Policy, 1978–1979* (Washington, D.C.: U.S. Government Printing Office, 1980).

16. Reviewed in Harding, pp. 107–72, and others.

17. See coverage in *Washington Post* and *New York Times* in the week prior to Shultz's late January departure for China. For background, see Jonathan Pollack, *The Lessons of Coalition Politics* (Santa Monica, Calif.: Rand Corp., 1984). See also Richard Nation's article in *Far Eastern Economic Review*, April 21, 1983, pp. 7–10.

18. See coverage in *Far Eastern Economic Review*, April 21, 1983, pp. 7–10.

19. See discussion in Robert G. Sutter and Larry Niksch, "China's Role in U.S. Security Policy," *Issues and Studies*, March 1984, pp. 42–60.

20. See coverage in *Far Eastern Economic Review*, April 21, 1983, pp. 7–10.

21. See U.S. Foreign Broadcast Information Service, *Daily Report—China (DR China)*, April–May 1983.

22. See O'Neill's official report on the visit to China, U.S. House of Representatives, *The United States and China* (Washington, D.C.: U.S. Government Printing Office, 1983). He found no interest in the Congress in amending the Taiwan Relations Act.

23. See China's reaction to the resolution in *DR China*, March 14 and November 21, 1983.

4

Nicaragua

National Reconciliation and
the Impatience of U.S. Policy

WILLIAM M. LEOGRANDE

The issue of how and under what circumstances to normalize relations with Nicaragua arose earlier than the election of Violeta Chamorro as president in 1990. It began with the question of how the United States should respond to the revolutionary government that came to power on July 19, 1979, when a broadly based insurrectionary movement led by the Marxist Sandinista National Liberation Front (FSLN) overthrew the dictatorship of Anastasio Somoza. Somoza's family had ruled Nicaragua since 1934 when his father, the commander of the U.S.-trained National Guard, ousted the civilian president. During its four decades in power, the family dynasty developed a reputation for enormous brutality and greed. Until running afoul of President Jimmy Carter because of the regime's human rights abuses, Anastasio Somoza had also been a long-standing ally of the United States. The Sandinistas, by contrast, blamed U.S. imperialism for the persistence of the Somoza dynasty. They identified with the Cuban revolution and international socialism. Just days after their triumph, senior Sandinista leaders celebrated with Fidel Castro in Havana.[1]

Nevertheless, the deterioration in relations between Washington and the Sandinistas was not immediate. The Carter administration sought to establish a modus vivendi with the new revolutionary government, hoping to influence it to adopt a moderate course by offering the incentive of U.S. economic assistance. Specifically, Washington hoped to dissuade the Sandinistas from providing significant military aid to other Central American revolutionaries (especially in El Salvador), as well as to prevent a military alignment of the Sandinistas with Cuba and the Soviet Union, or the creation of a Leninist state and centrally planned socialist economy at home. For the next decade, these same issues would remain at the heart of U.S. policy calculations about Nicaragua.[2]

Carter's policy had mixed success at best. It was hobbled at the outset when congressional Republicans balked at providing aid to an unabashedly revolutionary Marxist government that identified ideologically with America's cold war enemies. Republican resistance slowed congressional approval of Carter's request for a $75 million aid package for Nicaragua. After the bill was introduced, a year passed before the first funds flowed to Nicaragua, and even then the money was subject to sixteen restrictive conditions imposed by Republican lawmakers—terms that spoiled whatever good will the aid package might have purchased from the Sandinista government.[3]

Carter's policy of constructive engagement with the Sandinista government was ended by his defeat in the 1980 presidential election, so it is impossible to know whether it would have proven effective in the long run. By the time Carter left office, the internal political situation in Nicaragua was polarizing, and the Sandinistas had begun providing significant aid to their comrades in El Salvador, but Nicaragua had not yet become another Cuba.

THE NEW COLD WAR: PRESIDENT REAGAN AND THE CONTRAS

Ronald Reagan came to office convinced that the Sandinistas were irredeemable Marxist-Leninists whose revolutionary rule was inimical to U.S. interests. After two abortive diplomatic exchanges, the United States began, in December 1981, to provide aid to armed opponents of the Nicaraguan government—the "contras." Several small contra bands, no more than a few hundred men in all, were already operating in Honduras, receiving aid from the Argentine military government. The United States became their principal patron, forging unity among the disparate groups and financing their rapid expansion into a force of some fifteen thousand. In 1983 the CIA itself began paramilitary operations against Nicaragua, blowing up oil pipelines and storage facilities and mining Nicaragua's harbors. Concomitantly, the United States imposed economic sanctions against Nicaragua, cutting off bilateral aid in 1981 and trade in 1985, and invoking U.S. influence to halt loans from international financial institutions and private commercial banks.[4]

Through most of Reagan's eight years in office, senior administration officials were divided over the aims of U.S. policy. "Pragmatists," led by Chief of Staff (later Treasury Secretary) James Baker and Secretary of State George Shultz, saw the policy of hostility toward Nicaragua as a form of coercive diplomacy. Doubtful that the contras could ever win a military victory, they sought to apply pressure to the Sandinista regime in order to extract concessions at the bargaining table. The pragmatists were more concerned about Nicaragua's foreign policy than about its domestic political arrangements. If the Sandinistas would abandon support for other Central American revolutionaries and curtail their military ties with Cuba and the Soviet Union, the pragmatists were prepared to strike a deal.

Administration "hard-liners," on the other hand, insisted that no foreign policy accord was worth anything as long as the Sandinista regime remained in power. Led by CIA Director William Casey, United Nations Ambassador Jeane Kirkpatrick, and Defense Secretary Caspar Weinberger, they insisted that internal democracy must be the sine qua non objective of U.S. policy. At critical junctures in 1981, 1984, and 1987, the hard-liners were able to block the pragmatists' efforts to reach a diplomatic resolution of Washington's conflicts with the Sandinistas. At such moments of decision, President Reagan invariably sided with the hard-liners.[5]

Reagan's policy of hostility was one of the most controversial issues of his presidency, creating deep and bitter divisions between Republicans and Democrats. In 1982 the Congress tried to limit the purpose for which contra aid could be used to the interdiction of arms being smuggled by the Sandinistas from Nicaragua to El Salvador. As the war expanded in 1983, the House of Representatives voted to halt contra aid entirely, but the Republican majority in the Senate kept the program going. The mining of Nicaraguan harbors finally led Congress to prohibit contra aid in 1984. The administration nevertheless continued to assist the contras, using a variety of covert channels managed out of the National Security Council staff by Lt. Col. Oliver North.[6]

After Reagan's landslide reelection in November 1984, the pendulum began to swing back the other way. When Nicaraguan President Daniel Ortega made an ill-timed trip to Moscow in early 1985, Reagan convinced Congress to allow "humanitarian" aid (actually, nonlethal military assistance) for the contras. In 1986, by razor-thin margins in both chambers, Congress approved the president's full program of $100 million in unrestricted contra aid. The 1987 revelations of the Iran-contra scandal shifted the congressional balance yet again, finally ending U.S. military aid to the contras, although Washington would continue to provide the insurgents with food, clothing, and medicine until they finally disbanded in 1990.

Behind this see-saw battle between Congress and the executive lay a fundamental disagreement over the extent to which the Sandinista government threatened U.S. interests. Reagan saw Nicaragua as an arena of the cold war; the Sandinistas were Cuban and Soviet proxies who would inevitably threaten U.S. interests both locally and globally unless they were removed from power or were at least "Finlandized"—by severing their link to Havana and Moscow.[7] Congressional Democrats who opposed Reagan's policy of hostility regarded Nicaragua as a small, underdeveloped Third World country incapable of threatening the United States. A policy of diplomatic engagement, they believed, was more likely to reduce Nicaragua's military buildup and ease the constraints on democratic liberties introduced during the course of the contra war. Opponents also argued that by escalating the level of military conflict in Central America, U.S. policy risked engulfing the entire region in war and drawing the United States into direct combat involvement. That, in turn, would severely damage U.S. relations with Latin American nations such as Mexico, Brazil, and Argentina—nations vastly more important to the United States than the ministates of Central America.[8]

Perhaps the principal reason that Congress was willing to confront the president at all on the issue of Nicaragua was existence of widespread public opposition to Reagan's policy, opposition based largely in religious communities. The Catholic Church, virtually every major Protestant denomination, and many American Jewish organizations were outspoken in their opposition. Opinion polls consistently confirmed the public's reluctance to see the United States become more deeply involved in the Central American crisis.[9] Despite its best efforts, the administration was never able to rally public support behind its policy. Within the administration, the consistent opposition of such a large segment of the public was considered a major obstacle to the pursuit of a more aggressive policy.[10]

SEEKING A DIPLOMATIC SOLUTION: PRESIDENT BUSH AND ESQUIPULAS

In August 1987, the five Central American presidents meeting in Esquipulas, Guatemala, signed a regional peace accord drafted by Costa Rican President Oscar Arias. The Esquipulas agreement committed all the countries to free and fair elections, a reduction in conventional military forces, and an end to support for guerrillas operating in one another's territory. It also called for an end to extraregional support for insurgents, referring to U.S. support for the contras. The Esquipulas accord was notable in that the Sandinistas agreed, for the first time, to discuss their internal political arrangements. In previous peace negotiations mediated by the Contadora group (Mexico, Panama, Venezuela, and Colombia), the Sandinistas had agreed to foreign policy concessions but had adamantly refused to discuss domestic politics.[11]

The Reagan administration opposed the Esquipulas accord despite considerable pressure from Congress and from U.S. allies in Latin America and Europe. President George Bush, on the other hand, reassessed U.S.

policy when he took office in 1989. Bush did not seem to share Reagan's conviction that Central America was a crucial cold war contest of wills. As vice president, he had never taken a major role in promoting Reagan's policy to the public or to Congress, and he had not mentioned the region in his campaign against Michael Dukakis. James Baker, Bush's long-time friend and his secretary of state, regarded Central America as politically dangerous and strategically marginal.

Bush was mainly interested in removing Central America as a point of friction between the White House and the Democrat-controlled Congress. By supporting diplomatic processes in both El Salvador and Nicaragua, Bush diffused congressional opposition and refocused foreign policy on the great issue of the day—how to build a new world order on the rubble of collapsed Communist regimes in Eastern Europe and the Soviet Union. To this issue, Central America was irrelevant.

Shortly after Bush's inauguration, Baker opened a dialogue with congressional leaders to seek a bipartisan approach to the matter of Nicaragua. The resulting agreement, dubbed "the Treaty of Washington" by one senior administration official, did not resolve the policy differences, but both sides agreed to suspend the policy battle for a year, until the Nicaragua elections had taken place, scheduled for February 1990.[12]

The agreement represented a pragmatic compromise. Lacking the votes in Congress to resume military aid to the contras, the White House gave up the quest to make the Sandinistas "cry uncle," as Reagan had once described U.S. policy. Reagan's approach had failed, Baker admitted, because it was so divisive at home. Instead, Bush pledged sincere support for the Esquipulas peace process, applying diplomatic and economic pressure to move Nicaragua toward democracy and peace with its neighbors.

Unable to convince the administration to rely solely on diplomacy, congressional Democrats were forced to accept continued U.S. support for the contras, in the form of $4.5 million a month in nonmilitary aid through the end of February 1990. Thus the contras would be kept together, "body and soul" as Reagan used to say, in case the Nicaraguan elections went awry.[13]

The differences between the Bush and Reagan policies toward Nicaragua were subtle, but real. Bush had the same maximum objective as Reagan—to remove the Sandinista regime from power, replacing it with a conservative pro-U.S. alternative. Consequently, all aspects of Reagan's policy of hostility—the economic embargo, diplomatic efforts to cut off external financing from Europe and Latin America, threatening military exercises, and a refusal to engage in any serious diplomatic dialogue—continued unchanged.[14] Reagan's preferred policy instrument, the contras, were no longer available because of Congress's refusal to fund the war, but under the bipartisan agreement Bush was at least able to preserve them as a fighting force that might be reactivated later if political conditions changed.

Reagan's minimum and maximum objectives in Nicaragua were the same. The continued existence of the Sandinista government was simply unacceptable; nothing short of its removal would do. Not so for Bush; his minimum objective was containment of Nicaragua. He was prepared to accept coexistence if the Sandinistas would live up to their commitments under the Esquipulas agreement—that is, hold free elections and stop supplying aid to the Salvadoran guerrillas. Whereas Reagan resisted regional diplomatic efforts for fear they would produce an agreement that left the Sandinistas in power, Bush was more willing to support the peace process. Indeed, with no hope of removing the Sandinistas by military force, diplomacy was the only alternative. "We talked about diplomacy [during the Reagan years]," a senior administration official admitted, "but it began as a cover story for what we were really trying to do. What has happened since then is that the cover story has become real."[15]

THE TRANSITION

To run against Daniel Ortega in the February 1990 elections, the Nicaraguan opposition nominated Violeta Chamorro. Like Corazon Aquino in the Philippines, she was the perfect unity candidate. Drawn into politics by the murder of her activist husband who had long opposed the Somoza dictatorship, she carried none of the partisan baggage that weighed down other politicians. Even though she had resigned from the Sandinista governing junta in 1980 because of the leftward drift of the revolution, and even though her newspaper relentlessly denounced the Sandinistas, she nevertheless projected an aura of being above the political fray.

Still, the opposition was fractious and disorganized. U.S. officials expected the Sandinistas to win the election, despite more than $10 million in overt and covert support that Washington channeled to the Chamorro campaign.[16] In fact, Assistant Secretary of State for Inter-American Affairs Bernard Aronson had already begun discussions with Nicaraguan Vice Minister of Foreign Affairs Victor Tinoco about a step-by-step process for normalizing relations between the two countries after the anticipated Sandinista victory.[17]

To the surprise of most observers, Chamorro and the United Nicaraguan Opposition (UNO) coalition won a stunning victory. Chamorro received 54.7 percent of the popular vote, to Ortega's 40.8 percent, and UNO won fifty-one seats in the ninety-three-member National Assembly, to thirty-nine for the Sandinistas.[18] The decisive issues were the terrible state of the economy, the Sandinista refusal to end the highly unpopular military draft, and the public's doubt that the Sandinistas would be able to make peace with Washington and bring the war to a definitive conclusion.

After the election, Washington's first priority was to assure that the Sandinistas accepted the result and transferred power to Chamorro. The Sandinistas seemed to accept defeat and prepared to transform themselves from governing party into the opposition. Ironically, one of the main obstacles to a peaceful transition was the contra army that Washington had so vigorously resisted demobilizing.

Both the UNO transition team and the Bush administration urged the contras to disarm and repatriate to Nicaragua, but the contras themselves were reluctant to lay down their arms as long as the Sandinistas retained control of the armed forces. In March 1990 contra commanders signed an agreement with the Chamorro transition team in which they promised to demobilize their Honduran-based troops before inauguration. But simultaneously they began infiltrating most of their fighters back into Nicaragua, where they agreed in principle to disarm but procrastinated in accepting any specific deadline. Finally, the Sandinista government, the Chamorro transition team, and the contra commanders signed agreements for a ceasefire and full demobilization beginning on inauguration day and concluding three weeks later.[19]

The Bush administration responded to Chamorro's election by lifting the U.S. economic embargo that Reagan had imposed in 1985 and by requesting Congress to approve $300 million in economic assistance for the new government.[20] The request for economic aid was widely supported in Congress; members believed that the success of Nicaragua's unexpected transition to pluralist democracy would depend fundamentally upon reviving its moribund economy. Moreover, having financed the contra war for nearly a decade, many in Washington felt a responsibility to help pay for economic reconstruction.

It appeared, then, that Washington had realized its fondest wish: the Sandinistas had been ousted, replaced by a regime of pro-American conservatives whose campaign the United States had helped finance. As it turned out, the transition in bilateral relations from hostility to friendship would prove to be considerably less simple than either side expected in the jubilant days after Chamorro's victory.

CHAMORRO'S POLICY OF NATIONAL RECONCILIATION

Despite their electoral defeat, the Sandinistas retained important bases of power. They were still the largest single political party and by far the best organized. With supporters all across the country in trade unions, peasant associations, and student groups, the Sandinistas had the capacity to "govern from below," as Daniel Ortega put it.[21] They could mount mass demonstrations and strikes to force their demands on the UNO government and, in the event of confrontation, they could make Nicaragua ungovernable, as happened when Sandinista unions called general strikes in May and July 1990. The Sandinistas also retained considerable influence within the government bureaucracy, especially the judiciary and the military, much of which had been staffed by Sandinista loyalists after the fall of Somoza.

Despite opposition from hard-liners within her own UNO coalition and from the United States, Chamorro adopted a policy of "national reconciliation" toward the Sandinistas. Rather than trying to purge the Nicaraguan political system of Sandinista influence, she sought cooperation with her former adversaries in order to heal the deep wounds in the body politic and begin the gargantuan task of economic reconstruction.

Antonio Lacayo, Chamorro's son-in-law and her minister of the presidency (roughly equivalent the U.S. president's chief of staff), was the principal architect of the policy of reconciliation. It was Lacayo who negotiated the 1990 transition agreement with the Sandinistas, in which the Chamorro government agreed to respect the professional hierarchy of the Sandinista armed forces and police, and the Sandinistas affirmed the subordination of the military to civilian authority and the need for reducing its size.[22]

On inauguration day, Chamorro announced that she would retain Sandinista Defense Minister Humberto Ortega as chief of the armed forces. That decision opened the first rift between Chamorro and conservatives in the UNO coalition, led initially by her vice president, Virgilio Godoy, and later by National Assembly deputy and former contra leader Alfredo Cesar. The right criticized Chamorro for being soft on the Sandinistas, surrendering de facto control over the security forces to them. The Sandinistas, for their part, sought to strike a balance between cooperating with Chamorro, in order to stabilize the economy, and defending the interests of their poor constituents, who were hard hit by the government's economic policy.

Over the next several years, Nicaraguan politics evolved into a three-way struggle between Chamorro and her supporters, UNO's conservatives, and the Sandinistas. At times, Chamorro loyalists and Sandinista delegates in the National Assembly joined forces to defeat the conservatives. On other occasions, the original UNO coalition came back together to defeat the Sandinistas.[23]

Chamorro's appointment of Humberto Ortega was the first sign that

U.S.-Nicaraguan relations in the post-Sandinista era would not be entirely amiable. When U.S. officials learned of Chamorro's intention to retain Ortega, Bush dispatched Assistant Secretary Aronson to dissuade her. Chamarro was undeterred, convinced that her decision would foster reconciliation and was, in any event, the only plausible way to exert civilian control over a military whose officers' corps was composed entirely of Sandinista veterans.[24]

To be sure, Chamorro's election, coinciding as it did with the end of the cold war, radically transformed the issue agenda of U.S.-Nicaraguan relations. With the Sandinistas out of power and the Soviet Union disintegrating, there was no longer any danger that Nicaragua would act as a platform for the projection of Soviet power into Central America. Indeed, even the Cubans, suddenly bereft of allies and benefactors in the Eastern bloc, abdicated their support for revolutionary internationalism in a bid to reorient their economy toward the capitalist West.

Yet the Bush administration seemed to share the views of Chamorro's conservative critics, urging her at various junctures to be less accommodating to the Sandinistas on a wide range of issues. Three in particular dominated the bilateral issue agenda after 1990: civilian control over the armed forces, human rights, and compensation for nationalized property.

Civilian Control of the Military

U.S. officials in both the executive branch and Congress generally agreed with Nicaraguan conservatives that the transition agreement negotiated with the Sandinistas and the retention of Ortega as chief of the army severely limited civilian control of the military. The Chamorro government's dilemma in this regard was not fundamentally different from that faced by other newly elected civilians in the neighboring countries of El Salvador, Honduras, and Guatemala.

In the Nicaraguan case, however, Washington continued to worry about covert Sandinista support for the guerrilla movement in El Salvador. Although Chamorro certainly opposed such assistance, it was not clear that her control over the armed forces was sufficient to prevent it. On June 18, 1990, Chamorro informed Secretary of State James Baker that small arms were still being smuggled through Nicaragua to the Salvadoran guerrillas and pledged to seek ways to halt the trafficking.[25] Seven months later, in January 1991, four Sandinista military officers were arrested for having provided Salvadoran guerrillas with twenty-eight surface-to-air missiles from Nicaragua's inventory.[26]

The 1992 peace accord that ended the Salvadoran civil war reduced Washington's immediate worry that covert Sandinista aid to the Salvadoran guerrillas might destabilize the regime in San Salvador. But in May 1993, a large secret arms cache owned by one faction of the Salvadoran guerrillas exploded accidentally in Managua. Investigators concluded that it had been built in 1990 or 1991, after Chamorro became president. Since it seemed unlikely that such a cache could have been created without the knowledge of the Nicaraguan military, the discovery again raised the issue of whether the Sandinista army was operating autonomously.[27]

Human Rights

The issue of human rights was, in truth, another facet of the problem of civilian control over the military. No one accused the civilians in the Chamorro administration of ordering or condoning abuses. Yet reports of abuses mounted, particularly the intimidation and assassination of former contras by the police and armed forces. From the beginning of the Chamorro administration to the end of 1994, the Organization of American States International Support and Verification Commission (created to facilitate the demobilization and reintegration of the contras) estimated that some 270 former contras had died in violent circumstances. So few cases resulted in prosecutions that the U.S. State Department concluded, "A state of impunity for abuses committed against ex-RN [National Resistance members] can still be said to exist."[28]

Two of the most conspicuous assassinations were the murder on February 16, 1991, of former contra commander in chief Enrique Bermudez and the November 23, 1992, killing of conservative businessman Arges Sequeira Manga, director of the Association of Nicaraguan Confiscated Property Owners. Chamorro appointed a special presidential commission to investigate the Bermudez assassination, but it was unable to solve the case. British investigators invited by the government had no better luck.

Sequeira Manga was killed by a leftist paramilitary group, the Punitive Forces of the Left, for his work in lobbying the government to restore expropriated property to its original owners. Former Sandinista army Lt. Col. Frank Ibarra, leader of the Punitive Forces, was convicted of the crime, but he remained free while his lawyers argued that he qualified for immunity under an August 1993 amnesty.[29]

Another case that highlighted the problem of military impunity was the October 1990 killing of Jean Paul Genie, a teenager shot to death by Humberto Ortega's security guards because he passed their motorcade on the highway. In 1992 a criminal court judge ruled that eight of Ortega's bodyguards should be tried for murder and that Ortega himself should be tried for covering up the crime. The case was remanded to the military court system, as Nicaraguan law provided, which in June 1994 acquitted Ortega and his bodyguards of organizing or covering up the killing.[30]

Property Claims

During her campaign, Chamorro promised justice for those whose property had been confiscated unfairly by the Sandinistas, while at the same time promising not to dispossess the poor peasants and workers who had been given expropriated land and homes under the agrarian and urban reforms. The transition agreement negotiated between Chamorro and the lame-duck Sandinistas reiterated this dual pledge.[31] The property question ultimately evolved into one of the most complex and conflictual issues faced by the Chamorro government. It fractured both the UNO coalition and the Sandinista party, it provoked land and factory occupations, it spawned gridlock in the judicial and legislative branches of government, it dissuaded businesses from reinvesting, and it endangered U.S. economic aid.

Chamorro's challenge was to resolve the property issue while keeping her promises to both sides—the 5,288 owners who lost property under the Sandinistas and the 171,890 who received it.[32] UNO conservatives wanted to follow a simple, albeit conflictual, policy of returning all confiscated property to its previous owners. The Sandinistas warned that they would do whatever necessary to protect interests of the poor and prevent the reversal of the social gains of the revolution—most especially the agrarian reform. If she was to follow the conservatives' recommendation, Chamorro would have had to jettison her policy of national reconciliation.

Moreover, it was not clear that Chamorro could have successfully carried out a forced return of property even if she had wanted. Especially in rural areas, many civilians retained military weapons as a residue of the contra war, and many small peasants declared themselves prepared to defend their land against repossession. As the police and army were commanded by Sandinista officers, it was questionable whether the security forces could be relied upon to force peasants off their farms and workers out of their homes and factories. As one member of the Chamorro government put it, had the government embarked on a wholesale return of property, "We would be at war again."[33]

The Sandinistas' vehement opposition to returning expropriated property was not entirely selfless. During the lame-duck period between Chamorro's electoral triumph and her inauguration, the Sandinista government appropriated and distributed to its loyal cadres thousands of houses and farms comprising hundreds of thousands of acres.[34] This orgy of graft, dubbed "La Piñata," sullied the Sandinistas' reputation and prompted the formation of a "reform" wing of the party, which repudiated such banditry and ultimately split off to form a separate party.[35]

Chamorro's strategy on the property issue was to consult broadly with trade unions, small farmers' associations, and businesspeople in hopes of reaching some consensus on how to resolve nettlesome questions—specifically, how to decide which properties to return and which owners to be paid compensation, how to adjudicate the amount of compensation, and how to find the funds to finance the program. Chamorro's search for consensus was stymied by the main business association, the Superior Council of Private Enterprise (COSEP), which insisted on the rapid return of all expropriated property.

To Washington, the property issue was a prime example of the weakness of Chamorro's policy of national reconciliation. When conflicting sides had seemingly irreconcilable interests, conciliation produced stalemate. And stalemate on the property issue discouraged investment and slowed economic recovery. Moreover, a significant number of claimants were U.S. citizens, thus giving the U.S. government an immediate interest in the resolution of the issue. Of the 16,000 property claims filed with the Nicaraguan government, more than 1,487 had been filed by 506 U.S. citizens— many of them Nicaraguan-born immigrants who fled after the fall of Somoza. As more such immigrants were naturalized, the number of claims by U.S. citizens rose as fast as the Chamorro government could resolve them.[36]

Apart from the political shoals surrounding the property issue, the technical problems confronting the Chamorro government were mammoth in themselves. In many cases of expropriated property, the Sandinista government never acquired legal title or issued titles to the beneficiaries of the agrarian and urban reforms. Peasants without titles could not get credit, and new titles could not be issued until claims by previous owners were adjudicated and compensation paid. The adjudication of claims was stymied by the lack of adequate records of property boundaries and valuation. Values declared for tax purposes during the Somoza era were notoriously inaccurate. Moreover, some properties had appreciated considerably after expropriation because of capital improvements by either the state or subsequent owners. If such properties were to be returned, should the previous owner pay compensation for the improvements?

Finally, the Nicaraguan government did not have the resources to pay immediate compensation for even a small fraction of the properties in dispute. The total value of claims exceeded $650 million—twice the value of Nicaragua's annual foreign exchange earnings. The practice of issuing government bonds was highly unpopular among former owners, as reflected in the secondary market, where the bonds sold at about 15 percent of their face value in 1996.[37]

Not surprisingly, the complexity of the property issue made any simple formula for resolving claims untenable. In practice, resolution was achieved on a case-by-case basis, with negotiations over fair valuation and disposition. That, in turn, meant slow progress on a case load that involved nearly 16,000 properties, 25 percent of the arable farm land, and 177,000 people.

The Evolution of U.S. Policy in the Post-Sandinista Period

During the first two years of the Chamorro administration, Washington provided $442 million in economic assistance and generally expressed its doubts about Chamorro's policy of national reconciliation through quiet diplomacy. The lukewarm support of the Bush administration encouraged UNO conservatives to press their demands for the ouster of Humberto Ortega and the return of confiscated property.[38] On May 27, 1992, Senator Jesse Helms (R-N.C.) urged the Bush administration to hold up disbursement of further economic aid until Chamorro took effective action to reduce Sandinista control over the military and police and to compensate U.S. citizens for expropriated property. Bush agreed, freezing $104 million.[39]

The suspension of aid posed a serious threat to Nicaragua's economic recovery, and Chamorro acted quickly to mollify Washington. On September 22, she announced a series of measures. She pledged that all property claimants except those who lost property in the anti-Somoza nationalizations of 1979 would receive either their property or compensation. She announced the reactivation of the National Review Commission to expedite adjudication of property claims, and she created a mechanism for paying compensation in the form of twenty-year bonds with an interest rate of 3 percent (which claimants generally regarded as inadequate).[40]

On the human rights front, Chamorro established the Tripartite Commission, comprised of representatives from the Nicaraguan government, the Catholic Church, and the OAS International Support and Verification Commission. The commission's mandate was to investigate reports of human rights abuses and make recommendations to the government. On September 5, Chamorro fired the Sandinista chief of police and eleven other senior police officials.[41] These measures led President Bush to release about half the frozen aid ($54 million) in December 1992. A Helms staff assistant, James Nance, called the release "a disgrace and a national tragedy."[42]

In April 1993, President Bill Clinton released the remaining $50 million as part of a new policy of disengaging the United States from Nicaragua's partisan squabbles. The conflict between Chamorro and the conservative wing of UNO had mired the Nicaraguan political system in endless bickering, which gradually escalated into armed violence. In the countryside, groups of ex-combatants from both the contras and the Sandinista army ("recontras" and "recompas") dug up hidden arms and resumed their war against each other and the regular armed forces. Conservatives in Managua encouraged the "recontras" in order to put pressure on Chamorro, and many observers suspected the Sandinista-led army of encouraging the "recompas" as a counterweight.

Both sides looked to the United States for support. Alfredo Cesar, leader of the anti-Chamorro faction in UNO, traveled regularly to Washington to consult with Senator Helms and lobby against aid for Nicaragua. His brother-in-law Antonio Lacayo, Chamorro's principal adviser, also trekked north to lobby—or as he himself put it, "to panhandle"—for aid.[43]

The Clinton administration tried to end this unhealthy dynamic. By declaring its support for Chamorro as the elected president of Nicaragua, while at the same time declaring neutrality on Nicaragua's myriad policy battles, Clinton hoped to force the Nicaraguans to resolve their problems among themselves. "We are not going to play favorites," Ambassador John Maisto explained.[44]

But disengagement was not easy. Sparked by Senator Helms's activism, Congress became increasingly interested in Nicaragua. In October 1992, the House-Senate Conference Committee on the fiscal year 1993 Foreign Aid Appropriation conditioned Nicaragua's FY93 aid funds on judicial reform, a new human rights code of conduct for the police and armed forces, and an expeditious review of property claims.[45]

After the May 1993 arms cache explosion, Helms exploited congressional anger to win approval for a proposal freezing all aid to Nicaragua unless President Clinton certified that the Nicaraguan army was not engaged in international terrorism and that the government was making tangible progress in asserting civilian control over the military, resolving property claims, and improving human rights.[46]

Responding to Congress's disillusionment with Nicaragua (and perhaps recalling that Bush's aid suspension prompted quick action by the Chamorro government), Clinton imitated Bush, freezing $40 million in economic aid in July 1993. As the price of resuming assistance, Washington demanded a deadline for the removal of Humberto Ortega as armed forces chief and progress on the property issue, especially for U.S. citizens. "The basic theme was: How could we ever go back to the Hill for aid to Nicaragua?" an administration official explained. "We have nothing positive to report."[47]

As she had in 1992, Chamorro responded to the aid suspension with concessions. On the anniversary of her September 2 initiative on the property issue, she announced that she was firing the Sandinista head of military intelligence, Lenin Cerna. She also affirmed that she would replace Humberto Ortega as chief of the armed forces in 1994, and she sent to the National Assembly a new military code strengthening civilian control over the armed forces. That produced a strong statement of support for Chamorro from the White House.[48]

Two months later, after a December 1993 summit meeting with the Central American presidents, Clinton released the $40 million on the grounds that Chamorro had made substantial progress on the issues of concern to Washington. Congressional Republicans protested the decision.[49] In April 1994, they were able to add to the FY 1994–95 Foreign Assistance Authorization (PL 103–236) a prohibition on aid to any country that expropriated the property of U.S. citizens unless the president signed a waiver that continued aid was in the national interest. President Clinton signed waivers for Nicaragua in 1994 and 1995, arguing that continued aid was essential to consolidate Nicaraguan democracy.[50]

On February 21, 1995, Humberto Ortega retired as chief of the armed forces, replaced by the army's chief of staff, Maj. Gen. Joaquin Cuadra—also a Sandinista veteran but one with a reputation for political moderation.[51] Senator Helms nevertheless continued to press for a cut-off of aid to Nicaragua because Chamorro's government had not yet settled all the property claims of U.S. citizens—a cause he was able to press far more effectively as the new chairman of the Senate Foreign Relations Committee in the Republican-dominated Congress.[52]

Real progress began to be made on the property issue in the summer of 1995. As of June, the Nicaraguan government had approved compensation for 19 percent of all property claims, and fully 40 percent of claims by U.S. citizens had been resolved, as the government settled U.S. claims at the rate of about 50 per month.[53] In July former President Jimmy Carter hosted a conference of Nicaraguans from all the major political parties and interested social sectors, with the aim of establishing some consensual basis for moving forward. The participants generally agreed to safeguard the rights of small farmers and workers who benefited from the Sandinista agrarian and urban reforms, while compensating former owners of those properties.[54] President Chamorro responded warmly to the Carter initiative, incorporating most of his recommendations into draft laws that she submitted to the National Assembly.[55]

A compromise was finally achieved in November 1995 when the National Assembly passed a government-sponsored bill to safeguard the rights of small farmers and urban workers who benefited from Sandinista reforms, while at the same time guaranteeing that prior owners would be fairly compensated. The law ratified the titles of small holders and provided for compensating prior owners through government bonds backed by proceeds from the partial privatization of the telephone company. Larger holdings—typically properties handed out to Sandinista officials during "La Piñata"—would have to be purchased by the occupants within five years or they would be returned to the original owners.[56]

By mid-1995 Chamorro had also made considerable, albeit gradual, progress on civilian control of the armed forces. The replacement of senior Sandinista officials, including head of military intelligence Lenin Cerna and armed forces chief Humberto Ortega, removed people who were symbols of the politicization of the military during the conflicts of the 1980s. The people who replaced them, despite their own Sandinista roots, were less divisive personalities and took further steps to separate the armed forces from partisan politics. These personnel changes, combined with the new military code, gave the civilian government greater de jure and de facto control over the armed forces than at any time since 1990.

Without gainsaying the importance of the three issues that preoccupied U.S. policy toward Nicaragua in the post-Sandinista period—civilian control of the military, human rights, and property rights—many observers sensed that the debate was motivated at least in part by animosities dating back to the 1980s. Clinton's First Assistant Secretary of State for Inter-American Affairs Alexander Watson suggested as much when he referred to the conflict between Clinton and congressional Republicans over Nicaragua as "an old problem . . . which is, in many ways, an inheritance of the cold war."[57] Senator Helms, after all, had been trying to cut off U.S. aid to Nicaragua since President Carter's earliest efforts to assist the new Sandinista government in 1979.

The Clinton administration sought to disengage the United States from partisan domestic disputes within the Central American polities. In Nicaragua, that meant an unwillingness to take sides among bickering factions, and Clinton retreated from Bush's policy of trying to undermine the political influence of the Sandinistas. Congressional Republicans, by contrast, seemed intent on backing Nicaraguan conservatives.

Despite this ongoing policy dispute, one fact of U.S. policy was unavoidable: Whatever conditions Congress or the executive placed on U.S. aid to

Nicaragua, such aid became less and less. The Chamorro government, which received almost $300 million in 1990 after the Sandinistas lost the election, was slated for only $39 million in fiscal year 1996. Both Bush and Clinton used aid suspensions to extract concessions from Nicaragua, but the stick was getting smaller and smaller.[58]

The history of Violeta Chamorro's presidency was a cautionary tale for U.S. policy. A government initially sponsored to a significant degree by the United States nevertheless had serious policy conflicts with Washington. One lesson is that the transition from a socialist or quasisocialist regime to one committed to the market and private enterprise is complex and takes time to work through. The property issue is exemplary: Although the Sandinistas held power for only a decade and expropriated less than half the country's assets, sorting out the property issue has been fiendishly difficult, both technically and politically.

The pace of transition may be especially slow when socialists retain a significant popular constituency and important posts in the government bureaucracy, as the Sandinistas did during most of the Chamorro presidency. Under such conditions, change is likely to be incremental and the product of political compromises. It is likely to move much more slowly than the United States might prefer. If the United States pushes for an accelerated pace of change, it may risk upsetting the fragile political balance, with the attendant danger of political instability.

Finally, one of the hallmarks of a democratic polity is that leaders must be responsive to constituents on pain of political extinction. On a number of occasions, Chamorro crafted policies in ways designed to satisfy domestic constituencies, to maintain a working majority in the National Assembly, and to advance her overall goal of national reconciliation. Sometimes the result was policies that made the United States uncomfortable—especially her cooperation with the Sandinistas. To some in Washington, especially Senator Helms, Chamorro appeared to be consorting with the enemy. The lesson, however, is that democratic governments will almost always respond to domestic political dynamics first, international demands second. Washington would do well to practice patience and tolerance if it hopes to see such governments flourish.

Notes

1. On Sandino and the rise of Somoza, see Neill Macaulay, *The Sandino Affair* (Chicago: Quadrangle Books, 1971); Gregorio Selser, *Sandino* (New York: Monthly Review, 1981). The best history of the relationship between Somoza and the United States is Richard Millet, *Guardians of the Dynasty* (Maryknoll, N.Y.: Orbis Books, 1977). On

the ideology and background of the FSLN, see Dennis Gilbert, *Sandinistas: The Party and the Revolution* (New York: Basil Blackwell, 1988).

2. Robert A. Pastor, *Condemned to Repetition: The United States and Nicaragua* (Princeton: Princeton University Press, 1987).

3. On Carter's policy toward Nicaragua, see William M. LeoGrande, "The United States and the Nicaraguan Revolution," in *Nicaragua in Revolution*, ed. Thomas W. Walker (New York: Praeger, 1982), pp. 63–78.

4. On Reagan's policy, see William M. LeoGrande, "The United States and Nicaragua," in *Nicaragua: The First Five Years*, ed. Thomas W. Walker (New York: Praeger, 1985), pp. 425–46; Roy Gutman, *Banana Diplomacy: The Making of American Policy in Nicaragua 1981–1987* (New York: Simon and Schuster, 1988). On the contra war specifically, see Christopher Dickey, *With the Contras: A Reporter in the Wilds of Nicaragua* (New York: Simon and Schuster, 1985); Peter Kornbluh, *Nicaragua: The Price of Intervention* (Washington, D.C.: Institute for Policy Studies, 1987). On U.S. economic sanctions, see Michael E. Conroy, "Economic Aggression as an Instrument of Low Intensity Conflict," in *Reagan Versus the Sandinistas: The Undeclared War on Nicaragua*, ed. Thomas W. Walker (Boulder, Colo.: Westview, 1987), pp. 57–79.

5. Gutman, *Banana Diplomacy*, passim.

6. On congressional resistance to Reagan's policy, see William M. LeoGrande, "The Contras and Congress," in *Reagan Versus the Sandinistas*, ed. Walker, pp. 202–27; Cynthia J. Arnson, *Crossroads: Congress, the President, and Central America, 1976–1993* (University Park, Pa.: Penn State Press, 1993). On North's activities, see U.S. Congress, *Report of the Congressional Committees Investigating the Iran-Contra Affair*, H. Rept. 100–433, S. Rept. no. 100–216, 100th Congress, 1st session, November 17, 1987 (Washington, D.C.: Government Printing Office, 1988).

7. The National Bipartisan Commission on Central America, chaired by Henry Kissinger, presented the fullest rationale for administration policy, and it, too, focused most heavily on security as a rationale for U.S. involvement. *Report of the National Bipartisan Commission on Central America*, January 1984 (Washington, D.C.: Government Printing Office, 1983).

8. LeoGrande, "The Contras and Congress," pp. 202–27.

9. William M. LeoGrande, *Public Opinion and Central America* (Washington, D.C.: Washington Office on Latin America, 1984).

10. Reagan's Assistant Secretary of State for Inter-American Affairs Elliott Abrams said as much at a conference on Nicaragua at Princeton University in May 1990.

11. For a history of diplomatic efforts to resolve the U.S.-Nicaraguan conflict, see William M. LeoGrande, "Rollback or Containment: Nicaragua, the United States, and the Search for Peace," *International Security* 11, no. 2 (Fall 1986), pp. 89–120. The text of the Esquipulas agreement is in *Procedimiento para establecer la paz firme y duradera en centroamérica* (San José, Costa Rica: Oficina de Apoyo de la Presidencia de la República, 1987).

12. "U.S. Support for Democracy and Peace in Central America," *Selected Documents* no. 36 (Washington, D.C.: Department of State, 1989), includes the text of the

bipartisan accord and remarks by President Bush and Secretary Baker at the press conference announcing it. The senior official is quoted in Don Bohning, "On Latin Policy, the Administration Remains Adrift," *Miami Herald,* May 7, 1989.

13. Ann Devroy, "Bipartisan Accord Reached on Contras," *Washington Post,* March 25, 1989.

14. See, for example, Doyle McManus, "Baker Urges Western Europe to Pressure Nicaragua," *Los Angeles Times,* February 14, 1989.

15. Doyle McManus, "New U.S. Policy on Contras Told," *Miami Herald,* March 25, 1989.

16. Nina M. Serafino, "Nicaragua Chronology since the February 25, 1990, Elections: The Transition and President Chamorro's First 100 Days," *CRS Report for Congress,* September 5, 1990 (Washington, D.C.: Congressional Research Service, 1990), p. 1; Jacqueline Sharkey, "Nicaragua: Anatomy of an Election," *Common Cause,* May–June 1990.

17. Robert Pear, "Clash of Experts Blurs Policy on Central America," *New York Times,* August 24, 1989.

18. "Results of the February 25, 1990 Election," *Barricada International* (Managua, Nicaragua) March 10, 1990.

19. Mark A. Uhlig, "Cease-Fire Begins in Nicaragua as the Contras Agree to Disarm," *New York Times,* April 20, 1990.

20. Lawrence Eagleburger, "U.S. Assistance to Panama, Nicaragua," *Current Policy,* no. 1264 (Washington, D.C.: U.S. Department of State, 1990); Martin McReynolds, "U.S. Lifts Managua Trade Embargo," *Miami Herald,* March 14, 1990.

21. Lee Hockstader, "Chamorro Takes Office in Managua," *Washington Post,* April 26, 1990.

22. The key passages from the March 27, 1990, agreement are in Appendix V of Nina M. Serafino, "Nicaraguan Elections and Transition: Issues for U.S. Policy," *CRS Report for Congress,* (Washington, D.C.: Library of Congress Congressional Research Service, 1990).

23. George R. Vickers and Jack Spence, "Nicaragua: Two Years after the Fall," *World Policy Journal* 9 (Summer 1992), pp. 533–62. In 1995, the Sandinistas themselves split into two parties—see n.35.

24. Mark A. Uhlig, "Choice in Managua for Military Chief Sets Off Furor," *New York Times,* April 25, 1990.

25. Clifford Krauss, "Nicaraguan Says Arms Still Flow," *New York Times,* June 20, 1990.

26. Associated Press, "Arms to Be Returned, Managua Says," *New York Times,* February 3, 1991.

27. Tim Johnson, "Chamorro's Control Is Questioned," *Miami Herald,* May 25, 1993.

28. Report on Nicaraguan human rights practices during 1994, in U.S. Department of State, *Country Reports on Human Rights Practices for 1994* (Washington, D.C.: U.S. Government Printing Office, 1995); also available on-line as "Nicaraguan Human Rights Practices, 1994," on the Department of State Foreign Areas Network (DOSFAN) at gopher://dosfan.lib.uic.edu.

29. Shirley Christian, "Killing of Leader Angers Ex-Contras," *New York Times*, March 3, 1991; Tim Johnson, "Activists Murder Stuns Nicaragua," *Miami Herald*, November 24, 1992; "Nicaraguan Human Rights Practices, 1994," DOSFAN.

30. Shirley Christian, "Managua Army Chief May Face Trial in 1990 Killing," *New York Times*, July 4, 1992; "Nicaraguan Human Rights Practices, 1994," DOSFAN.

31. For an excellent history of the property issue through 1992, see Washington Office on Latin America (WOLA), "U.S. Policy and Property Rights in Nicaragua: Undermining the Search for Consensus," in *Nicaragua Issue Brief Number Two, December 1992* (Washington, D.C.: WOLA, 1992). Key excerpts from the Transition Protocol are in Serafino, *Nicaraguan Elections and Transition: Issues for U.S. Policy*, pp. 29–30.

32. Government of Nicaragua, Ministry of Finance, *The Property Issue in Nicaragua: Advances and Challenges* (Managua, Nicaragua: Ministry of Finance, July 1995), p. 3.

33. WOLA, "U.S. Policy and Property Rights in Nicaragua," p. 21.

34. Shirley Christian, "Chamorro Upholds Sandinista Giveaway," *New York Times*, September 13, 1991.

35. In February 1995, after several years of internal wrangling, the Sandinista party formally split when the reformists left to create a party of their own—thereby making Nicaraguan politics a four-way rather than a three-way contest. The reformists had been pressing the leadership for a number of policy changes—more internal party democracy, a less "orthodox" socialist appeal to potential voters, and repudiation of the "Piñata." After being defeated at the FSLN's May 1994 party congress, the reform wing was increasingly marginalized within the party by the orthodox wing, led by Daniel Ortega. Finally, Sergio Ramirez, Dora Maria Tellez, Luis Carrion, and others quit the party to form the Sandinista Renovation Movement. Francois Houtart, "Crisis in the FSLN: Class Conflict," *Envio* (Managua, Nicaragua) 13, no. 158 (September 1994), pp. 26–31; Tracy Wilkinson, "Post-Cold War Identity Crisis Locks Sandinistas in Bitter Power Struggle," *Los Angeles Times*, December 13, 1994; "Three Sandinista Moderates Resign, Join Rival Party," *Miami Herald*, February 4, 1995.

36. *Report of a Property Issues Conference*, Working Paper Series, Carter Center of Emory University (Atlanta: Carter Center, 1995), p. 4; U.S. Department of State, "Report on U.S. Investment Disputes in Nicaragua," Report to Congress pursuant to section 527(f) of the Foreign Relations Authorization Act, Fiscal Years 1994 and 1995, PL 103–236 (Washington, D.C.: typescript, 1994), pp. 1–2. See also Larry Rohter, "U.S. Prods Nicaragua on Seized Land," *New York Times*, July 25, 1995. International law does not allow a government to press the property claims of naturalized citizens who were not citizens when their property was expropriated. Nevertheless, U.S. policy has been to urge the Chamorro government to swiftly resolve all claims by U.S. citizens—and the Nicaraguan claims as well.

37. Government of Nicaragua, Ministry of Finance, *The Property Issue in Nicaragua: Advances and Challenges*, p. 5.

38. U.S. States Agency for International Development, *U.S. Overseas Grants and Loans and Assistance from International Organizations: Obligations and Loan Authorizations, 1945–1993* (Washington, D.C.: USAID, 1994), p. 105; Vickers and Spence,

"Nicaragua: Two Years after the Fall," *World Policy Journal* 9 (Summer 1992), pp. 533–62.

39. Letter to Ronald Roskens, U.S. Agency for International Development, from Senator Jesse Helms, May 27, 1992, reprinted in U.S. Senate, *Nicaragua Today, Republican Staff Report to the Committee on Foreign Relations,* S. Prt. 102–102, 102nd Congress, 2nd Session, August 1992 (Washington, D.C.: U.S. Government Printing Office, 1992), p. 142.

40. WOLA, "U.S. Policy and Property Rights in Nicaragua," pp. 24–25.

41. Douglas Farah, "Chamorro Replaces Sandinista Police Chief, 11 Others," *Washington Post,* September 6, 1992.

42. Tim Johnson, "Nicaragua: Saved by New U.S. Aid?" *Miami Herald,* December 4, 1992.

43. Christopher Marquis, "U.S. Releases Aid to Nicaragua, But Strings May Be Attached," *Miami Herald,* April 3, 1993; Christopher Marquis, "Nicaragua Still Looking to U.S. for Answers," *Miami Herald,* May 17, 1993.

44. Tim Johnson, "New U.S. Policy on Nicaragua: 'Fix Your Own Problems,'" *Miami Herald,* January 30, 1994. See also the speech by Assistant Secretary of State for Inter-American Affairs Alexander F. Watson, "Key Issues in Inter-American Relations," *U.S. State Department Dispatch,* January 17, 1994.

45. K. Larry Storrs, Mark P. Sullivan, and Maureen Taft-Morales, "Congress and Policy toward Latin America in 1992," *CRS Report for Congress,* October 15, 1993 (Washington, D.C.: Congressional Research Service, 1993), pp. 20–21.

46. PL 103–87 (September 30, 1993), described in K. Larry Storrs and Maureen Taft-Morales, *Nicaragua: Background and U.S. Policy Concerns"* (Washington, D.C.: Congressional Research Service, 1994), pp. 5–6.

47. Christopher Marquis, "U.S. Demands Nicaraguan Reforms as Condition to Aid," *Miami Herald,* August 13, 1993.

48. Tim Golden, "Nicaraguan Leader Reaffirms Plan to Oust General," *New York Times,* September 4, 1993; White House Office of the Press Secretary, statement of September 3, 1993, on Nicaragua, available on-line through DOSFAN at gopher://dosfan.lib.uic.edu.

49. White House Office of the Press Secretary, "Press Conference [President Clinton and the presidents of Central America]," November 30, 1993, available on-line through DOSFAN at gopher://dosfan.lib.uic.edu; "U.S. Senators Protest Freeing Aid to Managua," *Miami Herald,* December 16, 1993.

50. Storrs and Taft-Morales, "Nicaragua: Background and U.S. Policy Concerns," p. 6.

51. John Otis, "As Another Ortega Steps Down, Sandinistas' Old Guard Fades," *Miami Herald,* February 19, 1995.

52. Larry Rohter, "U.S. Prods Nicaragua on Seized Land," *New York Times,* July 25, 1995.

53. *Report of a Property Issues Conference,* p. 4.

54. Ibid.

55. Letter of transmittal from President Violeta Chamorro to President of the National Assembly Luis Humberto Guzmán, July 17, 1995, and accompanying draft laws

on urban property, rural property, and the privatization of the telephone company, TELCOR.

56. Dan Trotta, "Nicaraguan Leader Signs Compromise on Property Row," Reuters Wire Service, November 30, 1995.

57. Watson, "Key Issues in Inter-American Relations," *U.S. State Department Dispatch*, January 17, 1994.

58. U.S. Agency for International Development, *FY 1996 U.S. Economic and Military Assistance Request*, Table 4C, Congressional Presentation Documents for FY 1996, p. 26.

5

Vietnam

Detours on the Road to Normalization

RICHARD T. CHILDRESS AND STEPHEN J. SOLARZ

The difficulty in writing or speaking about Vietnam is its larger-than-life quality in the American psyche. The Vietnam experience has, like a metastasizing cancer, infiltrated our culture, our politics, and our policy in a way that many Americans do not even consciously recognize. Since the end of the Vietnam War, it has been a touchstone of every debate on the use of U.S. military force or political power internationally, and it has generated a rewrite of military strategy and tactics. The war spawned an entire Hollywood and television film type. It changed the way we view veterans and veterans' issues, and it created legislation. The Vietnam War also has been blamed variously for inflation, partisanship, the crime rate, drug use, and the destruction of civility in our political discourse. America has even extended this phenomenon internationally by defining the experience of others in terms Vietnamese. Afghanistan becomes Russia's Vietnam, and Cambodia was seen as Vietnam's Vietnam.

Culturally, Vietnam has almost become a hyphenated word. When the word *Vietnam* is used, it is almost invariably linked with the word *healing*. Refugee issues, humanitarian disaster relief, POW-MIA (prisoners of war and those missing in action), Agent Orange, nongovernmental projects in Vietnam, veterans' benefits, normalization of relations—even commercial and trade issues with Vietnam, which in any other context would be evaluated on their intrinsic merits—all become intertwined with the concept of healing. How much real healing is actually needed, as well as where and by whom, is seldom addressed. The process itself consumes more attention than the merits of the issues, whether referring to individual or group healing on either side of the Pacific.

It is beyond our scope here to deal with this phenomenon in detail, nor can we address in depth the intricate path of reaching a Cambodian settlement, Vietnam's relations with others, or Vietnam's own fears and challenges. These factors are discussed here only in the context of how they affected a stage of dialogue and negotiations between the United States and Vietnam on the normalization path.

Despite the significant steps taken by the Clinton administration, full normalization of relations still looks arduous to us, given the significant opposition in Congress and the continued reluctance by Vietnam to be fully forthcoming on the POW-MIA issue and to pursue political reform.

INTRODUCTION

In the sometimes arcane world of state-to-state relations, the media, the public, and some executive and congressional branch practitioners become confused over both the terminology and the context of "normal" relations. Various terms are sometimes used interchangeably in public policy debate: normalization, diplomatic recognition, and recognition of sovereignty; financial aid; commercial, trade, and consular relations; cultural exchanges; and gradients of each. The debate is often conducted with seemingly little or no regard to the significance of these relationships for the national interests or goals of the respective parties. The current or historical state of such relationships is not always considered rationally; how each nation views the relationship is not always judged objectively; and the mechanics of molding the relationship with policy tools are frequently misunderstood. The domestic pressures and subsequent policy decisions that result can have unintended consequences. Mistakes in the process may then become after-the-fact justifications for new policy steps.

In an ideal world, one might argue that a diplomatic presence does not imply approval of a state's policies and is no more than a channel for dialogue that could influence policy toward achieving U.S. objectives. But diplomatic recognition is, in reality, a powerful symbolic act that is interpreted in practice as partial approval, at least, of a receiving state's national policy, just as the withdrawal or withholding of recognition is seen as a statement of disapproval. After several interim steps, on July 11, 1995, President Clinton announced the establishment of diplomatic relations with Vietnam, but full normalization has not arrived.

The end of the Vietnam War resulted in the termination of almost all forms of recognition and official contact between the United States and Vietnam, and President Clinton's latest announcement was a part of a series of moves by the administration to normalize relations. After the imposition of a broad range of embargoes at the end of the war, U.S.-Vietnam negotiations had been based primarily upon the prospect of easing official U.S. restrictions as negotiating tools. Such movement was in the context of both actual and hoped-for positive responses from Vietnam on issues of concern to the United States, primarily the POW-MIA issue, on regional security matters affecting U.S. friends and allies in Southeast Asia, and on international negotiations.

The pace and scope at which incentives were provided by the United States was directly affected by real and perceived positive movement on U.S. objectives, changes in administrations, domestic and international pressures, and Vietnamese negotiating behavior, based on the view that negotiations are simply an extension of the revolutionary struggle. While popularly accepted commentary would lead to the conclusion that U.S.-Vietnam relations were essentially frozen from 1975 until the Clinton administration, significant dialogue was in fact conducted at high levels. It led to increased understanding on both sides concerning respective goals and strategies, progress on U.S. bilateral concerns, including POW-MIA accountability, the release of Vietnamese citizens in reeducation camps, orderly departure of Vietnamese refugees and Amerasians, the Vietnamese withdrawal from Cambodia, and development of a framework for a political settlement in that country in the early 1990s.

All of this progress took place in the absence of diplomatic, consular, or commercial relations. While these contacts brought significant forward movement on U.S. goals, progress was difficult. Interruptions were frequent, both because of U.S. naivete in acceptance of Vietnamese assertions of goodwill and because of Vietnamese intransigence. Further, even though the bilateral trade embargo has now been lifted, diplomatic relations established, and claims and property issues settled, significant challenges and obstacles remain.

THE HISTORICAL CONTEXT

The withdrawal of U.S. forces from Vietnam in 1973, followed by North Vietnamese violations of the Paris Peace Accords, the acrimonious debate in the United States on how to respond to the deepening crisis faced by the South, and the suspension of U.S. aid were obviously no match for the revolutionary and nationalist determination of North Vietnam. The combination led inexorably to the fall of Saigon in April 1975. North Vietnam confidently ignored protests against its military invasion of South Vietnam, and after the collapse it unrealistically called for fulfillment of U.S. pledges in the Paris Peace Accords. These demands included reconstruction aid from the United States, which had been linked to successful implementation of the agreements to end the war. Vietnam portrayed such pledges as deserved penance.

The Ford administration responded to the fall of South Vietnam by immediately applying the same level of wartime sanctions to the entire country that had been applied previously to the North: It seized all Vietnamese assets in the United States, rejected all calls for aid, and vetoed multiple Vietnamese requests for membership in the UN. Objections lodged by the United States included Vietnam's broad violation of the Paris agreements, highlighting the POW-MIA issue.

The events of 1975 also shook the confidence of the noncommunist Southeast Asia states as they collectively doubted U.S. resolve in the war's aftermath. They had a rational basis to suspect the long-range intentions of North Vietnam, as it crowed about its historic victory while maintaining the largest standing army in Southeast Asia, and support to regional insurgencies mushroomed. In response, some of the noncommunist countries in the region made various adjustments that included normalization of relations with the People's Republic of China (P.R.C.), a distancing from U.S. containment policy, and internal political change. Others outside Southeast Asia felt the effects as well and reevaluated their policies toward the Soviet Union, the P.R.C., and the United States.

The North's conquest of South Vietnam enabled the one-party totalitarian Marxist-based system in Hanoi to consolidate control throughout Vietnam. It also generated one of the most tragic human diasporas in history. Almost 2 million Indochinese fled by sea and land, and that number may be conservative. Summary executions ensued, an unknown number perished at sea or during overland flight, and tens of thousands were put into reeducation camps in Vietnam. The North Vietnamese march toward Saigon also accelerated the fall of Cambodia to Vietnam's Khmer Rouge allies, led by the infamous butcher Pol Pot, although Cambodia fell shortly before South Vietnam. The resulting tragedy was a genocidal policy in Cambodia in proportions that shook even the most ardent, idealistic supporters of the Vietnamese communists and the Khmer Rouge. These events also led eventually to a consolidation of political control over Laos by the Vietnamese-supported Pathet Lao Party.

This rolling tragedy had a major impact on the American body politic, generating the mostly unproductive debate over who lost Vietnam and turning policy making toward Vietnam into a continuing challenge for more than two decades. Those who supported U.S. involvement, and who had warned about the nature of international communist links and Hanoi's intentions toward the South and Indochina as a whole, pointed to the tragedy as predictable and placed blame on those who opposed U.S. involvement. Those in the opposition similarly pointed fingers, blaming U.S. policy for escalating what they viewed as a remote civil war centered on Asian nationalism into an East-West conflict that caused the ultimate cataclysm. However, most Americans, with the exception of the domestic political combatants, the families of those still missing, some veterans, and the new Indochinese refugees, tried to put the experience behind them and turned their interest to other issues.

THE NEGOTIATING GAUNTLET

"Healing the wounds of war" became a driving domestic and international imperative for the Carter administration as it assumed office in 1976. Domestically, President Carter's first major act was to pardon the ten thousand Vietnam War draft evaders and allow thousands to upgrade discharges that stemmed from protesting and resisting the war. Carter policy makers also believed that positive gestures from the United States, in response to calls from Hanoi for normalization, would heal domestic wounds, lead to greater regional stability, and limit Vietnamese ambitions.

Initiatives directed at both Vietnam and a domestic audience included appointing a POW-MIA commission, headed by United Auto Workers president Leonard Woodcock, which traveled to Vietnam. In a White House letter from the national security adviser on March 16, 1977, to the National League of Families, the mandate of the Woodcock Commission was "to obtain the best possible accounting for MIAs and the return of the remains of our dead." The commission also had a mandate "to receive from these governments [Vietnam and Laos] their views on matters affecting our mutual relations." Carter administration officials announced they would enter into bilateral talks with the Vietnamese. They also allowed the restrictions on travel to Vietnam to expire, informed the Vietnamese that the United States would no longer oppose their admission to the UN, and proposed reestablishment of diplomatic relations, to be followed by the lifting of the trade embargo.

Some warned that such a policy was fatally flawed from the beginning because the Vietnamese, flush with victory, would pocket the gains and demand more. Vietnamese intentions in the region were suspect, and Congress was deeply split. Further, the Woodcock Commission relied on the majority opinion of the newly published *Report of the House Select Committee on Missing Persons in Southeast Asia*. This report significantly downplayed Vietnam's ability to account for POW-MIAs, and the administration ignored a serious split in the committee over that question. Carter officials informed the National League of Families board of directors that POW-MIA accounting was a hoped-for byproduct of the normalization process. The administration raised domestic expectations that the Vietnamese would "come clean" to the Woodcock Commission. The White House letter to the National League of Families went so far as to express the hope that in a three-day trip to Vietnam, the commission would "bring back an adequate accounting of our fellow countrymen who were lost in the war."

A reading of the commission's conclusions indicate a clear acceptance of Vietnamese "goodwill and assertions." However, the only concrete response to the commission was the return of the remains of twelve servicemen, accompanied by denials that significant information was available on MIAs. (It was subsequently learned that the American PFC Robert Garwood, later convicted by court-martial for collaboration with the enemy, was alive in Vietnam at the time of the Woodcock Commission's visit in March 1977. Of the remains of thirty-three Americans returned in 1977, including the twelve turned over to the commission, all had been held in storage by the Hanoi government. In addition, Tucker Gougelmann and Arlo Gay, American civilians, had been in captivity when the House Select Committee traveled to Hanoi in December 1975. Gay was released the following year, but Gougelmann died of brutality and dysentery while in captivity between the Select Committee's visit and that of the Woodcock Commission.) In a press conference on March 29, 1977, President Carter then publicly stated that as far as he could discern, the Vietnamese "have acted in good faith."

The Vietnamese miscalculated badly during the 1977 bilateral talks with the commission. They initially refused to provide more information on MIAs or to establish diplomatic relations unless they received billions of dollars in reconstruction aid. Suddenly, the Vietnamese were the reluctant party and the United States was the supplicant. Congress reacted strongly against providing aid to Vietnam, and both houses of Congress passed resolutions to that effect.

In 1978 the worst fears about Vietnam's strategic intentions came to fruition as the Hanoi leadership fully aligned its political, military, and economic policies with Moscow. This move further disquieted the members of the Association of Southeast Asian Nations (ASEAN) and sent Sino-Vietnamese relations into a downward spiral. Unmoved, Vietnam began expelling several hundred thousand of its citizens. It invaded Cambodia and established its own Cambodian leadership in Phnom Penh in January 1979, replacing the infamous Pol Pot (whose allegiances by this time had shifted toward Beijing). In his place the Vietnamese installed former Khmer Rouge officials who had split from Pol Pot's faction.

Officials in the Carter administration were stung by Vietnamese rejection of initiatives they had developed in the face of domestic political opposition. Their attention turned toward organizing resistance (including the Khmer Rouge) to the Vietnamese occupation of Cambodia in coordination with ASEAN, the P.R.C., and the international community. Simultaneously, the administration had to cope with the Vietnamese-induced refugee crises engulfing all of Indochina and alarming the first ASEAN countries where refugees sought asylum. In the late 1970s, the United States became the leader of an international effort to resettle Indochina refugees, an effort that has spanned almost two decades. These developments effectively ended substantive U.S.-Vietnamese contact for almost two years until the Reagan administration.

The clear skepticism in the Carter administration that Vietnam could be still holding Americans captive was shaken by two events—the return of PFC Garwood alive, followed by congressional testimony in June 1981 by the retiring director of the Defense Intelligence Agency, Gen. Eugene Tighe. When pressed for his personal views at a hearing before the House Subcommittee on Asian and Pacific Affairs, General Tighe indicated that the weight of evidence had convinced him that Americans were alive and being held against their will in Indochina. Such testimony from a credible witness could neither be dismissed nor ignored by Congress. It also reinforced the new position of the Reagan administration that precluded ruling out the possibility that Americans were still held captive in Indochina.

No greater contrast in policy toward Vietnam could be drawn than a comparison of the first year in office of Presidents Carter and Reagan. Before assuming office, Reagan had publicly criticized the Carter administration policy toward Vietnam and viewed Vietnam in the cold war prism. Reagan opposed any normalization with Vietnam until the POW-MIA issue was resolved and Vietnamese forces had totally withdrawn from Cambodia. This stance reflected not only the administration's view of Vietnam in the cold war context but also the clearly held view that Vietnam was still a danger regionally and that the Vietnam War had been lost at home by incremental policy decisions and mismanagement.

Inherent in the administration's stance, however, was the willingness to reopen dialogue with Vietnam on POW-MIAs and on refugees, both as humanitarian issues unrelated to normalization. In 1981, after a three-year gap, Vietnam resumed cooperating on POW-MIAs by returning the remains of three Americans that also showed evidence of storage.

After a thorough National Security Council (NSC) staff study of the entire history of Vietnam-related issues, including a review of negotiations and other records in each of the presidential libraries, the Reagan administration implemented a multipronged strategy to resolve the POW-MIA issue and adopted a policy of presumptive refugee status for many of the Indochinese fleeing the region. The administration also provided humanitarian and other nonlethal assistance to the noncommunist elements resisting the Vietnamese-installed government in Cambodia, and it began to distance itself from the Khmer Rouge faction of the resistance.

The initial strategy on POW-MIAs included a public awareness program; full integration of the National League of POW-MIA Families' representative into the POW-MIA Interagency Group (IAG); a tripling of manpower in the Joint Casualty Resolution Center, the Defense Intelligence Agency POW-MIA office, and the Central Identification Laboratory; an upgrade in intelligence priorities; repeated diplomatic initiatives to other nations requesting them to urge greater Vietnamese cooperation; closer bipartisan consultation with the Congress; reopening of negotiations on a humanitarian basis with Vietnam and Laos; and opposition to private, irresponsible POW-MIA activities, such as cross-border forays. Negotiations were focused on resolving the live prisoner issue through an admission of their existence and on the repatriation of remains being held by Vietnam.

After interagency coordination, structured and limited talks were agreed upon, and in 1982 delegations at the deputy assistant secretary level went to both Vietnam and Laos. Unfortunately, the initial 1982 delegation led by Deputy Assistant Secretary of Defense Richard Armitage was received at a low level, and the Vietnamese did not respond to the modest requests for accelerated technical talks. That same year the administration supported the first National League of Families trip since 1975 to both countries. President Reagan then approved quiet dialogue in New York at the National Security Council staff level with politburo member and Foreign Minister Nguyen Co Thach, the highest-level meeting since 1977. The dinner meeting, facilitated by the League of Families, was intended to set the stage for serious policy agreements on the POW-MIA issue and for higher-level dialogue if it was determined that Hanoi had serious intentions of resolving the POW-MIA issue on a humanitarian basis. It was at this meeting that the Vietnamese first indicated they would treat the POW-MIA issue as humanitarian, and understandings were reached on the return of remains being held by Hanoi. This meeting led to a series of subsequent policy-level meetings in both Hanoi and New York City.

Overall, the first term of the Reagan administration was marked by significantly increased dialogue with the Vietnamese, on a disciplined and circumscribed basis, to resolve bilateral humanitarian issues and facilitate multilateral contacts on refugees. In addition, heightened public awareness of the POW-MIA issue became evident, Vietnam returned the remains of twenty-one servicemen, agreement with Vietnam for joint crash site investigations was reached, a road map to improve relations beginning with POW-MIAs was provided to the Lao, and the groundwork was established for what was hoped would be agreement by the Vietnamese to resolve the POW-MIA issue through a joint technical plan.

The internment of Vietnamese citizens in reeducation camps in Vietnam was particularly disturbing to Reagan officials, and securing their release became a major priority. Attempts made to structure an interview process, with orderly release and departure, were met with unacceptable conditions. The Vietnamese not only insisted on a public declaration to resettle everyone immediately in the United States but, further, that the United States would guarantee that those released and resettled would not oppose the Vietnamese government. The latter request was rejected out of hand by reminding the Vietnamese that the U.S. system of government precluded such restrictions. President Reagan announced in 1984 that the United States would accept all reeducation internees and their families. In addition, the administration designated special yearly quotas for reeducation inmates in reaction to Vietnamese objections that U.S. priorities would take quotas from other Vietnamese citizens who were not incarcerated but whom they wished to emigrate.

The Vietnamese began to release some internees, but restrictions on civil liberties and employment forced many to seek their way out of Vietnam through the Orderly Departure Program (ODP) or by land and sea. It was not until the late 1980s that the orderly release and interview process was firmly established.

Due to President Reagan's personal interest in POW-MIAs and fears in the Department of State that ASEAN and others might be misled into believing the United States was embarking on a normalization process, negotiations with Vietnam in the Reagan administration were led primarily by the White House NSC staff and the Department of Defense. However, they included strong support from and full coordination with the Department of State, which was represented on many of the delegations. Visible ranking emissaries from State or Defense were used only when the administration felt such trips were necessary to seal agreements or to demonstrate to the Vietnamese that there was interagency policy agreement. NSC dialogue through eleven meetings between 1982 and 1987 was focused on POW-MIAs, but it also included significant discussions with the Vietnamese leadership on Cambodia and the necessary preconditions for a positive U.S.-Vietnamese relationship in the future. The central message was that humanitarian issues, if addressed early, would not become obstacles to improved relations after a Cambodian settlement. This message was reinforced by a letter from Secretary of State Shultz to Foreign

Minister Thach, hand-carried by the NSC to Hanoi. A Special National Intelligence Estimate (SNIE) completed in 1987 concluded that Vietnam could unilaterally account for hundreds of Americans by returning stored remains.

Cambodia remained a central obstacle to normalization of relations during Reagan's second term. Reagan policy vigorously opposed both the Vietnamese occupation of Cambodia and the return of the Khmer Rouge. This policy was strongly supported in the Congress as well. It included initiatives for direct aid to the Cambodian resistance but did not prevent continued U.S.-Vietnamese bilateral dialogue and negotiations on humanitarian issues, especially POW-MIAs.

It was in this environment, after more than two years of NSC staff negotiations in Hanoi and New York and after the largest repatriation of stored remains to date, that Vietnamese leaders stated they were ready to conclude a joint plan on a humanitarian basis to resolve the POW-MIA issue within two years. The IAG recommended and the NSC approved an open high-level mission to Hanoi. The delegation of senior IAG principals consisted of Assistant Secretary of State Paul Wolfowitz, Assistant Secretary of Defense Richard Armitage, NSC Director of Asian Affairs Richard Childress, and the executive director of the National League of Families, Ann Mills Griffiths. This delegation went to Vietnam in January 1986. Despite Vietnamese pledges to conclude such a joint plan on a humanitarian basis, the Vietnamese reneged on the agreement and linked the plan both to the establishment of a Vietnamese MIA office in Washington and to a U.S. dialogue with the Vietnamese-installed Cambodian government. Following this disappointment and a flurry of message traffic, in October 1986 an NSC-led delegation met again with senior Vietnamese officials in Hanoi and New York to break the deadlock and revive the plan, but it then became obvious to all that the initiative was dead.

The Reagan administration again regrouped. The NSC staff recommended that President Reagan openly appoint an envoy as the president's special representative on POW-MIAs and other humanitarian matters, including refugees, Amerasians, and reeducation camp internees. (It was intended that such an emissary would need to serve only six months to a year to reinstitutionalize the effort. However, negotiations with Vietnam have a tendency to become a morass, and the emissary served through the Bush administration.) The NSC formally approved the emissary proposal and an initiative to respond to Vietnamese humanitarian concerns in a more formalized manner, to include a Washington-sponsored nongovernmental organization (NGO) survey of Vietnamese prosthetics needs, along with official encouragement of greater NGO effort to respond to other humanitarian concerns in Vietnam. Further, an internal review was undertaken of bureaucratic obstacles to NGO projects in Vietnam. These initiatives, under the rubric of humanitarian reciprocity, were approved as a way to meet Vietnamese accusations that their relationship with the United States was a one-way street. Hanoi's complaints summarily ignored the obvious subsidies already provided by the United States for POW-MIA and refugee programs, as well as previous proposals for U.S. support to a two-year plan on the POW-MIA issue.

President Reagan approved the initiative in October 1986, and former chairman of the Joint Chiefs of Staff (JCS), Gen. John Vessey, agreed to serve and was appointed in January 1987. Because of the previous attempts at linkage to political issues by the Vietnamese, the administration decided to approach renewed dialogue carefully. It was agreed that an NSC-led delegation would advance a Vessey trip by traveling to Hanoi, but the Vietnamese delayed acceptance of the advance delegation until May 1987. Upon arrival, the NSC delegation was treated to a hostile diatribe and an obstinacy never before encountered, and the Vietnamese said they "saw nothing new" in the U.S. proposal. The Vietnamese were promptly informed by the NSC representative that the meeting was over and the president would be informed that Vietnam refused the initiative. Only then did the Vietnamese indicate that the proposal would be considered. A mission led by General Vessey, with unanimous support from both houses of Congress, finally went to Hanoi in August 1987.

General Vessey was accompanied by a full interagency delegation (NSC, Defense, State, JCS, and the National League of Families' executive director). The Vietnamese agreed to resume cooperation on POW-MIAs, and unilateral repatriation of the remains of Americans in large numbers again resumed several months later. Hanoi agreed again to joint investigations of compelling POW-MIA discrepancy cases, including incidents of Americans last known alive, cases of discrepancy in remains of the dead, and others that clearly indicated Vietnamese knowledge. While 1988 became another high point in obtaining accountability, the Vietnamese again attempted linkage to political matters and scaled back the repatriation of remains in 1989, the first year of the Bush administration.

President Bush assumed office as it was increasingly evident that Vietnam was serious about a complete withdrawal from Cambodia. The broad political climate was also more conducive to the possibility of fashioning an acceptable political settlement among the Cambodian parties with international guarantees. This accelerated higher-level U.S.-Vietnamese dialogue on regional and bilateral issues.

For the first time since the end of the war, a president included Vietnam in an inaugural address. On January 20, 1989, while noting that Vietnam was the cause of much bipartisan division in the nation, President Bush expressed the belief that it was time to move on. He then sent a direct message to Vietnam, as well as to terrorists: "There are today Americans held against their will in foreign lands and Americans who are unaccounted for. Assistance can be shown here, and will be long remembered. Goodwill begets goodwill."

President Bush publicly stated at the beginning of his administration what negotiators since 1982 had been encouraging the Vietnamese to conclude—that resolution of the POW-MIA issue was in their long-term interest as it would remove a major obstacle, thus giving the United States the flexibility to normalize relations in the context of a Cambodian settlement.

Official Bush administration policy was clearly set out in congressional testimony on November 17, 1989, to the Subcommittee on Asian/Pacific Affairs. Normalization was directly linked to a Vietnamese withdrawal and a political settlement in Cambodia, but the "pace and scope" of that relationship would depend on POW-MIA accountability. Unfortunately, the Vietnamese missed another opportunity and took up a familiar and tiresome litany of complaints. "Pace and scope" at that time had been understood to be linkage of POW-MIAs to the trade embargo, not diplomatic recognition. This linkage was to be eroded later as negotiating energy turned more toward Cambodia and away from sustained policy attention to bilateral issues.

Reacting to revived Vietnamese assertions that U.S.-Vietnamese cooperation was a "one-way street" and that the United States was always "raising the ante," plus the threat by Vietnam to withdraw from Cambodia with or without a political settlement, the Bush administration began to develop an approach, referred to as the Vietnamese road map, toward normalization of economic and political relations. It included preconditions for a Cambodia settlement, all of the Reagan-era criteria on POW-MIAs and other humanitarian issues, and steps that the United States would take in response to Vietnamese actions. Despite the fact that the road map encompassed Vietnamese objectives, the Vietnamese indicated after it was presented in April 1991 that they would neither accept nor reject the plan. Regardless of this official stance, Vietnam did resume cooperation in some areas, but not without unique pressures.

A significant change in the Vietnamese leadership took place during the period as well. Nguyen Co Thach, vice premier, foreign minister, and politburo member, was retired in July 1991. Thach had been at the Paris negotiations on ending the war and was the primary interlocutor with U.S. negotiators in the 1980s, when significant progress was made on the POW-MIA issue through unilateral Vietnamese action. During this period, as a long-standing member of the politburo, he was able to influence government-wide responses to include the Ministries of Defense and Interior. He was replaced by Nguyen Manh Cam, who was not a politburo member but as foreign minister became the designated senior interlocutor with the United States. Interestingly, the unilateral Vietnamese return of remains halted after Thach's departure, and the pattern has continued despite Cam's later elevation to the politburo.

Meanwhile, at least two private researchers, apparently selected by Vietnam in preference to official channels and eventually subsidized by the United States, in 1992 were provided access to Vietnamese archival material, including a storehouse of official Vietnamese photographs of U.S. personnel, some obviously taken after their deaths but others of Americans alive and in captivity. Some speculate that the Vietnamese purpose in this case was to demonstrate they had more information that might be provided if the United States would further alter its policy. Others speculate that it was simply an economic opportunity for Vietnamese officials who enjoyed requisite access to official records and archival material. Whatever the reason, allowing access to the archives was clearly done with the knowledge of the politburo. Some in the Bush administration recognized this as confirmation of further intelligence assessments in the 1989–92 time frame regarding the availability of American remains not yet repatriated and the nature and extensive volume of Vietnamese archives being withheld, despite earlier denials to previous negotiators, including presidential emissary General Vessey. Secretary of Defense Cheney and Deputy Secretary of State Eagleburger confronted the Vietnamese directly with the evidence and asked for unilateral Vietnamese response.

The Vietnamese subsequently turned over thousands of photos (mostly duplicating those provided to the private researchers) and agreed to joint archival research and a full program of joint field investigations. Euphoria again developed in Washington, in the belief that this was finally the long-sought politburo decision to provide full cooperation. The Vietnamese moves on POW-MIAs, combined with the progress on Cambodia, were hopeful signs. The administration implemented its planned expansion of manpower and resources to meet agreements for joint operations regarding POW-MIAs. The Joint Task Force–Full Accounting was formally opened in Hawaii under Commander-in-Chief, U.S. Pacific Command (CINCPAC), and a reorganization of POW-MIA responsibilities in the Defense Department was carried out as well.

Although unilateral repatriation of remains from Vietnam had halted and the Vietnamese had not responded to interventions in this regard, administration officials confidently announced a major breakthrough that had turned accountability for POW-MIAs into more of an auditing issue.

It was in this environment that the Bush administration began movement on the road map. It turned out to be premature since analysis showed that only 1 percent of the material turned over by the Vietnamese correlated with missing Americans. Further, Hanoi refused to respond to requests for information on those photographs depicting Americans in their custody after death. The reality has been painful. The more the United States learned, the more it confirmed previous assessments that Vietnam had held back information for years and that it continued to do so. The joint effort was able to determine that some Americans categorized as last known alive had perished, but evidence to reach such determinations also reinforced intelligence judgments that Vietnam could account for many of the missing through the return of their remains.

Phase I Vietnamese actions, according to the road map, included full cooperation on resolving the "last known alive" discrepancy cases, and, through unilateral efforts, rapid recovery and repatriation of all "recovered and recoverable" remains. U.S. actions were specified in six reciprocal steps, to include lifting the twenty-five-mile ban on Vietnamese travel from their UN mission, initiation of talks on normalization, relaxing embargo travel rules for groups including business delegations, preparations for a liaison office in Phnom Penh, announcement of a plan to ease the Cambodian embargo, and stating publicly U.S. concerns about Khmer Rouge genocide in Cambodia. The Bush administration implemented all of these "reciprocal" steps without full Vietnamese compliance with their obligations on the POW-MIA issue.

This slippery slope became a water slide because subsequent phases were contingent on completion of phase I and continued Vietnamese action on POW-MIA benchmarks. The Bush administration rapidly moved on the remaining U.S. provisions of the road map in phase II. Significantly, phase II called for Vietnam to have resolved *all* last known alive discrepancy cases and to have repatriated all remains readily available to them. To this date in the Clinton administration, these phase I and II objectives still have not been met by Vietnam. Bush administration moves took place in the context of significant and welcome Vietnamese cooperation on a Cambodian settlement, and State Department policy makers made this element the driving force in the road map. Thus, the original integrated approach of the road map was lost. By late 1993, the United States had fulfilled all of its promised reciprocal steps in phases I and II.

The Clinton administration inherited a policy and a trend, but this administration's approach was quite different from that of the past decade and looked back to a different time. In a Little Rock Veterans Day ceremony on November 11, 1992, President-elect Clinton indicated that as he had pledged during the campaign, "there would be no normalization of relations with any nation that is at all suspected of withholding any information on POW-MIA" and that he would make resolution a national priority before normalizing relations with Vietnam. After assuming office in January 1993, the administration said it would only move forward when there was the fullest possible accounting. In February the administration said it generally supported the road map policy and wanted a full accounting. On March 22, 1993, Secretary of State Warren Christopher, in an address before the Chicago Council of Foreign Relations, said that, of the two preconditions for normal relations (Cambodia and POW-MIAs), Vietnam had fulfilled its obligations on the first and "our administration will be assessing that progress [on POW-MIAs] very carefully to determine whether we can move further down the road, or down the road map, to use the technical term, toward normalization with Vietnam."

At a White House press conference on April 23, 1993, President Clinton said he "had to be guided [on POW-MIAs] by people who know a lot about this, and I confess to being much more heavily influenced by the families of the people whose lives were lost there or whose lives remain in question than by the commercial interests or the other things that seem so compelling in this moment. I just am very influenced by how the families feel." In May, at the Vietnam Veterans Memorial, the president said that POW-MIA was the central outstanding issue in U.S.-Vietnamese relations and renewed his pledge to the families of MIAs.

Thus, throughout the first four months of his administration, President Clinton carried forward the public commitments of Presidents Reagan and Bush, reaffirmed his campaign commitments, and endorsed the road map approach. Further, in a July 1993 statement, the White House firmly indicated that there would be no change in the trade embargo or further steps toward normalization without tangible progress on POW-MIAs. It laid down four criteria from the road map: unilateral remains repatriations by Vietnam, continued resolution of last known alive discrepancy cases, assistance in implementing trilateral cooperation with Laos, and accelerated access to Vietnamese archives.

Despite these pledges and the clear lack of response by Vietnam, after a Senate delegation led by Senator John Kerry recommended that the United States should move forward with Vietnam, the administration removed longstanding U.S. objections to international lending to clear Vietnam's arrears to international financial institutions. The move was opposed by all of the major veterans' groups, the National League of Families, the business community (which wanted the bilateral trade embargo lifted first), and many former Reagan-Bush officials familiar with the negotiating history. The opposition was not against normalization per se, but against the rationale and the loss of leverage. President Clinton again reiterated to the families that there would be no more movement to improve bilateral economic or political relations without tangible POW-MIA results. In the fall, despite a complete halt to Vietnamese unilateral action, the president eased some provisions of the bilateral trade embargo. A February 3, 1994, White House announcement by President Clinton to lift the embargo fully also signaled a significant move to establish a consular-level office in Hanoi. He stated, "These actions do not constitute a normalization of relationships [with Vietnam]" and "before that happens, we must have more progress, more cooperation and more answers [on POW-MIA]."

In May 1994, the administration further announced that consular-level liaison offices would be established in Washington and Hanoi in a few months. Thus, in the space of barely fourteen months, the Clinton administration moved through all of the phase III U.S. reciprocal actions on the road map without expected Vietnamese actions or compliance on the four POW-MIA criteria that President Clinton had outlined seven months prior. The administration's rapid movement to meet Vietnam's most important priorities (economic) was then justified as the best way to resolve the POW-MIA issue. President Clinton justified the establishment of full diplomatic relations on July 11, 1995, in terms of significant progress on POW-MIA accounting and domestic healing. It is not known whether the administration actually believed this or if it was the result of business and international pressure to put the POW-MIA issue secondary to moves toward normalization. Clearly, many in Congress believe the latter, since accountability has decreased in the Clinton administration, and the Vietnamese continue to withhold answers on core POW-MIA discrepancy cases, which should be the easiest for them to resolve unilaterally.

It should be noted that despite the Clinton administration's public rhetoric concerning POW-MIAs, it omitted the POW-MIA matter from the July 1994 annual report National Security Strategy of the United States. It abolished the POW-MIA Interagency Group that had been a focal point of Vietnam policy making for well over a decade, and formed an Indochina working group that excluded the National League of Families. Reducing intelligence priorities on the POW-MIA issue and downplaying a decade of intelligence studies that concluded Vietnam was capable of solving hundreds of cases, the Clinton administration decoupled POW-MIAs from policy negotiations in favor of delegations led by the deputy secretary of veterans affairs, while awkwardly including the assistant secretary of state for East Asia and Pacific as a delegation member. This first presidential delegation, which included five major veterans' organizations, was scheduled to make the trip in the midst of the National League of Families' annual meeting. Despite pleas from the league, the schedule precluded their traditional participation and also precluded significant representation from the administration at the league's annual meeting of several hundred family members in Washington.

Publicly, the administration began praising "superb Vietnamese cooperation," as measured by the number of joint field activities, the return of unidentified fragmentary remains, and Vietnamese pledges to accelerate cooperation, rather than the traditional accountability through identifications of remains. The reality was the lowest level of accountability since the early 1980s and no unilateral repatriation of stored remains. The listed number of Americans accounted for during the Clinton administration has been the result of massively subsidized joint field activities viewed previously as adjuncts to negotiating for core discrepancy case resolution, including those "last known alive," achievable only through unilateral Vietnamese actions.

Having been a part of every policy-level delegation to Vietnam since 1982, the National League of Families was outraged by its exclusion from the 1993 delegation. The league funded its own trip to Hanoi in March 1994 and, using official U.S. government data, extracted pledges from the Vietnamese for unilateral action. The league was included in the next presidential delegation to Vietnam, led by the deputy secretary of veterans affairs. That trip finally reinstitutionalized the need for unilateral action by Vietnam, a focus strongly endorsed by all of the veterans' representatives on the trip. A policy-level DOD delegation followed in November 1994 and reiterated the need for unilateral action as a requirement, regardless of the level of joint field activities. In response to this renewed emphasis and to the unity of the veterans' groups, the families, and the Washington-based policy level of DOD, the Vietnamese acknowledged to U.S. officials, and in subsequent private meetings with the league's executive director and Clinton's national security adviser, that they could do more. The Vietnamese still have not responded with unilateral action.

While the U.S. agenda with Vietnam has been full, it has not fully addressed or adequately engaged the Vietnamese on another humanitarian issue of central concern—human rights.[1] Until recently, the human rights agenda was fully focused on the release and resettlement of reeducation camp internees, the fate of Amerasian children, and the establishment of an Orderly Departure Program to prevent deaths by pirates and drownings during attempts to leave Vietnam.[2] With agreements reached on these problems and with substantial progress made toward their resolution, the United States has recently been able to engage Vietnam in a formal human rights dialogue.

The Vietnamese constitution of 1992 proclaims a respect for human rights; however, the reality is arbitrary and warrantless arrests; coercion; a lack of legal safeguards; suppression of legitimate political dissent; religious persecution; denial of a fair trial; a general lack of civil liberties, including freedom of speech and the press and the right of assembly; and lack of an acceptable workers' rights regime. Vietnam's human rights record remains one of the worst in the world today.

While opening a formal human rights dialogue with Vietnam, the Clinton administration has rejected direct linkage to normalization, maintaining that economic development and broader contact have a greater chance to effect internal change. However, as relations continue to develop, pressures from labor, human rights organizations, the American-Vietnamese community, the Congress, and others continue. Within weeks of the announcement of diplomatic relations, the Vietnamese sentenced several people, including two U.S. citizens, to long terms and arrested prominent Buddhist clergy who advocated reforms. The Republican leadership in the House and Senate has introduced legislation to cut off funds for any expansion of the embassy beyond the levels of July 11, 1995, without unilateral action from Vietnam on POW-MIAs and real political reform. Key committee chairmen in both the Senate and the House also signaled their intent to block further economic steps, such as OPIC funds, Eximbank loans, and most-favored-nation status. Some of these proposed restrictions also are linked to receipt of the long-delayed requirement for the administration to provide a full evaluation of whether Vietnam continues to withhold POW-MIA remains and records. The 1997 appropriations language agreed upon by both the House and Senate required the president to certify Vietnam was cooperating in full faith on the POW-MIA issue. The president so certified, but the Senate put a hold on confirmation of the new U.S. ambassador pending an investigation by the Senate Select Committee on Intelligence as to the basis of such certification. The committee staff found that the certification was not based upon an intelligence assessment, and intelligence requirements on the POW-MIA issue were dropped in 1995. Compromise was reached in a letter dated April 10, 1997, from the president's national security adviser. The letter pledged to restore intelligence priorities and conduct a formal national intelligence estimate. The U.S. ambassador was then confirmed the same day.

Clinton administration efforts to establish liaison offices have required negotiations on a host of housekeeping matters and three major substantive issues: the treatment of Vietnamese-born U.S. citizens, outstanding issues of real property arising from the mutual seizures at war's end, and settlement of claims on seized Vietnamese assets. Although the media and the Vietnamese were tripping over themselves announcing that the liaison offices were a done deal in May 1994, the reality was different. Hard negotiations on the first issue were conducted from February to May 1994. The Vietnamese insisted that all those born in Vietnam to parents who were nationals were themselves citizens of the country and thus did not qualify for rights and protections extended to U.S.-born persons. Although they maintained this position, the Vietnamese finally agreed that U.S. officials would be notified and provided access to Vietnamese who might be detained if they held U.S. passports. Since this agreement was reached, flaws that concern administration officials have become evident. Vietnam also continues to impede efforts to interview returnees from third-country asylum camps.

The issue of real property—that is, the officially titled real estate of each government—was the second major problem to be resolved before the liaison offices could be established. Although the former South Vietnamese government owned only its chancery building in Washington, having rented the remainder of the properties it used, the United States held title to more than thirty properties in Vietnam, mostly in Saigon. The negotiations were complicated on the Vietnamese side, since some U.S. property was occupied through various arrangements with other parties, including another country.

In the cases in which such complications might have held up the establishment of liaison offices for an indeterminable period, U.S. officials agreed, based upon third-party professional appraisals, to accept property of equal value or greater, with future options for expansion in some cases. The actual turnover of these properties was scheduled to be done in phases. U.S. negotiators were fortunate to have learned, from the experiences of those nations who preceded them into Hanoi, what challenges Vietnamese authorities might bring to the table in this initial round.

When the United States established a consular-level liaison office in Vietnam, as stated in President Clinton's speech of February 3, 1994, the office would be focused only on the POW-MIA issue and other humanitarian concerns, and general services to United States citizens. However, despite this public portrayal, it was a major step toward full diplomatic normalization, an administration plan. The ODP is expected to continue in place, and the mechanism for Amerasian departures was planned as part of the ODP program. No new Amerasians are now coming forward for interview at U.S. facilities, but the potential exists for some to be found in the future in provincial locations. Reportedly, all reeducation internees arrested because of their association with the United States or the previous South Vietnamese government have been released or allowed to emigrate. However, those still in Vietnam suffer from various restrictions, and political arrests of other Vietnamese citizens continue, in many cases on an arbitrary basis.

The last issue, of greater concern to Vietnam because of U.S. leverage, was the liquidation of seized Vietnamese funds to satisfy American claimants. Public Law 96–606 set out the Vietnam Claims Program in order to adjudicate claims and awards under the Foreign Claims Settlement Commission of the United States. Payment of such claims is achieved by liquidation of assets held in the name of the South Vietnamese government, which have drawn interest since blocked in 1975. On February 26, 1986, the commission completed its adjudication and review, administratively recognizing 192 separate claimants owed more than $99 million. This total of seized assets has since increased to $350 million as the money draws 6 percent interest per annum. The current total of private claims was over $200 million plus claims of the Overseas Private Investment Corporation. An agreement on this issue was signed on January 28, 1994, awarding the private claimants $204 million. A repayment plan was negotiated for official debt.

THE DOMESTIC FACTOR

Much has been written concerning the influence of domestic pressure on U.S. foreign policy. Perhaps no single example is more striking than that of policy toward Vietnam. After the end of the war, domestic interest groups of all stripes lobbied the executive and legislative branches of government with varying success. As administrations changed, their advice was heeded, ignored, or integrated, depending on the overall political sympathy toward their stated goals or the general outlook on Vietnam. The Vietnamese propensity to include U.S. domestic opinion in their overall strategy gave even greater significance to domestic interest group behavior in the United States.

Aside from traditional think tanks of differing political persuasions, the most prominent issues-based organizations included the National League of Families, national veterans' organizations, refugee advocacy groups, reconciliation-oriented groups, humanitarian relief organizations, human rights groups, ethnic Vietnamese organizations, and, later, business-oriented lobby groups.

In addition, fringe groups made prominent by the media, frustrated by

Vietnamese stalling, began to blame Washington rather than Hanoi for the lack of an acceptable rate of progress. Extreme solutions advocated by some did more damage than good to their respective causes. Some recommended U.S. support for the overthrow of the Vietnamese government; some Rambo-oriented nonfamily groups peddled POW-MIA conspiracy and coverup theories, manufactured false POW-MIA "evidence," raised millions of dollars based on fraudulent information and photos, and smeared those who did not agree with them. At the other extreme, some went as far as dismissing U.S. policy objectives as primitive hangovers from the war, and they unequivocally advocated Vietnamese goals. The National League of Families was central in opposing such extreme "solutions."

U.S. public opinion on the POW-MIA issue has been greatly influenced by popular images in movies, books, and tabloid television. With some overlap, it has moved through distinct phases: the Rambo era of private rescues, from the late 1970s to the mid-1980s; the conspiracy era from the mid-1980s to the early 1990s, alleging U.S. government coverup; and lately a denial phase. Current entries into the debate react against past excesses but use them as a rationale to conclude the POW-MIA issue is a myth, rather than a serious issue. Although books written to cash in on the POW-MIA issue are hardly best-sellers and on the whole factually incorrect, reactions to them do serve as a bellwether of some public opinion. A factual book encompassing all aspects of the issue has yet to be written; most of those written to date tend to focus on U.S. actions or are self-serving.

President Carter assumed office before the Rambo phenomenon, and initially the administration's intent to heal and "put the war behind us" created a natural alliance with domestic-based reconciliation groups that downplayed the significance of the POW-MIA issue and the Vietnamese human rights violations. This emphasis began to shift at the very end of the administration because of Vietnam's rejection of Carter administration overtures, Vietnam's alignment with the Soviet Union, the administration's tilt toward the P.R.C., the outflow of refugees with their horror stories, and developments on the POW-MIA issue. These included the unexpected return of marine PFC Robert Garwood and the defection of the Vietnamese mortician who testified credibly on Vietnamese storage of American remains and on his sighting of Caucasian Americans in Hanoi. His "live sighting report" was buttressed by information on MIAs flowing from refugees as they left Indochina.

President Reagan entered office in this environment, but he had a long-abiding interest in POW-MIAs and a view of the Vietnam War as a noble cause gone awry because of Washington indecision and betrayal. The Vietnamese were still entrenched in Cambodia, and their politburo was still intent on dreams of an Indochina Federation.

Thus, the natural outgrowth of the Reagan administration's orientation toward Vietnam and the region included a priority on POW-MIAs, reeducation camp internees, an orderly refugee departure program, an aggressive and generous refugee quota for those who were persecuted for their association with the United States, safe havens for those who fled Pol Pot, and a determination to treat the three countries of Indochina separately. This view also led the administration to a Cambodia policy opposing the Vietnamese occupation and avoiding direct contact with the Khmer Rouge, to include urging a shift of existing military and economic support by the P.R.C. from the Khmer Rouge to the noncommunist resistance. Consequently, the Reagan administration was more sympathetic to the messages of refugee advocacy groups, the National League of POW-MIA Families, veterans, Vietnamese Americans, and those opposed to normalization as an objective unrelated to these issues.

The Bush administration carried forth the basic Reagan positions for the first two years. However, the long-anticipated withdrawal of Vietnamese forces from Cambodia and the need for intense negotiations to help facilitate a political settlement in that country led to a bureaucratic shift that gave primacy of Vietnam policy to the State Department. That shift brought new players in Vietnam policy at State whose focus was primarily Cambodia, which they felt should dictate U.S. incentives toward Vietnam and which they saw as more worthy of their diplomatic skills. Defense objected at the highest levels along with some at the NSC, believing that POW-MIA criteria were being given short shrift and that progress was achievable on both Cambodia and POW-MIAs.

Beginning with the development of the road map, bureaucratic tensions accelerated; some State Department officials saw POW-MIAs as an obstacle that needed to be managed rather than an issue that needed to be resolved, and refugee policy became secondary as well. The result was the internationalization of the refugee screening process under the United Nations High Commission on Refugees (UNHCR), where the criteria for status determination were less liberal than those of the United States. It downplayed the association of Vietnamese citizens with the United States during the war as a credible basis for fear of persecution.

Attention, resources, and responsibility for POW-MIAs were shifted from Washington to CINCPAC field operations, and the intelligence community became subject to bureaucratic and policy pressure to lower the expectations on POW-MIA accountability. A State-led strategy was implemented to circumscribe the POW-MIA Interagency Group, and State refused DOD requests to brief friends and allies on official assessments of Vietnamese knowledgeability. These tensions were exacerbated by a loss of continuity, through rotation or reassignment of State Department negotiators knowledgeable in the history of Vietnam negotiations. At the same time, experienced, language-qualified POW-MIA investigators were replaced in the field by inexperienced military personnel.

Thus, during the last two years of the Bush administration, the focus on Vietnam gradually shifted to a more internationalist and commercial perspective, as a Cambodian solution became more probable and as a new set of domestic pressures on Vietnam policy developed. Sensing possible commercial opportunities in the near future, business lobby groups became more active and secured a voice in some administration quarters. Similarly, fuzzy strategic thinking about Vietnam's potential role in Southeast Asia began to have a greater voice, originating in groups focused traditionally on diplomacy and statecraft. By the end of the Bush administration, interagency tensions over Vietnam were so high between State and Defense that a weak NSC did not choose to or was unable to resolve the conflicts. Despite interventions by Secretary Cheney and Under Secretary of Defense Wolfowitz (formerly assistant secretary of state), both insisting on adherence to the road map provisions, State's view prevailed—holding that the road map was a flexible tool, the Vietnamese commitments were real, and adjustments were needed.

In the final six months of the Bush administration, State abruptly quit calling IAG meetings on POW-MIAs. The other members of the IAG (Defense, NSC, League of Families) were forced to call meetings on their own to coordinate POW-MIA policy. They attempted to convince the rest of the administration that the government could pursue bilateral goals, reinforce a political settlement in Cambodia, and respond to Vietnamese humanitarian concerns through the road map. The assertion of State as the lead agency because of Cambodia led to a less effective POW-MIA strategy. Further, a shift toward near-total emphasis on field operations as the solution to the issue, rather than a simultaneous emphasis on pressing Vietnam for unilateral efforts to provide accountability, lessened accountability from Vietnam on priority cases.

As with previous administrations, the Clinton administration was influenced by its own domestic matrix. Appointed officials arrived with preconceived notions concerning Vietnam that they had nurtured for years while out of office. Many viewed the POW-MIA issue as an obstacle to be put behind them. Some officials were determined to proceed toward normalization, assuming validity in the steady stream of Vietnamese rhetoric concerning U.S. unfairness. It led to acceptance in some quarters that normalization itself was the goal and that bilateral problems would be resolved through Vietnamese responsiveness if incentives were provided in advance. In addition, because POW-MIA progress was being measured not in terms of accountability but in numbers of joint operations and the counting of unidentified remains, the system became self-reinforcing.

Few negotiators were in place when senior Clinton officials traveled to Vietnam and, by their own admission, did so without even reading the previous decade-long negotiating record. The administration aligned itself closely with the views of sympathetic think tanks as well as lobby groups pushing to lift the trade embargo. They made no attempt at jawboning U.S. friends and allies to delay providing bilateral aid to Vietnam or oppose aid and low-interest loans through international financial institutions (IFIs). The approval of loans through IFIs set in motion the inevitability of lifting the bilateral trade embargo, as the U.S. business community would not tolerate U.S. tax contributions to foreign competitors through such means while they were restricted on a bilateral basis.

In an attempt to make progress in POW-MIA accounting, a proposal to form a new POW-MIA Select Committee surfaced in the House, the major veterans' groups formed a joint ad hoc POW-MIA Committee, and the National League of Families' board of directors voted to seek funds to establish an oversight office in Vietnam. For the first time since the Carter administration, the league demonstrated at the White House during its annual meeting in July 1995.

The preceding sketch of some of the domestic forces at work since the end of the Vietnam War is not complete, but it is illustrative of the major influences and how they were integrated or ignored during each administration. Congressional policy and responses also reflected many of these same domestic factors.

Congressional interest in and oversight on Vietnam issues were to be of critical significance, since each of the constituencies brought their various pressures to bear on individual members, congressional leaders, and established committees.

Vietnam and Congress

The most steady oversight of Vietnam-related matters since the end of the Vietnam War has taken place in the House of Representatives. Aside from the House Select Committee on Missing Persons in Southeast Asia, the House Subcommittee on Asian and Pacific Affairs held frequent hearings on the gamut of Vietnam-related issues, such as Cambodia, refugees, POW-MIAs, human rights, and claims settlements. Further, that House subcommittee sponsored the only official body in the Democratic Congress chaired by a Republican—the POW-MIA Task Force. There was a consensus that the POW-MIA issue was of unique bipartisan concern. From the late 1970s until the early 1990s, well over fifty hearings were held and more than one hundred witnesses called. Subcommittee and task force witnesses included not only executive and legislative branch witnesses, but veterans' leaders, the National League of Families, refugee NGO leadership, human rights advocates, and Vietnamese witnesses. Hearings became more frequent in the 1980s, partly reflecting greater Vietnamese responsiveness. The Congressional Research Service finally updated its POW-MIA holdings during the first term of the Reagan administration, the first since the 1970s. The hearings were supplemented by regular informal dialogue and briefings in members' offices, at the White House, the State Department, the Department of Defense, and, on occasion, at executive branch POW-MIA interagency meetings.

By contrast, the Senate, after the end of the war, showed only sporadic interest, and those hearings it called were typically in response to anticipated major events regarding Cambodia or were general updates concerning Asia. On POW-MIAs, the Senate Veterans Affairs Committee held a series of hearings and investigations in 1985 focused solely upon private-sector claims regarding live prisoners and charges of U.S. government conspiracy and coverup. Despite cautions from the administration, the National League of Families, and others that disproving assertions without sources was an impossible task, the committee's expectation was that the Reagan administration could disprove many of the more outlandish claims. Predictably, the hearings reached no conclusion and simply spawned more accusations, many directed at the committee itself.

The next major effort by the Senate was the one-year probe into the POW-MIA issue by a Senate select committee during 1991–92. Although the committee held numerous hearings and took depositions from almost every U.S. official associated with the POW-MIA issue and Vietnam from the war through 1992, as well as many foreign officials, it had a fundamental flaw rooted in its origins. Public charges of government malfeasance, coverup, obstructionism, and worse had clouded the public debate over POW-MIA matters. Many who did not follow the issue closely felt that such investigations and hearings would put to rest domestic controversy and smooth the path toward normalized relations, but many who pushed for the effort felt that such charges would be confirmed and publicly exposed. Given these origins, committee energy was directed primarily toward U.S. government policy and practices and left gaping the critical hole of Vietnamese government policy, practice, and knowledgeability.

Senator John Kerry (D-Mass.) and Senator Robert Smith (R-N.H.) chaired the committee. The hearings dealt primarily with the viewpoints, almost polar opposites, of these two senators. Each embodied one branch of the public opinion toward Vietnam outlined earlier in this paper.

The POW-MIA issue was new to Senator Kerry, but Senator Smith had pursued it for several years, including his time as an ex officio but very active member of the House POW-MIA Task Force. Senator John McCain (R-Ariz.), a returned POW and advocate of normalized relations for many years, played a crucial role as well. While acknowledging Vietnamese flaws, his primary focus was on exposing the conspiracy theorists and moving the POW-MIA issue from a central position in Vietnam policy. The remainder of the committee members had been sporadically involved but were relatively uninformed about the details of the issue and the negotiating history. The two diverse philosophical perspectives toward Vietnam dominated committee staff work, selection of public witnesses, testimony, and conclusions.

The most emotional aspect of the issue, live prisoners, was central to many of the hearings. One side attempted to prove that there is a good case that Americans were alive, indeed abandoned, after the war and might still be alive. The other side attempted to discredit the claims of prisoners being held even today and to expose the most outrageous domestic claims and claimants. The latter effort, needed as it was, obscured the fact that rational people had testified to at least the possibility of Americans held alive after the war. Both sides pushed for a major declassification effort, each one believing it could buttress its own case: such openness would either reduce suspicion of the government or confirm it.

In the end, the committee's conclusion on live prisoners echoed the position of the Reagan administration—that the possibility could not be ruled out. The wholesale release of raw data has shed little light but much confusion, and it is still being exploited publicly by some to further their personal agendas regardless of the effects on the POW-MIA issue.

Unfortunately, the consequence of the committee hearings was a perception that complete answers on the POW-MIA issue could be reached by examining the domestic data base alone. The committee put into perspective some of the irrational claims made on the fringes, and it helped to establish joint mechanisms for field operations and archival research. It exposed the low priority given the issue by some administrations, publicly recording how POW-MIA policy suffered under changing political priorities. It also let Vietnam off the hook in terms of accountability and set the stage for further erosion of the unilateral POW-MIA conditions in the normalization road map, which demonstrably reduced accountability of POW-MIAs.

Since the committee could not prove, by using the U.S. data base, that Americans were being held against their will, the most emotional aspect of the issue was neutralized while the reality that only Vietnam could finally resolve the issue was essentially buried. The inconclusive closure was the basis for a Senate resolution to lift the trade embargo, supported by Senators Kerry and McCain, and the positive vote provided political justification for President Clinton to lift the embargo.

During the period of Senate select committee hearings, accountability almost halted as Hanoi responded to various missions, as well as executive and congressional requests. The entire executive branch POW-MIA bureaucracy did little but respond to the committee, while Vietnam anxiously awaited its conclusions, issued after the election of President Clinton, in order to incorporate the results into its own strategy. There was a delay of more than a year in a case-by-case report from the executive branch on missing Americans about whom the Vietnamese might have information. The report, requested by a Senate bill passed after the committee hearings, included a list of hundreds of names.

Leading up to its announcement about establishing full diplomatic relations with Vietnam, the Clinton administration developed a careful strategy to neutralize opposition. Of great concern was the almost unanimous opposition of the Republican leadership in the House and Senate and of the majorities in each of the relevant foreign affairs and defense committees, not to mention the opposition voiced by the announced Republican candidates for president, by the league, Rep. Sam Johnson, a returned POW, and by most major veterans' groups. Senator McCain, who had supported normalization since 1985, broke ranks as he had done on the trade embargo and supported the move along with the minority leadership. Since hearings had been scheduled on Vietnam, the administration moved quickly to preempt further opposition and announced McCain's decision the day before the full House Committee on International Relations held hearings. The returned POW community quickly responded and gathered sixty signatures on a letter to the president, dated July 10, 1995, opposing normalization without full cooperation on the POW-MIA issue, thus distancing themselves from McCain's views. As required by the Senate, in Presidential Determination 96-28, May 29, 1996, President Clinton provided a certification that the Vietnamese were "cooperating in full faith."

WHAT WORKED AND WHAT DID NOT?

The major approaches of each administration toward Vietnam are relatively clear, as is Vietnamese negotiating behavior. Significantly, U.S. policy had concrete successes over time:

- · the withdrawal of Vietnamese forces from Cambodia and a political settlement in that country without dominance by either of the communist protagonists;
- · the release of those Vietnamese imprisoned in reeducation camps, many of whom were resettled in the United States;
- · the resettlement of Amerasian children in the United States, along with many of their family members;
- · the successful implementation of a program for orderly departure from Vietnam; and
- · the accounting for 330 U.S. servicemen and civilians from Vietnam, the vast majority of whom were accounted for before lifting the trade embargo or granting diplomatic recognition.

As stated, getting this far was no easy trek for the United States, and analysis of the period provides insights into what kind of overall approach worked and what did not work. Conclusions about certain principles of U.S. negotiating behavior can be drawn on the basis of the experience gained in Vietnam.

Talk

It is clear that regardless of the severity of the U.S. embargo, no progress could be expected in the absence of structured dialogue between the United States and Vietnam. In fact, the Carter administration made no progress on any issues after the breakdown of normalization talks with the Vietnamese. Progress began again in the early 1980s when policy-level talks resumed, although the embargo was at its most restrictive.

Set a Narrow Agenda

Wide-ranging bilateral talks simply provided Vietnam an expanded "keyboard" for their negotiating strategy. The agenda must be limited to narrow issues, sequentially if possible. Broad normalization talks did not work.

As the wedge issue, POW-MIA dialogue and concrete results led to progress on refugees, ODP, Amerasian, and reeducation camp issues. These humanitarian talks were precursors to subsequent talks that addressed Vietnam's legitimate humanitarian needs. Throughout the dialogue, informal exchanges of views on Cambodia, on a normalization path, and on regional concerns built a base for broader economic and political discussions after the Vietnamese withdrawal from Cambodia.

Ask to Be Exploited

On the surface, this advice seems ludicrous; however, the Vietnamese sought to learn the top U.S. priority and exploit it, to the disadvantage of the United States. An understanding of this principle was a conscious part of the Reagan administration's strategy. Beginning in the early 1980s, for instance, POW-MIAs were once again made the clear priority of the United States. The Vietnamese attempted to link the matter to political issues such as diplomatic recognition, but when the United States refused to do so, they grudgingly cooperated by returning stored remains, but resisted agreement on a comprehensive plan, which was on the U.S. priority list. By doing so, the Vietnamese revealed that they could readily provide many more answers. In this regard, the families of POW-MIAs could depend on unilateral Vietnamese actions, including repatriation of identifiable remains, at times of high visibility—before the league's annual meetings, before Christmas, before POW-MIA Recognition Day, and at election time in the United States. Later, the pattern was extended to multilateral events related to UN activity or international discussions on Cambodia.

By focusing Vietnamese negotiating energy on exploitation of top U.S. priorities rather than on amorphous, multiple goals, U.S. negotiators made progress on the central bilateral issues that could collectively be defined as humanitarian.

Be Prepared to Walk Away

This principle does not conflict with the "talk" principle, but recognizes a core Vietnamese strategy. Vietnamese leaders knew that without dialogue, they lacked an important tool. If a complete breakdown of talks appeared likely, they worked to reestablish it relatively rapidly if the other party did not return to the table first.

After the breakdown of normalization talks in the late 1970s, the Vietnamese sent many signals of their desire to reengage the United States in dialogue. Similarly, when the NSC-led delegation in 1986 encountered heavy resistance in advancing the proposed trip by General Vessey, the

U.S. representatives informed the Vietnamese that Vessey was ready to abort the initiative. Hanoi immediately agreed to consider the initiative, fearful that their interruption of the talks could become permanent.

Present a United Front and Seek Friendly Support

Vietnamese negotiating behavior is replete with examples of attempts to "divide and conquer." This was evident throughout the Paris negotiations to end the war, during the aborted normalization talks of the late 1970s, through the Cambodian negotiations, and into the negotiations on bilateral issues from 1981 until today.[3] The Vietnamese have sought to put pressure on the U.S. executive and legislative branches through private U.S. groups, the media, individual members of Congress, overseas Vietnamese, the business community, and individuals. This has taken the form of public and private exhortation, as well as more nefarious means. The Vietnamese have also lobbied vigorously in the international community. Hanoi was viewed in the communist world as particularly adept and successful in this arena, and upon request it provided advice to Cuba, North Korea, and others on "how to handle the Americans." (Ironically, Russia, Kuwait, Israel, Iraq, and Croatia have also sought the National League of Families' advice on how to achieve an accounting for their missing nationals on a humanitarian basis.)

From the end of the war until the breakdown of normalization talks with the United States, Vietnam was confident of its position and predicted a bright future. Normalization and reconstruction aid from the United States appeared likely to them, especially during the early years of the Carter administration, given what the Vietnamese viewed as favorable conditions in the United States.

The Reagan administration attempted to present a united domestic front to Vietnamese strategy through a vigorous public awareness program on the POW-MIA issue that made use of statements at the presidential, cabinet, and subcabinet levels. The administration's approaches to veterans' leaders, the National League of Families, the Congress, POW-MIA activists, and the media were supplemented by briefings to friends and allies in Asia and Europe.

Domestically, the Reagan administration's message was that Vietnam's cooperation on the POW-MIA issue was inadequate; therefore, a united domestic front was needed to persuade the Vietnamese that unilateral responsiveness was in their long-term interest and would be the only path to normalization after a settlement in Cambodia. Internationally, friends and allies were informed that the United States did not want the POW-

MIA issue to be an obstacle in the Cambodia end game and that the international community could help by urging Vietnamese cooperation. The international contacts were supplemented by intelligence briefings on Vietnamese knowledgeability and consultations before and after each policy-level negotiation.

From 1981 to 1986, the effort paid off. Vietnam received messages and petitions by the millions from the United States, and interventions by the international community were common. The veterans' groups heretofore had expressed their interest in POW-MIA accountability by means of national resolutions, but they lacked an effective channel of communication. In consultation with the administration and the National League of Families, veterans' groups developed resolutions germane to ongoing negotiations that were brought to Hanoi by official delegations. The collective effort during this period, along with other elements of the strategy, brought more responses from Vietnam than at any time since 1977.

* * *

Adherence to the foregoing specific principles when negotiating with Vietnam worked on the whole, and ignoring them slowed progress perceptibly. Analysis of POW-MIA accountability and refugee issues shows that there was more real progress in a period when the embargo was at its tightest and there were no formal negotiations on normalization. Further, incentives provided *after* Vietnamese responses were more effective than those provided in advance. This statement does not suggest that incentives should be kept from the negotiating table; rather, it implies that the expectation of concessions proved a stronger incentive to the Vietnamese than their actual delivery.

BACKFIRE

The Reagan administration, however, failed to anticipate the extent to which the surge in public awareness would provide a fertile environment for a broad array of con artists, conspiracy theorists, authors, and Hollywood Rambo-genre movies. This domestic, populist reaction distorted public opinion to the point that many blamed the U.S. government instead of Hanoi for what was perceived as slow progress in negotiations. The administration declared that resolution of the POW-MIA issue was a matter of highest national priority, to signal the Vietnamese and the bureaucracy of President Reagan's serious intent to satisfactorily resolve the POW-MIA issue. Although more progress in accounting for missing Americans was made during 1981–89 than at any time before or since, the progress was not rapid enough to prevent the U.S. populace from becoming frustrated. It became clear that many veterans, the media, and some in Congress were focused solely on the live prisoner issue and had lost sight of accountability as another important way to address this issue.

U.S. officials became gun-shy of the public and defensive to Congress. In response to public pressures, the Senate held two series of hearings, in 1986 and from 1991 to 1992. The debate in the select committee reiterated the sentiment that it was time to "get the issue behind us." This attitude carried over into the executive branch strategies of both Bush and Clinton.

While the Vietnamese indicated to American negotiators that major POW-MIA progress would ensue in the normalization process, significant progress has not been evident. Current progress in accountability stems from agreements for joint operations reached before the lifting of the trade embargo, before the dropping of objections to international lending, and before the establishment of liaison offices or diplomatic relations. What has hampered progress, aside from the central issue of Vietnamese negotiating behavior, is the lack of continuity in U.S. policy and negotiators, historical domestic divisions stemming from the war, and a basic lack of in-depth understanding of Vietnam issues in the American body politic.

No Last Chapter

Though the bilateral trade embargo with Vietnam has been lifted and President Clinton has established full diplomatic relations, full normalization between the United States and Vietnam is not yet here. The major remaining bilateral obstacle, the POW-MIA issue, has affected the timing of congressional approval for an ambassador, as well as affecting economic initiatives. The delays are increasingly linked to congressional concerns over human rights as well.[4]

Multiple intelligence studies from the war through today conclude that Vietnam could easily account for hundreds of missing Americans if it unilaterally repatriated remains, opened its archives, and cooperated fully in cases where more than 80 percent of MIAs are in geographical areas of Laos and Cambodia that the Vietnamese controlled during the war.[5] While joint efforts to clean up the battlefield will continue to provide some accountability, there has not yet been a politburo decision to resolve the core cases, including those Americans last known alive in the custody or immediate vicinity of Vietnamese forces. Among the reasons that have been offered: a split in the politburo, a Vietnamese desire to exploit the issue for future financial or political advantage, a residue of hostility or hatred toward Americans in the Ministries of Interior and National Defense, fear of embarrassment, or fear that the United States will neglect issues of concern to Vietnam once the issue is resolved. Whatever the reason or reasons, Vietnam, in the current environment, has made a conscious decision to keep the issue alive, not to resolve it.

The fundamental Vietnamese emphasis on the POW-MIA issue has been central since the Paris negotiations, through every U.S. administration. Knowing it to be the most sensitive humanitarian issue to Americans, Hanoi has consistently attempted to use POW-MIAs for leverage, and it has been central to U.S. policy in dealings with Vietnam over the years.

The centrality of the POW-MIA issue to U.S. policy makers has engendered a variety of approaches, varying from concerted efforts at defining the issue away, on the one hand, to direct confrontations in order to resolve it, on the other. Even policy makers who viewed the POW-MIA issue as a hindrance to healing or normalization demonstrated its centrality by expending much political capital in a failed attempt to prove the contrary. Confronting the issue directly in negotiations has been the only demonstrable path to progress. Ironically, it is the path desired by the Vietnamese, for reasons that have been outlined here. When Reagan officials reopened dialogue with Vietnam on POW-MIAs, the politburo members were delighted and, referencing the 1978–81 freeze in talks, commented that they didn't know the U.S. still cared. That was also a challenge.

Although the Clinton administration has rejected direct linkage of human rights questions to normalization, Vietnamese human rights violations are also a potential obstacle. Strong feelings in favor of linkage exist in some human rights organizations, the American-Vietnamese community, and the labor movement, as well as in the Congress across the political spectrum. Linkage may not be desired as a matter of executive branch policy, but initiatives have been proposed in the current Congress.

Legislation proposed in the mid-1980s would have used blocked Vietnamese assets to pay private claims, and significant lobby pressure was put on the Reagan administration and Congress to liquidate the assets. The initiative was opposed by the administration and rejected by the Congress because of legitimate fears that it would interrupt humanitarian cooperation and that official claims of the U.S. government would become secondary. The thinking was that such transactions should be negotiated in the context of normalization discussions. Sufficient funds existed to cover the private claims, and the United States, as the custodian of the funds, was positioned to settle the claims from a position of strength and leverage.

High on Vietnam's list of near-term and long-term economic goals are most-favored-nation status (MFN) and favorable tariff treatment under the Generalized System of Preferences (GSP). In addition to Vietnam's primitive trade regime, which hampers accession to the World Trade Organization and limits U.S. flexibility, there are various legal and regulatory obstacles that will complicate the completion of a bilateral trade agreement.

The obstacles include Vietnam's communist status, the requirement for compliance with the U.S. Jackson-Vanik amendment (freedom of emigration), family reunification requirements, the potential for denial of MFN if the president determines a lack of cooperation in POW-MIA accounting, nonsettlement of claims, and a lack of workers' rights. Some of the requirements can be waived for Vietnam through U.S. executive action; under certain conditions legislation may be required. In any event, because it is Vietnam, Clinton should be reluctant to take significant steps without congressional approval.

Financial incentives to Vietnam could be used by the United States in negotiations to engender progress on issues of U.S. concern, but most of the programs of assistance are hampered by the same types of restrictions as apply to MFN and GSP. The programs include Eximbank financing of exports to Vietnam, OPIC insurance, bilateral aid, PL 480 provisions for agricultural commodities, and nonrestricted support for lending programs of multilateral agencies.

Soon after the United States lifted the bilateral trade embargo, the Vietnamese began lobbying vigorously for MFN and GSP through U.S. businesspeople and NGOs operating in Vietnam. If Vietnam develops into a significant site for U.S. firms manufacturing for the U.S. market in the near future (an unlikely prospect), additional pressures could be brought by U.S. business beyond those already felt by the administration. MFN will benefit Vietnam and other Asian investors significantly, since they will be the first to exploit Vietnam's cheap labor to access the huge U.S. market. Current pressures are primarily the result of Vietnamese veiled threats to U.S. business interests, warning that current conditions constitute a one-way street, and assertions from business interests that they cannot compete without U.S. government guarantees.

Despite a significant loss of leverage on bilateral issues that is the result of lifting the trade embargo and granting full diplomatic relations, one could argue that these actions allow the Clinton administration some breathing room to insist on meaningful Vietnamese unilateral action to meet the four POW-MIA criteria set forth by the president, to advance the bilateral human rights dialogue, and to further economic reform. Since Vietnam's priority is economic, leverage can still be used if the administration chooses this path. Precedent in the Clinton administration does not suggest this is a part of the overall strategy unless Congress carries out its threat of restrictions.

In the interim, it is in both countries' interest for Vietnam to proceed with internal economic reforms so that the country can be further integrated into Asia generally and ASEAN specifically. This long-term objective was shared in some respects throughout each American administration since the end of the Vietnam War and is common to ASEAN and broader international community objectives. Such integration provides greater exposure of the Vietnamese leadership to international economic and political norms, perhaps reduces some Vietnamese paranoia, and helps convince Vietnam that the POW-MIA issue is a "wasting asset" for them that needs to be resolved openly. Integration also meshes with Vietnam's desire to minimize its perceived isolation relative to the P.R.C.

However, U.S. policy makers need to view this from an internal Vietnamese perspective. They expect that integration into ASEAN will relieve U.S. pressure for internal political reforms and improved human rights. Vietnam has boldly endorsed universal declarations on human rights and has attempted to join the cultural argument between Asia and the West, as if its system were even comparable to the systems in ASEAN countries advancing the argument.

For the foreseeable future, Vietnam will have three major objectives: continued political control under the Communist Party, economic development that does not threaten such control, and a sense of security in its relationship to the P.R.C. While political change is inevitable over time, it will be due to internal factors, and U.S. leverage will be at the margins. Economic reforms have spawned divisions in the party and the government, as well as regional tensions between the North and the South. Recriminations are already evident between reformers and hard-liners, and without further reform the U.S. role in the Vietnamese economic future will be limited.

After listening to wishful speculation about a "new tiger" in Asia, spawned by young consultants, service industries, and lobby organizations with a vested interest in lifting the embargo, U.S. business is again looking at political and economic realities it tended to ignore for the past five years. Media stories of Vietnam's economic potential before and after the lifting of the trade embargo are strikingly different. While overblown stories of "the last frontier," "the emerging tiger in Asia," and the loss of business to foreigners have been common in the past, the media is beginning to report real investment numbers instead of reporting on corruption, unenforceability of legal codes, currency problems, bureaucratic hurdles, arbitrary decision making of government officials, the paucity of infrastructure, and the reality that Vietnam, with few exceptions, is almost a decade away from real profitability on a U.S. business scale. Black ink is not likely to flow from U.S. auditors' pens for several years in Vietnam. A lot of money is being spent and very little is being made.

Most long-time observers of Asia also recognize that Vietnam is not of real strategic relevance to the United States in the 1990s. However, worrisome statements are still being made by some members of Congress, armchair strategists, and military planners who looking for basing or geographical ports of call, and nascent military-to-military talks are underway. On the other hand, Vietnam is certainly looking for strategic solace, given their historic animosities with the P.R.C., conflicting claims in the South China Sea, and growing P.R.C. economic and political clout. Although elements of that agenda are variously shared by ASEAN, U.S. military power and political commitments are not designed to mediate arguments between the P.R.C. and Vietnam. The United States facilitated the end of the proxy war between the P.R.C. and Vietnam over Cambodia by opposing both unworthy claimants in an international and regional context, not by taking sides.

The reality of the economic and strategic conditions now and in the foreseeable future does not make Vietnam central to U.S. policy, certainly not as a counterweight to the P.R.C. The Chinese economic, military, and political clout now and in the future can only be dealt with at the regional and superpower level. The Vietnamese desire for full normalization with the United States is recognized, but the gap is wide and will remain so despite the wishful, almost romantic thinking of some.

Vietnam, the United States, and the people of both nations do have a unique relationship, forged through a unique history, and both sides can regret missed opportunities. The history of bilateral negotiations is tortured, and the historic antagonisms can be muted only by a credible effort to resolve the POW-MIA issue, the only path to real healing and full normalization.

In sum, despite the establishment of diplomatic relations, fully normalized relations between the United States and Vietnam are not on the immediate horizon, and Vietnam will remain, in an economic and strategic sense, of little importance to the United States. Future steps in the commercial sphere could conceivably take place in the absence of a major economic or strategic rationale if significant progress on POW-MIA accounting occurs through the unilateral return of remains by Hanoi. The longer Vietnam delays in this regard, the more likely it is that normalization would be linked to human rights concerns as well. If this occurs, it would be supported by those who, heretofore, believed Vietnam would be able to forge a real politburo consensus to resolve the uncertainty of the POW-MIA families.

Should the Clinton administration proceed with further elements of normalization as an objective, rather than as an instrument for resolving bilateral issues, congressional opposition is likely to increase, further reducing executive branch flexibility and creating a renewed round of recriminations as well as a new gauntlet for future negotiators, especially for the new ambassador in Vietnam.

The Vietnam experience has become central in Americans' definition of themselves, and this makes it unique. Whether the lessons drawn here are applicable to other normalization scenarios now or in the future is for others to judge. What is clear, however, is that the Vietnam experience will continue to have a place, one way or another, in decision making and at the negotiating tables for years to come.

NOTES

1. For a thorough review of the human rights situation in Vietnam, see *Country Reports on Human Rights Practices for 1996,* Committee on Foreign Relations of the Senate and Committee on International Relations of the House, 105th Congress, printed February 1997, USGPO. In addition, recent repression of religious freedom is described in a report by the Washington-based Puebla Institute.

2. Of the approximately forty thousand refugees still in Southeast Asia, almost fifteen thousand are former South Vietnamese or Lao military who face forcible repatriation under current policy. In addition, many former U.S. employees and political prisoners are mired in processing. The current administration policy of going along with UNHCR guidelines has led to violent resistance in the camps.

3. Aside from outright falsehoods to U.S. negotiators concerning remains of missing Americans or archival records, Hanoi's agreement that the POW-MIA issue was humanitarian was continuously violated. All of Hanoi's pledges of accelerated cooperation, joint operations, and additional technical meetings throughout the 1980s were broken or delayed on political grounds. After sustained formal negotiations on a comprehensive two-year plan, it was broken in the most egregious fashion by Hanoi's insistence on inserting political provisions.

4. For a detailed discussion of these legal impediments, see Congressional Research Service, *Vietnam: Procedural and Jurisdictional Questions regarding Possible Normalization of U.S. Diplomatic and Economic Relations,* Rept. no. 94-6335 (Washington, D.C.: Congressional Research Service).

5. Following are the major studies, now declassified, that document Vietnamese ability to account for missing Americans:

· *Hanoi and the POW-MIA Issue,* Special National Intelligence Estimate 14.3-87, Central Intelligence Agency, Washington, D.C., September 1987. (Key judgments are estimates of Vietnamese warehousing of the remains of four hundred to six hundred servicemen and use of the POW-MIA issue by Hanoi to achieve broader objectives.)

· U.S. Defense Intelligence Agency, *Americans Missing in Indochina: An Assessment of Vietnamese Accountability,* June 25, 1990. (A deliberately conservative study breaking down by categories the remains accountability potential, reaching into the hundreds.)

· Joint Casualty Resolution Center Study, September 26, 1990. (Key judgment: Uses the Remains Probability System to estimate continued storage and hundreds accountable.)

· U.S. Defense Intelligence Agency assessment of JCRC study, September 27, 1991. (Key finding: The remains of five hundred to seven hundred bodies collected by Vietnamese and easily retrievable.)

· Revisions to 1990 DIA assessment, May 1993. (Estimate: The remains of 435 to 560 bodies are in storage.)

6

Iraq
The Failure of a Strategy

BRUCE W. JENTLESON

This is a case study of what *not* to do. While U.S. policy was not the only factor that went into Saddam Hussein's calculation to invade Kuwait, it surely was a key factor. We take nothing away from the achievements of Operations Desert Shield and Desert Storm if we are willing to see how this war could have been avoided, and how its occurrence demonstrated the failure of the policies begun by the Reagan administration and intensified by the Bush administration. It thus is a case in which we seek to learn from failure, not success, in keeping with Santayana's classic dictum that "those who do not learn from history are condemned to repeat it."[1]

HISTORICAL BACKGROUND

In the 1950s Iraq was the closest ally the United States had in the Arab world. It was a charter member (in fact, the only Arab member) of the Baghdad Pact, godfathered by Secretary of State John Foster Dulles in 1955 as the Middle Eastern component in his global system of anticommunist regional alliances.[2] But when the old Iraqi monarchy was overthrown by a leftist military coup in 1958, the new regime of General Abdul Karim Qassim withdrew from the alliance—leaving the Baghdad Pact without Baghdad and thus precipitating a restructuring of the alliance under a new name, the Central Treaty Organization (CENTO). The new regime in Baghdad opened diplomatic relations with the Soviet Union.

Iraq threatened a total break in diplomatic relations with the United States when in 1961 the Kennedy administration joined Britain in recognizing Kuwait as an independent state. Prime Minister Qassim claimed that Kuwait was an "integral part of Iraq" based on their common Ottoman Empire provincial boundaries.[3] The U.S. Central Intelligence Agency reportedly was involved in numerous attempts to overthrow Qassim, including an assassination plot using a poisoned handkerchief, which failed, and then in a successful coup, which brought the Arab Socialist Renaissance, or Ba'ath, party to power in 1963.[4]

Nevertheless, under the Ba'athists, U.S.-Iraqi relations were further strained. Following the 1967 Arab-Israeli war, Iraq severed diplomatic ties with the United States. And like their predecessors, the Ba'athists proved to be pro-Soviet. They signed numerous trade and military agreements with Moscow, culminating in the April 1972 Treaty of Friendship and Cooperation. At the time, relations between the United States and Iran were growing closer. The Shah of Iran was cast by President Richard Nixon and his national security adviser, Henry Kissinger, as the key "regional pillar" upholding U.S. interests in the Persian Gulf.

Thus, the U.S.-Soviet superpower rivalry and the Iran-Iraq regional one fed into each other. The Arab-Israeli conflict made it a three-sided dynamic. Iraq again fought on the side of the Arabs in the 1973 war (as it had in 1948 and 1967). When the path-breaking Camp David Accords were brokered by the Carter administration and signed by Egypt and Israel in 1978, it was Iraq that led the "Rejectionist Front." Iraq also was one of the major sponsors of terrorism, providing funding, training, safe haven, and other assistance to the Palestine Liberation Organization (PLO) and other terrorist groups. The Carter administration made Iraq one of the first countries on its newly established list of state sponsors of terrorism, against which tough economic sanctions were imposed.

However, in 1979–80, the strategic scenario was rocked by a series of shocks. In January 1979 the Shah of Iran, that pillar of U.S. policy, was brought down by the Islamic fundamentalist revolution led by the Ayatollah Khomeini. In November seventy-six Americans were taken hostage at the U.S. Embassy in Teheran. In December the Soviet Union invaded Afghanistan. And in September 1980 Iraq launched a war against Iran. Throughout this period there were also signs of strains in Iraqi-Soviet relations. It was beginning to appear that perhaps there might be a basis for a U.S.-Iraqi relationship.

Phase One: The Iran-Iraq War and the Alliance-of-Convenience Strategy

Before the Iran-Iraq war started, the Carter administration had made some very preliminary overtures to Saddam Hussein. But while there have been varying accounts and allegations of U.S. collusion in Saddam's initiation of the war with Iran in September 1980, the evidence seems to support President Carter's claim that "we had no previous knowledge of nor influence over this move."[5]

Initially the Reagan administration maintained neutrality, but by early

1982, with the war turning in Iran's favor and with the Ayatollah becoming increasingly aggressive in fomenting Islamic fundamentalist threats throughout the region, the "tilt" to Iraq was begun. A first key move was taking Iraq off the list of state sponsors of terrorism. The statement for the record was that this policy shift was "intended both to recognize Iraq's improved record [on terrorism] and to offer an incentive to continue this positive trend."[6] Privately, though, as the leading Defense Department counterterrorism official later conceded, "no one had any doubts about his [Saddam's] continued involvement with terrorism. . . . The real reason [for taking Iraq off the terrorism list] was to help them succeed in the war against Iran."[7]

The practical significance of Iraq's removal from the state terrorism list was that countries on the list were prohibited from receiving U.S. government-financed export credits and were subject to highly restrictive controls on arms sales and technology exports. Once off the list, export credits could be offered and export controls loosened. In fiscal year 1983 Iraq was granted over $400 million in U.S. Agriculture Department Commodity Credit Corporation (CCC) guarantees with which to purchase U.S. agricultural exports. Iraq then was dependent on imports for about 75 percent of all its food supply. Yet the disruption of its oil production, two years into the war, was leaving it strapped for cash. Oil revenues had plummeted from $22 billion in 1980 to $9 billion to $10 billion. The CCC financing thus provided much-needed purchasing power for food for the war-torn Iraqi people. In FY 1984, CCC guarantees increased to $513 million and by FY 1987 to $652.5 million, which was almost one-fourth of the total CCC guarantee program.

While the Reagan administration did not directly sell Iraq weapons, it did engage in a policy that an NSC aide later conceded was one of "nods and winks" toward third-country arms sales to Iraq.[8] And the administration did begin to sell equipment and technology of a "dual use" nature (that is, having both civilian and military applications and uses), which the Iraqis pledged (ostensibly) to use only nonmilitarily. Perhaps even more militarily valuable to the Iraqis were the intelligence data that the Reagan administration started supplying, including satellite reconnaissance photos of strategic Iranian sites for targeting bombing raids, data on Iranian air force and troop positions gathered from U.S.-manned AWACS based in Saudi Arabia, communications intercepts, and other vital military information. "My sense," recalled another Reagan official, "was that such U.S.-provided intelligence saved the Iraqis from being overrun in several key battles."[9] It was supposed to be "the bait on the hook," as a Reagan official later phrased it, showing Iraq how valuable an ally the United States could be.

Starting in late 1983, feelers about restoring U.S.-Iraqi diplomatic relations went back and forth between Washington and Baghdad. The restoration came in November 1984, right after Ronald Reagan's reelection. There were, of course, the for-the-record assertions that this did not signal any change in the official policy of neutrality. The tilt to Iraq, though, could hardly be denied any longer. In fact, Reagan administration officials waxed on about how "Iraq no longer regarded itself as a 'front-line Arab state'," and that Saddam now believed that a Middle East peace "should include security for Israel." Cables came back from the region approvingly quoting Saddam as speaking of "the beautiful atmosphere between us." "We were convinced," a key Reagan Middle East expert said, "that Iraq was changing."[10] The new Iraqi ambassador, Nizar Hamdoon, quickly established himself as a popular figure in Washington, working the party circuit and writing op-ed articles in the *Washington Post* on "How to Survive in Washington." "Everything and everyone is workable," Ambassador Hamdoon wrote, "depending on how you approach them and how much time you spend."[11]

Despite the closer relations with and increasing economic and military assistance from the United States, the war with Iran still was not going well for Iraq. In July 1986, Assistant Secretary of State Richard Murphy expressed concern that "the longer the war continues, the greater the risk of an Iraqi defeat." [12] But what Assistant Secretary Murphy did not appear to know was that the latest Iranian military advances had been made possible in part by U.S. arms sales.

At one point in the Iran-Contra affair, when despite U.S. arms shipments the Iranians still had released only two of the American hostages being held in Lebanon, the Reagan administration calculated that maybe the Iranians needed to feel a greater need for U.S. arms. CIA Director William Casey sent a message to Saddam Hussein, via Vice President George Bush and through King Hussein of Jordan and Egyptian President Hosni Mubarak, that Saddam should step up his bombing attacks on Iran. To help the effort, Casey provided Saddam with additional military intelligence, including satellite photographs of bombing sites. Sure enough, in just the two days following Bush's meeting with Mubarak, the Iraqi air force flew 359 missions, many of which struck more deeply into Iranian territory than ever before.[13] Now perhaps Iran would want U.S. arms enough to release all the hostages.

On yet another track, though, Oliver North was not carrying merely cakes and Bibles to the Iranians. In a secret meeting on October 29 in Mainz, West Germany, with the Iranian intermediaries, North went so far as to promise to help Iran get rid of Saddam: "We also recognize that Saddam

Hussein must go. . . . I cannot tell you exactly day by day or step by step. . . . Yet the general outline follows those steps that I gave you last night."[14]

But none of this strategy worked—and soon the whole operation unraveled. One of the effects of the revelations of the arms-for-hostages deal was to make the Reagan administration move even closer to Iraq. It did so in part to relieve the political fallout at home, in part to regain credibility with Saudi Arabia and other Arab allies, and in part to assuage "the sense of betrayal felt by the Iraqis." "It is difficult to refute the Iraqis' underlying accusation," Assistant Secretary Murphy wrote Secretary Shultz, "that the U.S. has armed Iran to kill Iraqis."[15]

It was around this time that concerns intensified about Iranian efforts to expand the war against Iraq's neighbor Kuwait. Its attacks on Kuwaiti-bound shipping had escalated.[16] It also had increased covert efforts to foment unrest among Kuwait's Shia minority. In February 1987 U.S. intelligence picked up evidence of sites being constructed along the Iranian coast near the Strait of Hormuz for new Silkworm antiship missiles obtained from China.

Another contributing consideration was the fear of "losing the Gulf" to the Soviet Union. In fact, it was only when the Reagan administration learned of a Soviet offer to reflag Kuwait's tankers that it decided to make its own reflagging offer. Protecting Kuwaiti oil tankers under the American flag and with U.S. Navy escorts thus was consistent with the long-standing U.S. commitments both to contain Iranian aggression against moderate Arab states and to defend the principle of freedom of the seas and the vital economic interests at risk from another major disruption of world oil supplies. Yet it also should be acknowledged that the reflagging of Kuwaiti oil tankers amounted to a de facto military alliance between the United States and Iraq. While Kuwait was not a declared party to the war, it also was not an innocent bystander. It was, after all, providing billions of dollars in financing to Iraq. Such assistance did not justify Iranian aggression against Kuwait, but it did mean that coming to Kuwait's defense was not simply standing up for a neutral.

Moreover, the threat to Persian Gulf oil shipping was coming not only from Iran but also from Iraq. Iraq had launched more attacks than Iran in the "tanker war" in the period immediately leading up to reflagging. It then used the U.S. naval presence as a protective shield behind which it increased its attacks on shipping almost threefold. Even Saddam's claim of "friendly fire" in the May 1987 attack on the U.S.S. *Stark*, killing thirty-seven American sailors, was readily accepted by the Reagan administration.[17] Nevertheless, the general sense was that this strategy was successful. Kuwait was protected, the sea lanes were kept open, the Soviet Union was kept out, and Iran was contained. In July 1988 Iran agreed to a United Nations–monitored cease-fire, ending the eight-year-long war on virtually the same terms it had previously rejected. There were costs, such as an estimated $250 million for the Pentagon to run the naval operations. There were casualties, including the 290 passengers on a commercial Iran Air flight mistakenly shot down by the U.S.S. *Vincennes*. And there were risks at a number of junctures "of becoming trapped in a process of escalation it [the Reagan administration] could not control."[18] But, overall, making the enemy of an enemy a friend appeared to have worked.

Still, though, there was substantial basis for questioning just how much of a friend Saddam had become. First of all, while Iraq had been removed from the state terrorist list, the Reagan administration's own intelligence indicated that "Baghdad's retreat from terrorism was painfully slow."[19] For example, on June 5, 1982, just a few months after Iraq was taken off the state terrorist list, Saddam had a hand in the attempted assassination in London of Israeli ambassador Shlomo Argov, the event that precipitated the Israeli-Palestinian-Syrian war in Lebanon. There also was the October 1985 hijacking of the cruise ship *Achille Lauro* and the murder of a U.S. citizen, the elderly wheelchair-bound Leon Klinghoffer, in which the main perpetrator, Abu Abbas, escaped capture with Iraqi assistance.[20] A few months later came the attempted terrorist attack at the Rome airport, about which one of the terrorists later confessed that they had come to Rome from Baghdad and that their mission was "to attack an American target, 'any one'."[21]

The point is not whether antiterrorism was a more or less important security concern than averting an Iranian victory over Iraq. A more balanced strategy could have pursued both objectives together. It was one thing to make the initial concession of taking Iraq off the terrorism list, but given the asymmetry of the relationship, the United States should have been able to hold Iraq to its commitment not to threaten the interests of its new and vital supporter—if not as a precondition then at least subsequently as a mandatory reciprocation. The economic benefits that Iraq was reaping from being off the terrorism list were quite substantial: over $5 billion in agricultural credits on very favorable financial terms, at a time when it was having trouble feeding its people; machinery and technology exports, of which 85 percent would have been unavailable had Iraq been on the terrorism list. It should have been made clear to Saddam that the United States was serious about both objectives, and that if he valued the economic benefits Iraq was receiving, then he needed to take that into account in setting his priorities. Instead, it was difficult for Saddam not to conclude that the United States was so fixated on the anti-Iran objective that Iraq was safe from reinclusion on the terrorism list no matter what he did. So he went on with terrorism—and stayed off the list.

A second major criticism focuses on the Reagan administration's excessive loosening of export controls on dual-use technologies. It was one thing to feed the Iraqi population while it was at war with Iran, or to provide some industrial equipment, or even to share military intelligence and to bolster Iraqi defensive military capabilities. It was quite another matter to loosen controls on dual-use technology and equipment to a degree that significantly and substantially contributed to Iraqi development of offensive military capabilities, especially in nuclear, biological, and chemical weapons. Iraq developed such capabilities far beyond the needs of its war with Iran—indeed, to the point where Iraq became the principal threat to the regional balance of power and to U.S. interests in the region.

Specific dual-use technology exports in particular exacerbated the effects of the misguided policy, despite the warnings available.[22] In one particularly salient case, Defense Department officials, such as Assistant Secretary Richard Perle, sought to block many of these technology exports because of concerns regarding Iraqi nuclear weapons, chemical weapons, and ballistic missile development. "There is a body of evidence," Perle warned, "indicating that Iraq continues to actively pursue an interest in nuclear weapons."[23] But Perle lost the bureaucratic battle. Indeed at a July 1986 NSC meeting, the Defense Department was given "a severe dressing-down for its 'obstruction' of Iraqi high technology applications." A new National Security Directive was issued "enjoining all government agencies 'to be more forthcoming' on Iraqi license requests."[24]

Following the Iran-contra fiasco, the Reagan administration loosened dual-use export controls even further, in an effort to refurbish their bona fides. "The instruction was issued," according to an internal Commerce Department memo, "to treat Iraqi applications favorably."[25] A Pentagon official claimed that, in reviewing the license applications for dual-use exports to Iraq, the Defense Department objected to about 40 percent of the applications.[26] (By way of comparison, the DOD objection rate at that time for dual-use export license applications to the Soviet Union was about 5 percent.)

What concerned some officials about the license applications was not only the nature of the exports involved but also the identity of the Iraqi customers. Exports "were knowingly sent," according to a former White House official, "to Iraqi nuclear installations." One of them was Sa'ad 16, said by Saddam's government to be simply a university research unit and industrial facility, but which proved to be Iraq's largest and most important site for missile and nonconventional weapons development. As an analysis by the Defense Department's Office for Non-Proliferation concluded, "almost all of the labs named deal with areas applicable to missile research and production. . . . A lab for 'seismographic soil test' was also listed, possibly indicating nuclear research." Then there was the Nassr State Establishment for Mechanical Industries (NASSR), known since the 1970s to be a key military installation. When Commerce was considering a dual-use export application in July 1988, DOD stated in no uncertain terms that this was a "bad end-user." The export application and numerous others were licensed anyway.[27] When it could not stop the exports, DOD tried at least to require verification of nonmilitary end uses. They proposed an agreement with the Iraqi government allowing on-site inspections for a four-year period, but the proposal was turned down.

In sum, the basis for the alliance of convenience that the Reagan administration struck with Iraq was the shared, or at least coinciding, interests of those who had mutual enemies. Given the severity of the Iranian threat and continuing U.S.-Soviet global competition, the basis was unquestionably a strong one. But even then it was not complete. Issues such as terrorism still were points of tension. There were signs of Iraqi military ambitions exceeding mere survival of the war with Iran. Meanwhile, Saddam Hussein had some praise—but still mostly virulent rhetoric—for the United States and mostly repression for his own people.

Phase Two: "The Foot Not Put Down"

The chemical bombs began to fall on the Iraqi Kurds on the morning of August 25, 1988. Villagers later would tell investigators flown in by the U.S. Congress of "yellowish clouds," of gruesome human deaths, of dead livestock, even of birds that had "fallen out of the sky."[28] With the Iran-Iraq war over—indeed, it had ended only five days earlier—Saddam Hussein was wasting little time in mounting his "final offensive" against the Iraqi Kurds.

The U.S. Senate swiftly and unanimously passed the Prevention of Genocide Act of 1988 calling for tough economic sanctions against Iraq. "Iraq's campaign against the Kurdish people," the Senate bill stated, "appears to constitute an act of genocide, a crime abhorred by civilized people everywhere and banned under international law."[29] The Reagan administration, however, strongly opposed the Senate bill and managed to defeat it. The attacks on the Kurds were "abhorrent and unjustifiable," Secretary of State

George Shultz declared. But to impose sanctions was "premature," one of his deputies argued. We need "solid, businesslike relations" with Iraq, said another. The bottom line, as laid out in an administration memorandum, was that "there should be no radical policy change now regarding Iraq."[30]

This position was curious in a number of respects:

· With the Iran-Iraq war over, the enemy-enemy-friend rationale for looking the other way in the name of the alliance of convenience had become less pressing.

· Amidst the debt and devastation wrought by eight years of war, the Iraqi economy was potentially quite vulnerable to economic sanctions.

· The disinclination to use economic sanctions for foreign policy purposes in this instance was out of character for an administration that had so vehemently opposed "solid, businesslike relations" as a strategy of influence when it came to sanctions against the Soviet Union, Nicaragua, or Libya.

· Not only was chemical warfare morally reprehensible but also a clear and blatant violation of the 1925 Geneva Protocol Banning the Use of Chemical Weapons in War, to which Iraq was a party.

Why, then, were there no U.S. sanctions? The 1988 sanctions debate was a key transitional stage in U.S.-Iraqi relations, which can help in understanding both the strategy and the politics of the policy course on which the Bush administration would embark in 1989.

One of the main arguments all along for increasing trade with Iraq had been that expanded economic relations would be a source of U.S. political leverage. The more Iraq came to value and depend on trade with the United States, the greater the purported potential U.S. influence on Iraqi policies. As proponents of sanctions saw it, now was the time to tap that potential. The Iraqi economy was in dire straits, and the toll from eight years of war was an estimated $450 billion. To be sure, with his police state apparatus at his disposal, Saddam did not have to worry about Iraq's consumers marching in the streets. But Ba'athist party political domination traditionally had been part of a Faustian-like bargain that the Iraqi people had been willing to make in return for a much higher level of public services and standard of living than in most other Arab countries. After the deprivations and disruptions of eight years of war, there was an expectation of a "peace dividend."

Yet burdened with $80 billion of debt, the country's availability of new credit was tight. Western commercial banks, if they were willing to lend at all, were asking interest rates as high as 15–20 percent. Most Western governments had put Iraq "off cover" for medium-term and even short-term financing. Nor was there much relief in sight from world oil markets. The combination of declining world prices and the disruptions of the war had pushed Iraqi oil revenues down from $22 billion in 1980 to a low of $7.8 billion in 1986. In 1988 they still were only $11 billion, or half of the pre-war level, not even taking inflation into account.

Therefore, the relative value to Iraq of its trade with the United States was quite significant. U.S. Commodity Credit Corporation (CCC) credits had not followed the general pattern of tightening credit; in fact, they had grown to exceed $1 billion per year. The United States also had become a major customer for Iraqi oil. In 1981, before the tilt to Iraq began, the United States did not import a single barrel of Iraqi oil. Even as late as 1987, U.S. imports of Iraqi oil were no more than 30 million barrels. But in 1988 this figure increased more than 400 percent, to 126 million barrels, amounting to one of every four barrels of Iraqi oil exports.[31]

As U.S.-Iraqi trade expanded, not only the Iraqis derived economic benefits. There are, after all, at least two parties to every economic transaction. One of the parties was an American farmer, an American worker, an American corporation. Their interests lay in the continuation if not the expansion of this trade—surely not in its disruption by economic sanctions. This was especially true for U.S. agriculture. The very mention of sanctions evoked bitter memories of the 1980 grain embargo (the "Carter embargo," as Ronald Reagan called it during the presidential campaign) against the Soviet Union following its invasion of Afghanistan. In 1988 the Iraqi market was the twelfth largest overall market for U.S. agricultural exports. For some crops, such as rice, it was the number one export market. Iraq was second only to Mexico as a recipient of CCC export credit guarantees. Another $1.1 billion in guarantees were slated for fiscal year 1989, on top of $1.1 billion the previous year and $3.4 billion cumulative since fiscal year 1983.

The Iraqis were quick to recognize the potential for reversing the direction of who had leverage over whom in the U.S.-Iraq trade relationship. They threatened both to turn elsewhere for their future agricultural imports and to renege on the roughly $1.5 billion in outstanding CCC debt. The Reagan administration did less countering of such threats than conveying them to Capitol Hill. The message was received. Iraq was "a large and growing market for U.S. agricultural exports," noted House Agriculture Committee chairman E. ("Kika") de la Garza (D-Texas). "In light of the difficulties our nation's farmers have faced over the past few years, I am deeply concerned over any possible loss of a major market for U.S.

agricultural commodities." Of course, de la Garza added, "at the same time I in no way wish to condone the use of chemical weapons by Iraq, or any other country."[32] Agriculture chairman de la Garza and other Democrats from agricultural districts joined with Republicans in the House to block the original Senate sanctions bill, which would have suspended the CCC program. This coalition ensured that the closest that the House bill came to agricultural sanctions was a loose requirement that the president impose "appropriate additional sanctions" if Iraq again used chemical weapons.

It also was business as usual on the manufacturing and dual-use technology export side. Trade with Iraq in manufactured goods was not as high as in agriculture, but exports were growing. Billions of dollars in contracts had been signed in such Iraqi sectors as petroleum, electricity generation, petrochemicals, steel, and transportation.[33] Not only would these be lost if sanctions were imposed, but U.S. companies would also be excluded from the anticipated boom in Iraqi reconstruction from the war with Iran. The Commerce Department estimated the potential for $3 billion of U.S. nonagricultural exports annually for the foreseeable future.

The U.S. Chamber of Commerce urged House Foreign Affairs Committee chairman Dante Fascell to "set aside the emotions of the moment" and ponder the economic costs of sanctions against Iraq.[34] Particularly active in antisanctions lobbying was the U.S.-Iraq Business Forum, which had been established in 1985.[35] Members included numerous oil companies heavily involved in importing Iraqi oil (Amoco, Mobil, Exxon, Texaco, Occidental), defense contractors (Lockheed, Bell Helicopter-Textron, United Technologies), and other Fortune 500 companies (AT&T, General Motors, Bechtel, Caterpillar).

The Business Forum exemplified the reverse leverage phenomenon even more graphically than the CCC credits lobby. While not formally a lobbyist for the Iraqi government, its ties to the Iraqi Embassy in Washington had been quite close. Even before the forum had its own office, Iraqi Ambassador Nizar Hamdoon had written to the chief executive officers of several major American corporations on its behalf: "Any United States company interested in doing business with Iraq . . . would do well to join the Forum." Ambassador Hamdoon later made the link tighter, telling a group of CEOs that "our people in Baghdad give priority—when there is competition between the two companies—to the one that is a member of the Forum."

The U.S.-Iraqi Business Forum also had close ties to the Reagan administration. "I talked to senior officials in the administration," forum president Marshall Wiley later stated. "I asked if they had any objections to what we were doing. We were told that not only were our goals consistent with U.S. policy, but what we were endeavoring to do served to enhance their policy. The administration wanted closer diplomatic and commercial ties to Iraq, the very same things are wanted."[36] And the Business Forum weighed in heavily both in Congress and with the press on the sanctions debate.

All told, as one congressional staff aide put it, the lobbying against sanctions "was obscene." All "the special interests," one senator lamented, "got into the act."[37] Whatever leverage the sanctions may have brought the United States over Iraq was being constrained by the leverage that groups with vested interests in trade with Iraq were exerting in reverse.

It would be simplistic, though, to reduce the Reagan administration's opposition to sanctions against Iraq simply to economic interest group politics. There also was the geopolitical calculus that, as one internal analysis put it, Iraq's foreign policy was moving "deeper into the mainstream." Numerous Iraqi actions and attitudes were cited in a key State Department study as evidence of a "moderating policy trend":

Iraq's shift toward moderation, cooperation with neighbors and mainline Arab positions on Palestine seems *permanent and deepening.*

In the likely case that the Iran-Iraq war ends in an armed truce rather than a peace treaty or a decisive victory, Iraq will be vulnerable, hence *unlikely to embark on foreign adventures* in the Gulf or against Israel.

Iraq has developed good working relations with Kuwait and is no longer trying to encroach on Kuwaiti territory.[38]

While this study was written before the chemical weapons attacks on the Kurds, its analysis was based on trends that it identified as dating back to 1978. Moreover, other administration analyses contemporaneous with the chemical weapons attacks took the conclusions even further, arguing that even Saddam himself was changing. He was deemed the type of leader with whom one could pursue a strategy of "persuasion," to whom one could make the case that he "has more to gain from conforming to international standards than [from] flouting them."[39]

However, at least two major dissents were mounted in the Reagan State Department. One was a paper written by a member of the Policy Planning Staff, questioning how much Saddam had changed and whether he might now need to be "contained" to keep him from taking advantage of the regional power imbalance left by such a weakened Iran.[40] The United States therefore needed to be prepared "to punish Iraq." But the paper took the balance-of-power logic even further, arguing that the United States also needed to "bolster an economically and militarily strained Iran from Iraqi exploitation."[41]

Clearly, given the continued intensity of anti-American sentiment and radical Islamic fundamentalism in Iran at the time, there is room to question whether any retilt toward Iran would have worked. A more nuanced policy of wariness and firmness toward both Iran and Iraq may have made more strategic sense. But what is striking is that the whole argument was dismissed less by any analytic refutation of its strategic logic than on political grounds. In the wake of the Iran-contra scandal, anything that could be interpreted as "soft on Iran" was politically untenable. The Policy Planning paper was leaked to the press in mid-September, likely intentionally, and high administration officials rushed to disown it. Whatever strategic debate there might have been was cut short by political considerations. The "soft on Iran" brush could tar a policy proposal in the same way that "soft on communism" had done for so long.

In the end, President Reagan had no need to veto the sanctions bill because it got tied up in the end-of-session maneuvering and gridlock on Capitol Hill. But the pen was ready. There would be no sanctions. Indeed, quite to the contrary, new licenses for dual-use technology exports were being granted at a rate more than 50 percent greater than *before* Saddam's gassing of the Kurds. One Reagan Commerce Department official gave sworn testimony to a congressional committee that when he proposed that sanctions be imposed, he was told that the policy was to continue to be one of "normal trade." Reagan administration records show that between September and December 1988, 65 licenses were granted for dual-use technology exports. This averages out as an annual rate of 260 licenses, more than double the rate for January through August 1988 (85 licenses, for a 128 annual rate).[42]

Later, following the Iraqi invasion of Kuwait, one former Reagan official would lament that "it would have been much better at the time of their use of poison gas [in 1988] if we'd put our foot down."[43] What was a dictator such as Saddam to think, when even the use of chemical weapons fell within the bounds of behavior that the United States considered tolerable? If this new relationship with the United States was not conditional on an issue as salient as chemical warfare, then what would it be conditional upon? And how credible could future threats be if they needed to be made?

Phase Three: The "Family of Nations" Strategy

National Security Directive (NSD) 26, signed by President George Bush on October 2, 1989, established the goal, stated the rationale, and defined the strategy. The goal: to achieve "normal relations between the United States and Iraq." The rationale: This "would serve our longer-term interests and promote stability in both the Gulf and the Middle East." The strategy: Use "economic and political incentives for Iraq to moderate its behavior and to increase our influence with Iraq."[44]

The essence of the Bush strategy as manifested in NSD-26 was a belief in both the value of and the possibilities for moving beyond the wartime alliance of convenience to a more enduring *accommodation* between the United States and Iraq. The Iran-Iraq war was over, but the bases for a U.S.-Iraqi relationship—strategic, political, and economic—were seen as more robust after six years of nurturing and amidst the continuing changes in global and regional geopolitics than when the Reagan administration had initiated the opening to Iraq in 1982. While this strategic assessment was not without its cautions and caveats, the overall thrust was toward building a fuller, deeper, and more lasting accommodation with Iraq—at least a "limited detente," as one White House official put it, with Saddam Hussein.[45]

Based on interviews, declassified documents, and other sources, four core concepts emerge as key to the "logic of accommodation" embodied in NSD-26: (1) the persistence of the threats from Iran and the Soviet Union; (2) a view of Iraq as a force for regional stability and peace; (3) gains both political and economic to be made from increased trade with Iraq; and (4) relegating human rights issues (including the Kurds) to "low-politics" status.

Persistent Threats

U.S.-Iranian relations at the end of the Iran-Iraq war were in many respects worse than when the Reagan administration first tilted toward Iraq in 1982. As bad as relations had been then, there were no direct military hostilities between U.S. and Iranian forces until the numerous incidents of 1987–88, including the U.S.S. *Vincennes*–Iran Air tragedy. Iran also was continuing to aid Hizbollah and other terrorist groups in Lebanon still holding Americans hostage. Then there was the death sentence pronounced in February 1989 against British author Salman Rushdie for his "blasphemous" book, *The Satanic Verses*. Even when the Ayatollah Khomeini died in June 1989, he left in his last will and testament a call for "fierce animosity to the West, a militant assertion of Iran's Islamic identity."[46]

As to the Soviet Union, the other original member of the enemy-enemy-friend calculus, its threat was diminished but still not to be dismissed by the Bush administration. Recall that the Bush administration's initial approach to U.S.-Soviet relations was extremely cautious, no more than "status quo plus," in its own terms. The question of the day was still whether Gorbachev was "for real." In the Persian Gulf and Middle East, the Soviets were even then seen as very much the formidable rival they had been for decades.

Iraq as a Force for Regional Peace and Stability

The Bush administration saw the "deeper-into-the-mainstream" trend pointed to by the Reagan administration in Iraqi foreign policy as continuing. Some caution was counseled "because Iraq's postwar intentions are still evolving." But the possibility was pushed that "the lessons of war may have changed Iraq from a radical state challenging the system, to a more responsible, status-quo state working within the system and promoting stability in the region."[47] The goal was to reform and "resocialize" Saddam into "the family of nations."[48]

Part of the reasoning was what some referred to as the "exhaustion" thesis; that is, after eight years of war, Saddam and his people had little endurance left for further aggression, and with their huge war debt and economic reconstruction needs, were primed to be responsive to inducements to moderation. Some of this reasoning was based on interpretations of signs of moderation in Saddam's recent regional policies. In February 1989 Iraq joined with Egypt, Jordan, and North Yemen to create the Arab Cooperation Council (ACC) as a new regional economic and nonmilitary grouping. Saddam reestablished diplomatic relations with Egypt and provided key sponsorship for getting Egypt invited in May 1989 to its first Arab League summit in almost a decade. Saddam also signed bilateral non-aggression pacts with Saudi Arabia and Bahrain, ostensibly to allay any fears they might have of Iraq's regional ambitions now that its war with Iran was over. The accord with Saudi Arabia established the principle of "non-use of force and armies between the two states."[49]

Of all the regional issues, the main one on which the Bush administration wanted Iraqi cooperation was the Arab-Israeli peace process. Saddam was supporting PLO chairman Yassir Arafat in his recognition of Israel's right to exist and the opening of an official PLO-U.S. dialogue. The initial breakthrough had been achieved in December 1988 in the closing days of the Reagan administration. It was up to the Bush administration to sustain and develop the dialogue. Given the opposition of other longtime rejectionist forces (for example, Iran, Syria, radical PLO factions), Saddam's support was considered crucial.

Gains from Trade

One set of gains to be made from increased trade with Iraq was political.

"Trade is the best key to political influence," as one report held. "Economic incentives," NSD-26 affirmed, were to be proposed "for Iraq to moderate its behavior and to increase our influence." CCC credit guarantees continued to be one of the principal economic incentives. Iraq's need for agricultural imports kept increasing, but not its ability to pay for them. There also was a sense that nonagricultural trade could, and should, take off. "*To Iraq, technology is our most important asset.*"[50] Postwar reconstruction was expected to set off a boom in Iraqi demand for industrial equipment and technology, construction projects, oil equipment, and other sectors in which U.S. companies were highly competitive.

The other gains to be made from trade were of course economic. "I'd be very wealthy," an NSC aide later remarked about interest group pressure, "if I could have a dollar for every company that called me [during the drafting of NSD-26]." She added that "the same was true for members of Congress," pushing the interests of constituents and political supporters.[51]

The Kurds and Human Rights: Low Politics

Human rights considerations are included in NSD-26 as a subject that "should continue to be an important element in our policy toward Iraq." This, however, is a statement that cannot be accepted at face value. First, it is difficult to see from whence this continuation was to be—from the Reagan-Bush opposition to the chemical warfare sanctions? Second, other Bush administration documents indicate much less importance being given to human rights.

The resemblance to the Bush policy toward China following the June 1989 Tiananmen massacre is strong: Geopolitical factors took precedence; quiet diplomacy was preferred to sanctions; expectations were limited; and the main concern was to prevent human rights from becoming an obstacle to the strategic and economic bases for accommodation.

Yet during the period leading up to the signing of NSD-26 on October 2, 1989, repeated warnings were sounded about Iraqi actions, capabilities, and intentions. These warnings were quite inconsistent with the logic of accommodation, and they went unheeded.

Some examples:

· In mid-January 1989 ABC News broke a story about Iraq's development of biological weapons. Despite being a signatory to the 1972 Biological Weapons Convention, Iraq had programs under way to develop weapons capable of spreading typhoid, cholera, and anthrax massively throughout a targeted population. The news reports were confirmed by U.S. government and other sources.[52]

· Testimony on continuing Iraqi chemical weapons programs came from top U.S. intelligence officials. CIA Director William H. Webster pointed to Iraq as the single largest producer of chemical weapons in the Third World.[53]

· Rear Admiral Thomas A. Brooks, director of Naval Intelligence, testified to Congress that Iraq was among those states "actively pursuing a capability" for nuclear weapons. Even more urgent concerns were being expressed by key officials in the Department of Energy's Proliferation Intelligence Program.[54]

· In late February 1989, Amnesty International issued a report on Iraq ("Children: Innocent Victims of Political Repression") that should have shocked even those who might have grown immune to stories of human rights violations. Even in the world as imperfect as Amnesty knew it to be, "we can think of none which cries out more for international attention and action."[55]

· Saddam again moved against the Kurds. An estimated half a million Kurds were being forcibly relocated. The Senate Foreign Relations Committee proposed economic sanctions. The Bush administration opposed them.

· The First Baghdad International Exhibition for Military Production was held in April, commemorating Saddam Hussein's birthday.[56] "Defense equipment for peace and prosperity" was the official slogan. But the military exhibition was a shock even to many of the arms traders and government officials who had been dealing with (and selling to) Iraq for a long time. On exhibit were not only foreign weapons but also Iraqi-made weapons of surprising sophistication and quantity. They included at least ten Iraqi-built ballistic missiles; a new transporter for mobile SCUD missile launchers that so closely resembled commercial vehicles as to make surveillance more difficult; French Mirage jets modified to carry Soviet-style laser-guided missiles; three types of fuel-air explosives; new ground-based and airborne radar systems; long-range artillery rockets; and a prototype of the "Super Gun." This giant piece of artillery was designed to "shoot" thousand-pound bombs—including chemical, biological, and possibly small nuclear warheads—over distances greater than six hundred miles.[57]

· A series of top-secret high-level intelligence reports from the U.S. Defense Intelligence Agency (DIA) and the CIA in June and September 1989 provided extensive evidence that Saddam Hussein had developed a network of front companies across Europe and in the United States through which he was acquiring key technology for building his weapons arsenal, including nuclear, chemical, and biological weapons and ballistic missiles.[58] Yet the Bush administration continued to license dual-use exports to Iraq. Nor does it appear to have been a question of these reports not reaching top Bush administration officials. The June DIA report, according to the *Los Angeles Times,* went to "high level Administration officials." The *Los Angeles Times* reporters were even more specific with respect to the CIA report of September 3. It went "to 38 administration officials, including seven at the National Security Council and 10 at the State Department," including Secretary of State James Baker. Another CIA report the very next day (September 4) was written in "stronger and more definitive" language, apparently because of concern that the prior version had not made it clear that the report was principally about Iraqi development of nuclear weapons. This, too, went to Secretary Baker and other top officials. And two *New York Times* reporters state that evidence of the Iraqi arms buildup was presented directly by President Bush at an NSC meeting.[59]

· On August 4, 1989, acting on tips from informants, the FBI raided the Atlanta branch of the Italian Banca Nazionale del Lavoro (BNL). What they found was evidence of the largest bank fraud in U.S. history (a record later broken by the Bank of Credit and Commerce International, or BCCI). Far beyond the $720 million in CCC credits for Iraq that it had been guaranteeing, BNL-Atlanta had made over $4 billion in unauthorized and largely unsecured loans to Iraq—and not simply to buy wheat, rice, and corn. Much of this money was used by Iraq to acquire materials, equipment, and technology for nuclear and chemical weapons and ballistic missile programs. BNL had been acting as the principal banker for Saddam's global network of front companies.

DOD officials informed the FBI of their own suspicions of BNL's role in Iraq's procurement network. The Customs Service wrote the U.S. attorney, Northern District of Georgia, who was charged with the legal investigation, about their suspicions that BNL had "provided loans to various U.S. firms for the illegal export to Iraq of missile related technology to be used in the Condor II project." The assistant U.S. attorney prosecuting the case told Federal Reserve officials that "she believes that BNL-Atlanta made loans to finance the purchase by Iraq of missile casings."[60] A State Department briefing memo acknowledged that "the money does appear to have been used to finance a wide range of imports and projects, probably including the acquisition of sensitive technology."[61] The Agriculture Department's inspector-general was so concerned about the revelations of corruption in the CCC program that he advised scaling back the upcoming fiscal year 1990 CCC program, at least on an interim basis. The Iraqi government expressed "surprise" at the whole outcry. All its financing arrangements with BNL, it insisted, were "correct and legal." And the money was spent "purely for civil use."[62]

Nevertheless, NSD-26 was sent to the president and signed by him on October 2, 1989. The point, of course, is not merely that a piece of paper was signed by the president. National Security Directives are the *end products* of extensive and high priority deliberative processes, and as such, though often relatively short, they reflect more complex and complete strategies. Also, once promulgated, they become *instruments* to be invoked as authoritative sources of support and justification in intra-administration policy disputes. As one veteran State Department official observed, "Once it [an NSD] is signed by the president, opposing the policy is no longer a matter of bureaucratic in-fighting but willful opposition to the President."[63] The argument that a particular position is consistent with the mandate established by the president in a National Security Directive can often be the margin needed to prevail over a contending position. This is very much what NSC-26 manifested, and how it was used.

The other key decision made by the Bush administration around the same time involved the allocation of $1 billion in new CCC credit guarantees to Iraq for the new fiscal year 1990. Earlier, at the August 10 meeting of the National Advisory Council on International Monetary and Financial Policy (NAC), the interagency group with jurisdiction over CCC and other international financial policies, the Agriculture Department had proposed the additional $1 billion for Iraq for fiscal year 1990. But this NAC meeting took place less than a week after the BNL raid. At the insistence of the representatives of the Treasury Department and the Federal Reserve Board, the NAC deferred any recommendation.

It took almost three months for even a compromise FY 1990 CCC package to be approved for Iraq. Even USDA began to have its doubts, fearing that the BNL case might engulf the CCC program in a scandal that could have broader reverberations. But the key pushes came from the State Department, including direct action by Secretary of State Baker. At one interagency meeting, the State representative "was particularly forceful in arguing that [CCC] programming should go forward," stressing that Iraq had great strategic importance to the United States.[64] On the eve of another meeting, Baker personally called Agriculture Secretary Clayton Yeutter to make the case.[65] Similar efforts were made by Deputy Secretary of State Lawrence Eagleburger and other Baker State Department officials.

The NAC finally gave approval. Iraq was to receive $1 billion in fiscal year 1990 CCC credit guarantees, split into two $500 million tranches. "Your call to Yeutter and our subsequent efforts with OMB and Treasury paid off," one of Baker's top aides wrote him. You should "break the good news to Foreign Minister Tariq Aziz, since he raised the issue with you, and you promised to take a personal interest in it."[66] Baker's telex to Aziz stated that the decision to grant the full $1 billion in new CCC credits "reflects the importance we attach to our relationship with Iraq."[67]

In that same cable, Secretary Baker laid out a quid pro quo. It would "be useful," he told Aziz, "if you could weigh in with [the Palestinians] and . . . urge them to give a positive response [to the Baker plan]. . . . We are at a critical point in our diplomacy." But far from providing the "weighing in" quo for the $1 billion CCC quid, shortly after the Baker cable the Iraqis announced the creation of the Popular Arab Front, dedicated to supporting the intifada. On even this issue, of such importance to the Bush administration, the Iraqis were not being accommodating. Not to mention the global front company network, or the BNL scandal, or the treatment of the Kurds. None of these developments squared with the logic of accommodation. And they were all quite visible at the very time that the die was being cast.

Phase Four: The Enemy of My Enemy . . . Is Still My Enemy, Too

The whole idea, President Bush would later contend, was to bring Saddam Hussein "into the family of nations." That was what the Reagan administration had started trying to do. That was what NSD-26 was all about. And that was what the Bush administration tried to do, right up to August 2, 1990, when Saddam invaded Kuwait and showed how far outside the family of nations he was intent on remaining.

In December 1989, only two months after NSD-26 was promulgated and one month after the new $1 billion CCC commitment, U.S. intelligence picked up evidence of Iraqi tests of two new long-range ballistic missiles. There also were further reports on Saddam's nuclear weapons programs. The interagency Subcommittee on Nuclear Export Controls (SNEC), chaired by the State Department, recently had received intelligence briefings leading it to conclude that "Iraq is acquiring nuclear related equipment and materials without regard to immediate need." SNEC members were informed of the intelligence community's presumption that "the Iraqi government is interested in acquiring a nuclear explosive capability." They also were shown supporting evidence that "Iraq is acquiring nuclear related equipment and materials without regard to immediate need."[68] Yet, as Alan Friedman recounts, such doubts were "brushed aside" by Baker's State Department, and "within twenty-four hours of the intelligence briefing, State . . . recommended seven of the nine exports [then under consideration] for immediate approval."[69]

Nor were the signs from Baghdad particularly encouraging on the Arab-Israeli peace process. Iraq convened the Popular Arab Front's first "intifada support" meeting in Baghdad, which issued a communique in support of "the brave Palestinian intifadah" (as well as expressing "solidarity with the heroic people of Vietnam . . . Namibia, South Africa and Nicaragua").[70] This was followed by broadcasts from PLO central radio, transmitting from Baghdad, assailing the U.S.-led peace talks as having reached a "level of absurdity." In his Army Day speech, Saddam warned against "hostile, aggressive and usurpist Zionism," and implicated the United States directly, asserting that "if Israel carries out an act of aggression, the United States will not be able to deny the charge of encouraging Israel to carry out such an act."[71]

Yet the Baker State Department continued to push ahead with the second $500 million tranche of CCC credit guarantees. "We want to move ahead on the second tranche this month, as the Iraqis have requested," a January 4, 1990, memo stated.[72] Others, though, were not quite so dismissive. The BNL investigations had been uncovering numerous irregularities and possible illegalities. The U.S. Attorney's Office in Atlanta indicated that it anticipated its first indictments by early February. The USDA, with the support of Treasury, was willing to continue the first tranche without suspension but was resisting the release of the second tranche.

There was also some dissent from within State. A paper entitled "Containing Iraq" was prepared by two members of the Policy Planning Staff. The analogy as reflected in the title was to Kennan's original strategy for dealing with the Soviet Union. Saddam's regime had to be viewed as inherently and continuingly expansionist by nature, irrespective of how exhausted it might be at any particular moment. As with Stalin's Russia, if Saddam's Iraq was forced to make choices, the regime's internal contradictions would be exacerbated. The policy being proposed was for firmer, more vigilant policies: not necessarily a return to pre-1982 strict adversarial relations, but having an element of containment to firm up and balance the overly accommodationist NSD-26 approach. One proposal, with its own touch of historical irony, was that Iraq be put on the agenda for the upcoming Soviet-U.S. ministerial meeting in pursuit of something of a joint containment effort.[73] But the paper had little impact.

On February 15, 1990, the Voice of America (VOA) aired an editorial transmitted into a number of Arab countries, including Iraq, reflecting on the implications of the recent freedom wave that had swept away the dictators of Eastern Europe.

A successful tyranny requires a strong, ruthless secret police. A successful democracy requires the abolition of such a force. That is a lesson the people of Eastern Europe have learned well. . . . Secret police are also entrenched in other countries, such as China, North Korea, Iran, *Iraq*, Syria, Libya, Cuba and Albania. The rulers of these countries hold power by force and fear, not by the consent of the governed. But as East Europeans demonstrated so dramatically in 1989, the tide of history is against such rulers. The 1990s should belong not to the dictators and the secret police, but to the people.[74]

The broadcast was almost routine for the times. Not, though, to the ears of Saddam Hussein. Deputy Foreign Minister Hamdoon "convoked" U.S. Ambassador April Glaspie to protest such "a flagrant interference in the internal affairs of Iraq and the direct official [by the U.S. government] instigation against the legitimate authority [Saddam's regime]." Of course, Hamdoon didn't mention that Saddam was said to have ordered the heads of his security services to watch videotapes of the fall of Romania's Nicolae Ceausescu, so as to learn from his mistakes.[75]

But instead of expressing outrage at the outlandish "flagrant interference" charges, or using the incident to raise human rights and democratization issues, the Bush administration sought mostly to assuage Saddam's hurt feelings. The message of apology from Washington was delivered by Ambassador Glaspie:

President Bush wants good relations with Iraq, relations built on confidence and trust, so that we can discuss a broad range of issues frankly and fruitfully. I am sorry that the Government of Iraq did not inform me of its concern about the editorial sooner, so that I could have provided you with the official assurance of our regret without delay.[76]

All future VOA editorials were to be cleared by the State Department, by order of Secretary Baker.

Yet, even by his own standards Saddam had been quite strident of late. He used the first anniversary of the Arab Cooperation Council, the founding of which the Bush administration had pointed to as an indicator of

Iraqi moderation, as the occasion for launching a series of attacks on the United States. Indeed, Saddam went so far as to say that there was no room among "good" Arabs for "the faint-hearted who would argue that, as a superpower, the United States will be the decisive factor and others have no choice but to submit."[77] Saddam also used the ACC's first anniversary summit to issue demands on his fellow Arab states. For one, he demanded a moratorium on the $40 billion debt—about half Iraq's total debt—that Iraq owed to other Arab states in the wake of the Iran-Iraq war. In the ensuing months the proposed moratorium hardened to demands for outright debt forgiveness. "Let the Gulf regimes know," he told President Mubarak and King Hussein, "that if they do not give this money to me, I will know how to get it."[78]

In late March an Iraq-destined shipment of 95 krytrons, also known as nuclear triggers, was seized in London in a joint British-American "sting." Official denials were of course the order of the day. One of Saddam's ambassadors claimed that the incident was but the latest foray of an anti-Iraq campaign run by Britain, the United States, and "the Zionist entity." "Everybody knows that the Iraqi nuclear program is for peaceful purposes," he continued. The Zionists and their allies were simply trying "to find the necessary justifications or atmosphere for a new Israeli military aggression against Iraq."[79]

Saddam further demonstrated his disregard for world opinion when on March 15 he executed Farzad Bazoft, an Iranian-born British journalist falsely accused of spying. British consular officials were refused access to the prisoner. Prime Minister Margaret Thatcher strongly protested. When government-to-government negotiations made no progress, she appealed to U.N. Secretary General Javier Perez de Cuellar to intercede. But Saddam hanged his "spy." He and his henchmen were described as "gloating" in their defiance. "Thatcher wanted him alive," said Minister of Information Latif Nussayif Jassim. "We sent him home in a box."[80] It truly was a "spring of bad behavior," as one Bush administration official termed it.[81] The question remained what the Bush administration intended to do about it.

On April 2, at a ceremony honoring his armed forces and military-industrial complex, Saddam launched into a diatribe more sweeping and scathing than even his February ACC speeches. On the United States: "Present-day America is a great nation—a great nation by material standards not by moral standards. A great person is judged by his manners. The United States is a superpower in accordance with material yardsticks. It is not a superpower in accordance with moral and ethical yardsticks. In practice, they are hypocrites. They are using it as a slogan for neo-imperialism, for meddling in the internal affairs of others."

To Israel, Saddam boasted that "we have the binary chemical" weapon, the most lethal of all chemical weapons, otherwise possessed only by the United States and the Soviet Union, and he threatened that with this weapon *"we will make the fire eat up half of Israel."*[82] The State Department immediately denounced the speech as "inflammatory, irresponsible and outrageous." A White House statement called it "particularly deplorable and irresponsible." President Bush himself stated, "This is no time to be talking about using chemical or biological weapons. This is no time to be escalating tensions in the Middle East. And I found those statements to be bad. . . . I would suggest that those statements be withdrawn."[83]

On April 16 a key meeting was convened in the White House Situation Room. The group was the interagency Deputies Committee, chaired by Deputy National Security Adviser Robert Gates. This was the first meeting at such a senior level to assess relations with Iraq since the issuance of NSD-26. But although positions had begun to shift, and working groups were tasked to come up with proposals for policy revisions, the April 16 meeting ended with "nothing decided" in any definitive sense, according to a Commerce official. Key top foreign policy officials still were reluctant. A *Wall Street Journal* reporter quotes sources pointing to Gates as "leery about moving too quickly." A *Los Angeles Times* story citing the notes of participants in the meeting quotes both Under Secretary of State Robert Kimmitt and a top NSC official on the matter of export controls: "the President doesn't want to single out Iraq."[84]

The Bush administration also continued to oppose congressional proposals for sanctions. It opposed one bill that would have imposed sanctions because of Iraqi human rights violations, even though part of the evidence of human rights violations was drawn from the administration's own official report. Nor had a final decision yet been made on the second CCC tranche.

On May 29 the Deputies Committee met again. This meeting, according to one participant, was "initiated by NSC staff because they want to prevent the CCC program from being canceled as it would exacerbate the already strained foreign policy relations with Iraq."[85] Again, the action taken was limited. The second CCC tranche remained suspended but was not terminated. The press announcement cited the allegation of fraud and abuse but made no linkage to foreign policy concerns. Export-Import Bank lending was to be subject to project-by-project review, but the presidential waiver of restrictions on lending was kept in place. Export controls were to be tightened but were not targeted against Iraq, being instead an effort to strengthen the multilateral nonproliferation regimes generally.

Yet at the time of the latest export control review, the Bush administration gave approval to export a shipment of glass-fiber technology, which could be used either for commercial manufacturing or for ballistic missiles and nuclear weapons. A year later, UN inspectors would find it as part of Iraq's nuclear weapons complex.[86]

In the predawn hours of May 30, Israeli forces intercepted a small flotilla of speedboats carrying armed terrorists toward the Israeli coast. The terrorist operation was targeted at the beaches near Tel-Aviv—beaches frequented by tourists from the United States and elsewhere, as well as by Israelis—and also at the U.S. Embassy. Any doubt as to the identity of the terrorists was removed when the Palestine Liberation Front (PLF) faction of Abu Abbas issued a communiqué *from its Baghdad office* proudly claiming responsibility. It was Abu Abbas who had been responsible for the *Achille Lauro* hijacking and the murder of Leon Klinghoffer in 1985, aided in his escape by Saddam Hussein.

Nor was Saddam limiting his support of terrorism to Abu Abbas. The State Department cited "disturbing reports that Iraqi officials have been in contact with members of the notorious Abu Nidal organization . . . and a number of other Palestinian groups and factions which we believe have representatives in Iraq."[87] The *New York Times* had run a story in May citing Arab diplomats as sources that Yassir Arafat had ordered "several thousand guerrillas" to relocate from Jordan and other Arab nations to Iraq. By August, according to a report by the Rand Corporation, there were some fourteen hundred terrorists operating out of Iraq—a substantial number in itself and about a 100 percent increase over the previous year.[88]

The State Department cable traffic shows that by late June a somewhat tougher line was being taken with Saddam on terrorism, but not tough enough to put Iraq back on the state terrorism list, which would have hit the country hard. Had the U.S. government not removed Iraq from the list, the country would have been disqualified for nearly 85 percent of the exports that had been licensed for Iraq since 1982.

In May 1990 two Rand Corporation analysts circulated a draft paper assessing the threat posed by Saddam Hussein. On the one hand, it offered an "optimistic view" that Saddam "has learned his lesson from the Iran-Iraq war and would not return to his 'bad old days' of threatening Iraq's neighbors"; its "pessimistic view," on the other hand, was that "historically, Saddam Hussein has been ambitious and ruthless" and that "given the current regional power balance—and the past pattern—Iraq is likely to use its power overtly or implicitly to achieve regional domination." The conclusion: "At present the Iraqi policy direction appears closer to that seen in the pessimistic view than the optimistic one. Should Iraqi preponderance of relative power in the region continue, Iraq ambitions are likely to grow. . . . If, however, Iraqi power can be balanced without threatening Iraq's core interests, Saddam . . . might adopt policies more consistent with the optimistic perspective."[89]

This paper was the basis for a Rand workshop sponsored by the Pentagon. Participants included officers of the U.S. Central Command (CENTCOM), representing its commander, Gen. H. Norman Schwarzkopf, as well as officials of the Pentagon's Joint Staff, the CIA, the DIA, and the State Department. The workshop originally had been scheduled as a gaming exercise, "to experiment with political-military contingency analysis that would adamantly push ahead with 'But what if?' questions." As events had it, the first day of the workshop also turned out to be the day Saddam Hussein deployed the first contingents of what within two weeks would be 150,000 Iraqi troops along the Kuwaiti border. The what-if questions no longer were hypothetical.[90]

It would be going too far to say that as of July 17, when Saddam made his initial direct threats against Kuwait and started mobilizing troops along the border, the Bush administration should have assumed an invasion to be probable. But as the threats intensified and the troop mobilization escalated on an almost daily basis, the prospect of an invasion no longer should have been taken to be as improbable as it was viewed. Numerous general statements were made about principles and expected behavior, but not once during the crisis period did a Bush administration official state that the United States would defend Kuwait if it came under attack.

By July 25 the evidence that Iraq was planning to invade Kuwait was considered "convincing" by the CIA's chief national intelligence officer (NIO) for warnings.[91] While others in the intelligence community disagreed, a warning at this level should have been credible enough to prompt at least a hedging of bets—a firming up of the deterrence posture in addition to the reassurances still being extended. Yet it was on the same date, July 25, that Ambassador Glaspie met with Saddam and delivered her "direct instruction from the President to seek better relations with Iraq."

The total available record of the Glaspie-Saddam meeting—not merely the Iraqi transcript but also the ambassador's congressional testimony, cables leaked to the press, and statements by other administration officials—indicates that her warnings were not as "crystal clear" as claimed.[92] Three days after the Glaspie-Saddam meeting, President Bush cabled his own less-than-firm personal message to Saddam. Some within the administration first tried to toughen the message up, and then to block it, but failed on both counts. Some of these officials had participated in the Rand crisis simulation group, which had concluded "that the only way to forestall such a situation would be to get the President of the United States to warn

Saddam that if he stepped over the border, the United States was going to come get him."[93] But President Bush's message stopped well short of such firmness and clarity.

Nor had U.S. actions since the Iraqi troop buildup done much to firm up the deterrent. Secretary of State Baker later would stress two major signals supposedly sent to Iraq during the crisis period. "Signal No. 1," Baker said, "was to slap foreign policy export controls on exports to Iraq." Yet while tighter than before, export controls still were loose enough that some dual-use export licenses were being granted even in these last pre-invasion days. "Signal No. 2 was to cancel or suspend the CCC program."[94] Yet this step, too, was very little very late, especially since the Bush administration at the time was again opposing an economic sanctions bill Congress was seeking to pass.

By most accounts (including the Pentagon's post–Gulf war studies), Saddam had already made the decision to invade Kuwait before the eleventh-hour talks at Jiddah. The collapse of the talks was more pretext than precipitant. Saddam's accusation of an economic "dagger in the back," leaving no other choice but to take what Kuwait would not give, and more, was but a cover story, and a transparent one at that. There *were* other options. Saddam could have continued to try to coerce Kuwait. Or he could have seized only the Rumaila oilfield along with Bubiyan and Warbah islands, an act of aggression that he may well have gotten away with. He also could have cut his huge military spending, which was eating up 42 percent of his oil revenues. But the Iraqi military had already run its computer simulations and war games. Military exercises, including even a dress rehearsal for a heliborne assault on Kuwait City, had been staged. On August 2 Saddam moved.

ANALYSIS AND LESSONS

In testimony at a May 1992 congressional hearing, a top official of both the Reagan and Bush administrations defended their policy toward Iraq as "prudent at the time . . . a subtle leaning toward Iraq . . . seeking to probe, test and encourage the Iraqis while being wary of their intentions . . . to engage Iraq and to offer the Iraqis a mix of incentives and disincentives, but without any illusion."[95] Had the actual policy lived up to this characterization, it may well have been more successful.

Only "with the benefit of 20/20 hindsight," Secretary of State Baker would later assert, were there "some things that we might have done differently if we had known that this was going to happen."[96] In fact, though, warnings were sounded early and often. They were issued while the Iran-Iraq war alliance of convenience was being built and maintained; in the wake of the August 1988 chemical weapons attacks on the Kurds; in 1989 amidst the formulation of NSD-26; during the 1990 "spring of bad behavior"; and as the crisis over Kuwait built up. The warnings came both from within the Reagan and Bush administrations and from Congress, foreign policy analysts, journalists, and other governments. They emphasized Saddam's actions as well as his rhetoric, his capabilities as well as his ambitions. Indeed, the problem was not simply a matter of *some* things that *might* have been done differently *if* only Saddam Hussein's true colors *could* have been known. Rather, *many* things *should* have been done differently based on information and analysis that *were* available at the time.

One of the key failings of U.S. policy toward Iraq was that it did not meet basic standards of reciprocity. While measures of reciprocity are often imprecise and somewhat subjective, what is needed is a "rough equivalence" in the benefits derived by the respective partners to the relationship. For example, the Reagan and Bush administrations repeatedly contended that reciprocation for U.S. support would come on other issues on the foreign policy agenda, such as terrorism and Middle East peace. In fact, though, on both issues, Iraqi moderation was limited at best.

Under the immediate circumstances of early 1982, when Iraq was genuinely near defeat, taking it off the state terrorism list as a means for making it eligible for U.S. economic assistance did have sound enemy-enemy-friend logic. But Iraq never seriously reciprocated with substantial lasting reductions in its support for terrorism. Nor was terrorism only a peripheral concern to the United States in these years. In the 1986 Chicago Council on Foreign Relations public opinion survey, terrorism ranked behind only the nuclear arms race among the biggest foreign policy problems.[97]

As to the strong U.S. interest in Iraqi support of the Arab-Israeli peace process, the problem was that tactical maneuvers were taken for strategic shifts of position. One example is Saddam's support for PLO Chairman Yassir Arafat's December 1988 decision to recognize Israel's right to exist, a move that was undoubtedly helpful to U.S. interests at the time in establishing a dialogue with the PLO. What was questionable was the interpretation of this support as an indicator of a trend toward Iraqi moderation. Saddam supported Arafat not because Saddam had moderated toward Israel but because his main Arab rival, Syrian President Hafez Assad, opposed Arafat. The same motivation also prompted Saddam to send arms to the Lebanese Christian general, Michel Aoun, who was seeking to drive Syria out of Lebanon, in the face of stiff opposition from the United States (and also from France and the Arab League).

When moderate positions toward Israel did not serve such ulterior motives, Saddam did not take them. Secretary Baker's October 1989 request for Iraqi cooperation was met with the curious claim, from Foreign Minister Aziz, that it was Iraqi policy "to refrain from public statements on the peace process."[98] Yet Iraq had hardly refrained in the past, such as its 1978 hosting of the Rejectionist Front denunciations of the Camp David Accords. Moreover, Baghdad was the site of the meeting of the PLO Central Council which rejected the Baker Plan and called for an escalation of the intifada. In other words, Saddam's interests still dictated support for the PLO, but this no longer coincided with support for the peace process. Indeed, it was his support for the May 30, 1990, Palestinian terrorist raid on Israel that led to the breakdown of the U.S.-PLO dialogue—that same dialogue of which his support supposedly was such a telling sign of his moderation. These were not exactly mainstream, moderate, or reciprocating actions. "The danger of mistaking a leader's tactically motivated good behavior as a sign of more fundamental change," as Alexander George observes, "is a familiar one in international relations."[99] Iraq was manipulating more than moderating, but the Reagan and Bush administrations failed to see the difference.

Another example concerns U.S.-Iraqi trade. The main rationale cited by both the Reagan and Bush administrations for increasing trade with Iraq amounted to an assertion of political reciprocity. "Trade is the best key to political influence," Bush's transition team asserted. "Economic incentives," NSD-26 affirmed, were the best instrument the United States had for getting Iraq "to moderate its behavior and to increase our influence."

Yet at other times there were almost plaintive pleas as to how little political reciprocity could be expected in return. When antiterrorism sanctions were proposed following the *Achille Lauro*, the Reagan administration opposed them for fear that they would be "resented in Baghdad." When the Senate overwhelmingly approved sanctions following the August 1988 chemical weapons attacks on the Kurds, the objection was that such action would "reduce" U.S. influence.[100] Nor were sanctions to be imposed during Saddam's 1990 "spring of bad behavior," including his threat to "make the fire eat up half of Israel." A Republican-led Senate delegation visiting Iraq even assured Saddam that President Bush likely would veto any sanctions bill passed by Congress.

Other policy experiences, as well as the scholarly literature, are sobering as to the difficulties in using sanctions to convert economic vulnerability to political influence.[101] But between talk of sanctions that can bring a country to its knees and a strategy that simply writes off the possibilities of sanctions, there is plenty of middle ground for realistic assessments of vulnerability. An economy such as Iraq's, burdened by eight years of war debt, hampered in its reconstruction by low world oil prices, short on food and tight on credit, can reasonably be put in this middle ground. Thus there was no objective basis for dismissing the sanctions option out of hand.

Nor can the Reagan-Bush claim of "quiet diplomacy"—that is, a commitment to exerting economic pressure through diplomatic channels and at the administration's discretion rather than through congressionally imposed mandates—be accepted at face value. Quiet diplomacy works best when the target believes that the sender is discreet but serious, rather than keeping things quiet to prevent them from getting serious. Neither administration at any point gave Saddam any reason to think that they disagreed only on the method of sanctions but were serious about even an implicit requirement of genuine political reciprocity in exchange for the economic benefits being proffered. In effect, the Reagan and Bush administrations were trying to have it both ways. They argued that trade should be increased because it would bring leverage over Iraqi political behavior, but when moderation was not forthcoming in Iraqi political behavior, they insisted there was too little leverage to do anything about it. When policy needed to be justified, leverage was invoked. But when leverage was needed, there was none.

Moreover, the extension of trade and other economic benefits can have political influence only if the reverse leverage paradox can be averted. A strategy cannot be based on the utility of trade as leverage over another state if, when it comes time to exert that leverage, groups interested in the continuation of that trade are likely to exert domestic political pressures so great as to be constraining if not prohibitive.

In the end, Saddam Hussein calculated, as a distinguished bipartisan study group put it, "both that the regional balance of power stood in his favor and that local and outside powers would not react vigorously."[102] U.S. policy was not the only factor in such a calculation. It was, however, a critical one. The United States lacked deterrent credibility in the eyes of Saddam Hussein.

One of the falsest of the false dichotomies that have plagued U.S. foreign policy in both theory and practice is that between deterrence and cooperation. A "viable theory of deterrence," as Alexander George and Richard Smoke argued over twenty years ago, requires less of an "exclusive preoccupation with threats of punishment" as the sole means for influencing an adversary's behavior, and more of "a broader theory of processes by which nations influence each other, one that encompasses the utility of positive inducements as well as, or in lieu of, threats of negative sanctions."[103] The falseness of the dichotomy works in the other direction as well—that is, against theories of cooperation that focus too exclusively on positive inducements and that fail to encompass the utility that threats and negative actions can have for building cooperation. Nor is this true only with respect to U.S. foreign policy. "The record demonstrates," British diplomat and scholar Evan Luard wrote in 1967 with more general historical reference, "that neither a policy of conciliation or deterrence can ever be successful if conducted in isolation from one another."[104]

This pertains to efforts to forge cooperation among allies as well as efforts at accommodation between states that have been adversaries and that still have significant conflicts and tensions in their relationship. As long as reasonable doubt remains about the prospective new friend's intentions, the leader of that state must know both that cooperation has its benefits *and* that noncooperation has its consequences. In sending the latter message and affecting cost-benefit calculations accordingly, the deterrent component can serve as its own inducement, while also guarding against the possibility that the accommodation strategy will fail.

This amounts to what might be called a "flexible-but-firm" accommodation strategy, analogous to the "firm-but-flexible" deterrence strategy shown by Paul Huth and others to be quite effective in the prevention of war.[105] The firm-but-flexible strategy is distinguished from harder-line deterrence strategies by its keeping the door open to cooperation while maintaining a credible deterrent. The flexible-but-firm strategy analogously differs from softer-line accommodation strategies in pursuing cooperation but at the same time maintaining the credibility of its deterrent posture to convey a willingness and ability to slam the door shut if necessary.

CONCLUSION: THE SOURCES OF FOREIGN POLICY FAILURE

In his classic work *American Diplomacy*, George Kennan offers a useful way of thinking about the reasons for foreign policy failure. One possibility is that it was a failure but not a failing, that the situation was "outside the range of our influence" and that nothing we could have done could have altered the outcome.[106] This is quite a useful perspective (for scholars and policy makers alike) as a recognition that even great powers are not omnipotent—that is, as long as delimitation does not become a cover for denial, as some sought in the U.S.-Iraqi case.

"To the extent that it [a foreign policy failure] was the fault of American diplomacy," Kennan goes on to ask, "what went wrong—the concepts or the execution?" Kennan meant these as analytically distinct but not mutually exclusive categories. The "concepts" dimension gets at flaws in the substance of policy and strategy, the "execution" at mistakes in the decision-making processes, policy formulation, and policy implementation.

U.S. policy toward Iraq from 1982 to 1990 failed. It failed because it was flawed in both its concepts and its execution. But it did not have to fail.

And there are lessons to be derived from the reasons why it failed, so that we may learn from history rather than being condemned to repeat it.

NOTES

1. This chapter is drawn from my book *With Friends Like These: Reagan, Bush and Saddam, 1982–1990* (New York: W. W. Norton, 1994).

2. The other members were Turkey, Pakistan, Iran, and Britain. The United States was not a formal member.

3. U.S. Department of Defense, *Conduct of the Persian Gulf War, Final Report to Congress under Title V of the Persian Gulf Conflict Supplemental Authorization and Personnel Benefits Act of 1991* (PL 101–25), 1992, p. 6. See also Dilip Hiro, *Desert Shield to Desert Storm: The Second Gulf War* (London: HarperCollins, 1992), chap. 1.

4. Judith Miller and Laurie Mylroie, *Saddam Hussein and the Crisis in the Gulf* (New York: Times Books, 1990), pp. 141–42.

5. Jimmy Carter, *Keeping Faith: Memoirs of a President* (New York: Bantam Books, 1982), p. 506.

6. Letter, 1982, to members of Congress from Kenneth Duberstein, Reagan administration chief of congressional relations, cited in "Congress and Iraq: A Chronology," *Congressional Quarterly Weekly Report*, April 27, 1992, p. 1070.

7. Former Assistant Secretary of Defense Noel Koch, quoted in Guy Gugliotta et al., "At War, Iraq Courted U.S. into Economic Embrace," *Washington Post*, September 16, 1990, p. A34.

8. Howard Teicher, quoted in Douglas Frantz and Murray Waas, "Secret Effort by Bush in '89 Helped Hussein Build Iraq's War Machine," *Los Angeles Times*, February 24, 1992, p. A6.

9. Bob Woodward, *Veil: The Secret Wars of the CIA* (New York: Simon and Schuster, 1987), pp. 439, 480; statement by Congressman Henry Gonzalez, *Congressional Record*, March 9, 1992, pp. H1107–12; Jim Hoagland, "America's Frankenstein Monster," *Washington Post*, February 7, 1991, p. A19.

10. Bernard Gwertzman, "U.S. and Iraq Reported Ready to Renew Ties after 17 Years," *New York Times*, November 13, 1984, p. 14; Bernard Gwertzman, "U.S. Restores Full Ties with Iraq But Cites Neutrality in Gulf War," *New York Times*, November 27, 1984, p. 1; Kenneth R. Timmerman, *The Death Lobby: How the West Armed Iraq* (Boston: Houghton Mifflin, 1991), p. 193.

11. Nizar Hamdoon, "Ambassador's Diary: How to Survive in Washington," *Washington Post*, August 30, 1987, pp. C1, C4.

12. U.S. State Department memorandum, "Iraq: CPPG Meeting of Wednesday July 23" (1986).

13. Murray Waas and Craig Unger, "In the Loop: Bush's Secret Mission," *New Yorker*, November 2, 1992, pp. 74–80.

14. "Transcription of Meetings with Albert Hakim, Richard Secord, Oliver North and Iranian Intermediaries in Mainz," *The Iran-Contra Affair: The Making of a Scandal, 1983–1988* (Alexandria, Va.: Chadwyck-Healey, 1990), Document no. 3563. North later acknowledged having concurred with the Iranians that "there is a need for a non-

hostile regime in Baghdad" and having led them to believe that "we can bring our influence to bear with certain friendly Arab nations" to get rid of Saddam; Christopher Hitchens, "Realpolitik in the Gulf: A Game Gone Tilt," in Micah L. Sifry and Christopher Cerf, eds., *The Gulf War Reader: History, Documents, Opinions* (New York: Times Books, 1991), p. 114.

15. U.S. State Department memorandum, "U.S.-Iraqi Relations: Picking Up the Pieces," December 3, 1986.

16. Iranian attacks on Persian Gulf shipping increased from 14 in 1985 to 41 in 1986 and 22 in the first three months of 1987. As earlier in the war, this was part of an escalating cycle in which Iraqi attacks were still greater: 33 in 1985, 66 in 1986, and 24 in the first three months of 1987. Congressional Research Service, "Ship Attacks in the Persian Gulf," 1987.

17. On doubts as to how accidental the attack on the U.S.S. *Stark* may have been, see Amacia Baram, "Iraq: Between East and West," in Efram Karsh, ed., *The Iran-Iraq War: Impact and Implications* (New York: St. Martin's, 1989), p. 86; Elaine Sciolino, *The Outlaw State: Saddam Hussein's Quest for Power and the Gulf Crisis* (New York: John Wiley, 1991), pp. 169–70.

18. Janice Gross Stein, "The Wrong Strategy in the Right Place," *International Security* 14 (Winter 1988–89), p. 148.

19. U.S. State Department memorandum, "Iraq's Retreat from International Terrorism," July 1, 1986.

20. Abu Abbas's escape route also took him through Yugoslavia. However, as Secretary of State George Shultz stated at a press conference, "With respect to Yugoslavia, he [Abbas] passed through. With respect to Iraq, he seems to have been welcomed there. That is different and it constitutes more of a problem"; George P. Shultz, *Turmoil and Triumph: My Years as Secretary of State* (New York: Scribner's, 1993), p. 676.

21. U.S. State Department, "Chronology: October 4 through December 6, 1985," p. 1.

22. See, for example, Jentleson, *With Friends Like These*, pp. 48–56, 62–65, 88–89, 105–27, 139–42, 152–53, 220–26.

23. U.S. Defense Department memorandum, "Subject: High Technology Dual Use Exports to Iraq," July 1, 1985.

24. Timmerman, *The Death Lobby*, p. 241.

25. U.S. Commerce Department memorandum, "The NSC and Iraq," May 27, 1991.

26. U.S. Congress, House of Representatives, Committee on Banking, Finance, and Urban Affairs, *Banca Nazionale del Lavoro (BNL)*, Hearing, 102nd Congress, 1st Session, April 9, 1991, p. 79.

27. Statement by Congressman Gonzalez, *Congressional Record*, July 21, 1992, pp. H6338–46.

28. Eyewitness accounts, recounted to staff of the Senate Foreign Relations Committee, *Chemical Weapons Use in Kurdistan: Iraq's Final Offensive*, S. Rpt. 100–48, 100th Congress, 2nd Session, October 1988, p. 12.

29. The Genocide Convention defines genocide as "any of the following acts committed with intent to destroy, in whole or in part, a national, ethnical, racial or religious group as such: (a) killing members of the group; (b) causing serious bodily or mental

harm to members of the group; (c) deliberately inflicting on the group conditions of life calculated to bring about its physical destruction in whole or in part."

30. Shultz, *Turmoil and Triumph*, p. 241; Pamela Fessler, "Congress' Record on Saddam: Decade of Talk, Not Action," *Congressional Quarterly Weekly Report*, April 27, 1991, p. 1072; Frantz and Waas, "Bush Secretly Helped Iraq," p. A12; State Department memorandum, "Administration Policy on Proposed Iraq Sanctions," October 18, 1988.

31. U.S. Department of Energy, "Petroleum Supply Annual," Energy Information Administration, Office of Oil and Gas, 1981–90; "Discount Prices on Imports of Iraqi Oil, 1988–1990," document provided by U.S. Congress, House of Representatives, Committee on Energy and Commerce, Subcommittee on Energy and Power.

32. Fessler, "Congress' Record on Saddam," p. 173.

33. State Department memorandum, "U.S.-Iraqi Relations: Implications of Passage of Economic Sanctions Bill," October 18, 1988.

34. Letter from William T. Archey, Vice President, International Affairs, U.S. Chamber of Commerce, to House Foreign Affairs Committee Chairman Dante B. Fascell, September 15, 1988.

35. This account is drawn from three interdependent sources: Joe Conason, "The Iraq Lobby," *New Republic*, October 1, 1990, pp. 14–17; Murray Waas, "What We Gave Saddam for Christmas," *Village Voice*, December 18, 1990, included in U.S. Congress, House of Representatives, Committee on Government Operations, Commerce, Consumer and Monetary Affairs Subcommittee, *U.S. Government Controls on Sales to Iraq*, 101st Congress, 2nd Session, September 27, 1990, pp. 300–310; Timmerman, *The Death Lobby*, pp. 219–23, 305–8.

36. Waas, "What We Gave Saddam for Christmas," p. 309.

37. Douglas Waller, "Glass House," *New Republic*, November 5, 1990, pp. 13–14; Sciolino, *The Outlaw State*, p. 171.

38. U.S. State Department memorandum, "Iraq's Foreign Policy: Deeper into the Mainstream," March 3, 1988 (emphasis added).

39. Letter from Assistant Secretary of State for Legislative Affairs J. Edward Fox to House Foreign Affairs Committee Chairman Dante B. Fascell, September 13, 1988.

40. Paul A. Gigot, "A Great American Screw-Up: The U.S. and Iraq, 1980–1990," *National Interest* (Winter 1990–91), pp. 3–10; Don Oberdorfer, "Missed Signals in the Middle East," *Washington Post Magazine*, March 17, 1991, pp. 19–41; former Reagan administration official, interview by author, March 9 and April 22, 1993.

41. Zalmay Khalilzad, "A Geo-Strategic Overview: Stability or New Aggressive Coalitions," in *Proceedings of the Washington Institute*, 3rd Annual Policy Conference, "U.S. Policy in the Middle East: Toward the Next Administration," September 16–18, 1988 (Washington, D.C.: Washington Institute for Near East Policy: 1988), pp. 12–13.

42. "Approved Licenses to Iraq, 1985–1990," U.S. Department of Commerce.

43. Anthony Lewis, "Paying for Reagan," *New York Times*, October 5, 1990, p. A15.

44. National Security Directive 26, declassified version, October 2, 1989.

45. Miller and Mylroie, *Saddam Hussein and the Crisis in the Gulf*, p. 151.

46. Shaul Bakhash, "What Khomeini Did," *New York Review of Books*, July 20, 1989, p. 17.

47. "Guidelines for U.S.-Iraq Policy," U.S. Department of State, p. 1.

48. Alexander L. George, *Bridging the Gap: Theory and Practice in Foreign Policy* (Washington, D.C.: U.S. Institute of Peace Press, 1993), pp. 45–60.

49. Hiro, p. 56.

50. "Guidelines for U.S.-Iraq Policy," p. 5 (emphasis in original).

51. Sandra L. Charles, NSC director for Near East and South Asian Affairs, quoted in R. Jeffrey Smith, "Selling to Scoundrels: Why We Won't Stop," *Washington Post,* November 15, 1992, pp. C1, C4.

52. Stephen Engelberg, "Iraq Said to Study Biological Arms," *New York Times,* January 18, 1989, p. A7; David B. Ottaway, "Official Denies Iraq Has Germ Warfare Plant," *Washington Post,* January 19, 1989, p. A36.

53. U.S. Congress, Senate, Committee on Foreign Relations, hearings, *Chemical and Biological Weapons Threat: The Urgent Need for Remedies,* 101st Congress, 1st sess., March 1, 1989, pp. 27–45.

54. U.S. Congress, House of Representatives, Committee on Armed Services, Subcommittee on Seapower and Strategic and Critical Materials, *Department of Defense Authorization for Appropriations for Fiscal Year 1990, Title 1,* HR 2461, 101st Congress, 1st sess., February 22, 1989, pp. 39–41. See also Glenn Frankel, "Iraq Said Developing A-Weapons," *Washington Post,* March 31, 1989, pp. A1, A32, citing Israeli sources.

55. U.S. Senate, Committee on Foreign Relations, U.S. Policy toward Iraq: Human Rights, Weapons Proliferation, and International Law, 101st Congress, 2nd sess., June 15, 1990, pp. 56–70.

56. Timmerman, *The Death Lobby,* pp. 331–41.

57. William Lowther, *Arms and the Man: Dr. Gerald Bull, Iraq and the Supergun* (Novato, Calif.: Presidio Press, 1991); William Scott Malone, David Halevy, and Sam Hemingway, "The Guns of Saddam," *Washington Post,* February 10, 1991, pp. C1, C4; Congressman Henry Gonzalez, testimony and documents submitted to the Senate Banking Committee, *United States Export Policy toward Iraq;* Timmerman, *The Death Lobby,* pp. 70, 160–62.

58. The full reports remain classified. Portions were released in the *Congressional Record* by Congressman Henry Gonzalez. See especially the *Record* for July 27, 1992, pp. H6696–H6704; August 10, 1992, pp. H7871–82; and September 21, 1992, pp. H8820–19.

59. Dean Baquet with Elaine Sciolino, "European Suppliers of Iraq Were Known to Pentagon," *New York Times,* November 2, 1992, p. A3; Douglas Frantz and Murray Waas, "CIA Told White House of Iraqi Arms Efforts," *Los Angeles Times,* August 6, 1992, pp. A1, A3.

60. Letter dated September 21, 1989, in *Congressional Record,* February 3, 1992, p. H213; *Congressional Record,* July 27, 1992, p. H6700.

61. U.S. State Department information memorandum, "Subject: The Banca del Lavoro Scandal and Trade with Iraq," September 22, 1989.

62. Communique issued by Iraqi Embassy in Rome, cited in Laura Colby, "Iraq Voices 'Surprise' in BNL Scandal, Says Export-Credit Pacts Date to 1982," *Wall Street Journal,* September 12, 1989, p. A8.

63. Bernard Roshco, *When Policy Fails: How the Buck Was Passed When Kuwait*

Was Invaded, Harvard University, John F. Kennedy School of Government, Discussion Paper D-15, 1992, p. 10.

64. U.S. Treasury Department memorandum, "CCC Credit Guarantees for Iraq" (no date); Minutes, NAC Staff Committee, October 3, 1989.

65. U.S. State Department, "The Iraqi CCC Program," October 26, 1989.

66. U.S. State Department, "Message to Iraqi Foreign Minister on CCC Credits," November 9, 1989.

67. U.S. State Department, "Message from Secretary to Iraqi Foreign Minister on CCC," November 9, 1989.

68. Memorandum dated November 21, 1989, included in *Congressional Record,* July 21, 1992, p. H6344.

69. Alan Friedman, *Spider's Web: The Secret History of How the White House Illegally Armed Iraq* (New York: Bantam Books, 1993), pp. 149–50.

70. Foreign Broadcast Information Service, Near East Section (hereinafter FBIS NES), December 7, 1989, pp. 28–29, and December 11, 1989, pp. 22–23.

71. *Keesing's Record of World Events,* "Middle East-Arab World," January 1990, p. 37199; FBIS-NES, January 5, 1990, p. 18.

72. U.S. State Department memorandum, "Second Tranche of CCC Credits for Iraq," January 4, 1990.

73. Oberdorfer, "Missed Signals in the Middle East," March 13, 1991, p. 22; interview, former Bush administration official, April 4, 1992.

74. "No More Secret Police," text included in Stanley Kober, *Appeasement and the Gulf War* (Washington, D.C.: Progressive Policy Institute, 1992) (emphasis added).

75. Karsh and Rautsi, *Saddam Hussein: A Political Biography,* p. 208.

76. Letter dated February 28, 1990, in Kober, *Appeasement and the Gulf War.*

77. FBIS-NES, February 20, 1990, pp. 1–6, and February 27, 1990, pp. 1–5; "Kuwait: How the West Blundered," *Economist,* September 29, 1990.

78. Lawrence Freedman and Efraim Karsh, *The Gulf Conflict: Diplomacy and War in the New World Order* (London: Faber and Faber, 1993), p. 45.

79. Timmerman, *The Death Lobby,* pp. 378–79.

80. *Keesing's Record of World Events,* March 1990, p. 37332; Nigel Hawkes, "Major in Plea for Observer Reporter," *Observer,* October 1, 1989, p. 1; Timmerman, *The Death Lobby,* p. 376.

81. Oberdorfer, "Missed Signals in the Middle East," p. 36.

82. FBIS NES, April 3, 1990, pp. 32–37 (emphasis added).

83. Bob Woodward, *The Commanders* (New York: Simon and Schuster, 1991), p. 201.

84. Oberdorfer, "Missed Signals in the Middle East," p. 36; Robert S. Greenberger, "How the Baker Plan for Early Sanctions against Iraq Failed," *Wall Street Journal,* October 1, 1990, pp. A1, A12; *Los Angeles Times,* February 24, 1992, pp. A1, A6; Friedman, *Spider's Web,* pp. 161–62.

85. *Congressional Record,* July 9, 1992, p. H6241.

86. *Congressional Record,* July 27, 1992; R. Jeffrey Smith, "U.S. Cleared Factory Sale to Iraq Despite Own Ban," *Washington Post,* July 17, 1992, pp. A1, A14.

87. June 27 cable from U.S. Secretary of State to U.S. Embassy, Baghdad, "Iraq and Terrorism."

88. Ishan A. Hijazi, "PLO and Iraq Cooperate on Hard-Line Strategy," *New York Times*, May 13, 1990; Bruce Hoffman, *The Ultimate Fifth Column: Saddam Hussein, International Terrorism and the Crisis in the Gulf*, P-7668 (Santa Monica, Calif.: Rand Corporation, 1990), p. 2.

89. Paul K. Davis and John Arquilla, *Deterring or Coercing Opponents in Crisis: Lessons from the War with Saddam Hussein* (Santa Monica, Calif.: Rand Corporation, 1991), pp. 5–7.

90. Ibid., p. 5; Woodward, *The Commanders*, p. 217.

91. U.S. Senate, Select Committee on Intelligence, Nomination of Robert Gates, 102nd Congress, 1st sess., September 24, 1991, pp. 29–30.

92. Aside from the innumerable articles and commentaries on the Glaspie-Saddam meeting, the key sources for the primary documents are as follows. Excerpts from the Iraqi version of the transcript were published in the *New York Times*, September 23, 1990, p. 19; excerpts from the July 24 cable from Secretary of State Baker and the July 25 cable from Ambassador Glaspie reporting on her meeting with Saddam were published in the *Washington Post*, October 21, 1992, p. A17. See also Ambassador Glaspie's testimony, U.S. House of Representatives, Committee on Foreign Affairs, Subcommittee on Europe and the Middle East, *United States–Iraqi Relations*, 102nd Congress, 1st sess., March 12, 1991, and the "informal public discussion" with the Senate Foreign Relations Committee on March 20, 1991, never officially published but available through the Federal Information Systems Corporation data base.

93. Woodward, *The Commanders*, p. 217.

94. Douglas Frantz and Murray Waas, "U.S. Loans Indirectly Financed Iraq Military," *Los Angeles Times*, February 25, 1992, p. 7.

95. Testimony of Lawrence Eagleburger, U.S. Congress, House of Representatives, Committee on Banking, Finance, and Urban Affairs, *Banca Nazionale del Lavoro (BNL) Scandal and the Department of Agriculture's Commodity Credit Corporation (CCC) Program for Iraq*, part 1, 102nd Congress, 2nd sess., May 21, 1992, pp. 29–39.

96. Baker's statement on October 29, 1990, cited in Thomas L. Friedman, "Baker Seen as Balancing Bush's Urge to Fight Iraq," *New York Times*, November 3, 1990, p. 6; Bush statement during the third presidential debate, transcript, *New York Times*, October 20, 1992, p. A24.

97. John E. Reilly, "America's State of Mind," *Foreign Policy* 66 (Spring 1987), p. 42.

98. U.S. State Department, "Secretary's October 6 Meeting with Iraqi Foreign Minister Tariq Aziz," October 13, 1989, *Congressional Record*, March 1. 1992, pp. H864–66.

99. George, *Bridging the Gap*, p. 47.

100. Letter dated June 20, 1985, from Secretary of State George Shultz to Congressman Howard L. Berman (D-Calif.); State Department memorandum, "Administration Policy on Proposed Iraq Sanctions," October 18, 1988.

101. Johan Galtung, "On the Effects of International Sanctions, with Examples from the Case of Rhodesia," *World Politics* 19 (April 1967), pp. 378–416.

102. Washington Institute for Near East Policy, Strategic Study Group, *Restoring the Balance: U.S. Strategy and the Gulf Crisis* (Washington, D.C.: Washington Institute on Near East Policy, 1991), p. 13.

103. Alexander George and Richard Smoke, "Deterrence and Foreign Policy," *World Politics* 41 (January 1989), p. 182. See also their earlier, classic book, *Deterrence in American Foreign Policy: Theory and Practice* (New York: Columbia University Press, 1974), especially chap. 21.

104. Evan Luard, "Conciliation and Deterrence: A Comparison of Political Strategies in the Interwar and Postwar Periods," *World Politics* 19 (January 1967), p. 185. Luard applies this to the 1938 Munich agreement, arguing that "the fault was that the British and others attempted conciliation without a sufficient reserve of deterrence as an inducement against alternative courses. Conceivably, it is true, no degree of armed strength on their part could have convinced Hitler that they really meant business or could have deterred him from war. . . . On the other hand . . . conciliation unbacked by strength was certain to fail."

105. Paul Huth and Bruce Russett, "Deterrence Failure and Crisis Escalation," *International Studies Quarterly* 32 (March 1988), pp. 29–45; Paul Huth, *Extended Deterrence and the Prevention of War* (New Haven: Yale University Press, 1988); Noel Kaplowitz, "Psychopolitical Dimensions of International Relations: The Reciprocal Effects of Conflict Strategies," *International Studies Quarterly* 28 (December 1984), pp. 373–406.

106. George F. Kennan, *American Diplomacy, 1900–1950* (Chicago: University of Chicago Press, 1951), p. vii.

7

U.S.-Cuba Negotiations
The Continuing Stall

PAMELA S. FALK

U.S. interest in establishing a road map for policy makers to negotiate successfully a democratic transition in Cuba dramatically increased in the summer of 1994, when there was a threat that Cuban rafters would repeat the
mass exodus of 1980. Since Cuban President Fidel Castro's revolution was
launched in December 1958, the United States has had nine presidents,
along with their casts of negotiators. A case study of the series of pro-
tracted U.S.-Cuba negotiations over that period is timely. During the thirty-
five years of U.S.-Cuba negotiations, both U.S. and Cuban interests have
shifted significantly, but the lessons that may be gleaned from three decades of negotiations provide insights for future negotiating efforts. Moreover, pressure for a transition to democracy in Cuba has been strength-
ened during the five years since the Soviet Union collapsed.

In diplomacy the golden rule in complex international negotiations is
that negotiation will be successful only if each side gains something it wants.
To date, both U.S. and Cuban negotiators have concluded—after approaching the precipice of normalization several times since the early 1960s—
that there is more to lose than to gain.[1] For its part, the Cuban government has found it useful politically during the past thirty-five years to
have a Goliath against whom Fidel Castro could play David, in the true
spirit of Cuba's legendary Jose Martí. Given this scenario, the Cubans have
passed up several opportunities to negotiate an end to the U.S. embargo.[2]

As for Washington, no aspect of its foreign relations has stirred more
domestic passion nor brought the United States closer to a nuclear confrontation. Documents declassified during the past few years, regarding
the collapse of Fulgencio Batista during the Eisenhower administration and
secret negotiations during the administration of President Gerald Ford,
have opened up new information about how bilateral relations were con-

ducted, how negotiations to build a relationship in the early days were stalled, and how opportunities were lost.[3] The details and the process of the negotiations are as instructive as the changing checklists of demands by both sides: The controversial round of secret shuttle diplomacy during the spring of 1995 by the Clinton administration is reminiscent of clandestine meetings in crowded airport lounges twenty years earlier by the Nixon and Ford negotiators led by Henry Kissinger. Both produced significant interim agreements. In the case of the Kissinger negotiations, relations took a rapid nosedive as a result of unrelated policy shifts by the Cuban government; for the Clinton administration, relations with Cuba remain tense principally because of embargo-tightening legislation, despite significant accords reached on immigration.

Some negotiators argue that the issues in 1995 are the same as during the 1975 negotiations.[4] More to the point, the list of bilateral demands has changed, but the fundamental U.S. and Cuban differences remain the same.[5] The United States desires democratic political reform in Cuba and compensation for the seized property of Cubans who are nationalized U.S. citizens—both individual and corporate; the Cuban priority remains the lifting of the embargo. Despite these core differences, the intervening three decades have produced scores of additional issues, from Cuban support for revolutionary movements in this hemisphere and in Africa, to Cuban involvement in the Puerto Rico independence movement, to Cuba's economic and political alliance with the former Soviet Union.

The study of the public debate and negotiated resolution or attempted resolution of these issues offers today's analyst or negotiator insight into the approaches that can work and those that will not. Perhaps the most important factor for U.S. observers is the strength of the Cuban-American community in the United States, while U.S. policy makers have historically been concerned about the danger of an economically weak Cuba; after all, Cuba has already hosted nuclear missiles. The history that follows is intended to put today's dilemmas and competing domestic concerns into perspective and to demonstrate that appropriate negotiations can advance U.S. interests without forsaking U.S. values.

HISTORY OF NEGOTIATIONS

President Dwight D. Eisenhower had just completed six months in office and the Senate had nearly completed the confirmation of his secretary of state, John Foster Dulles, when an unknown guerrilla commander, Fidel Castro, on July 26, 1953, launched an unsuccessful military assault against an army barracks of then-President Fulgencio Batista, known as the Moncada barracks.[6] Communism was seen, in the words of the new secretary, as a rising menace in Latin America. But in light of cable traffic from the era and memoirs written about the period by former presidents and secretaries of state, it is clear that few policy makers took much note of Castro's failed attack on the Moncada barracks. Captured and sentenced to fifteen years in prison, Castro had served two years when he was released by Batista in a general amnesty for the Moncada rebels.

Responding to Batista's dramatic increase in human rights abuses and the growing opposition to his iron-fisted rule, the Eisenhower administration stopped the shipment of arms to Cuba in March 1958; nine months later, on December 31, 1958, Castro's 26th of July movement overthrew Batista.[7] In April 1959, Castro arrived in New York City on his infamous trip to Harlem's Hotel Teresa at the invitation of a newspaper organization, the American National Society of Editors. He spoke in Washington and at Harvard and Princeton and met with Henry Luce of *Time* magazine and Frank Bartholomew of UPI. He met with Acting Secretary of State Christian Herter and the Central Intelligence Agency's Latin America expert Frank Droller, but President Dwight D. Eisenhower snubbed Castro in favor of a golfing trip and sent Richard Nixon, vice president, in his stead. Castro was accompanied by Ernesto Betancourt, Washington representative of the 26th of July Movement.

On his return to Havana, Castro found himself under attack from the left for being conciliatory to U.S. business interests and from the right (including Cuba's president, Manuel Urrutia Lleo) for cooperating with the communists. The next step toward a collapse in relations with the United States was the lightning-quick transformation of private ownership to state authority in Cuba, formalized by the Institute of Agrarian Reform (INRA), the government agency responsible for nationalizations of U.S. property. The personal fortunes that Castro nationalized included the estates of the U.S. owners of the United Fruit Company and King Ranch.[8] President Urrutia Lleo was among the first loyalists to abandon the cause. He angrily denounced the regime before he fled to the United States.[9]

In January 1960, senior Washington policy makers organized Committee 5412 in part to plan ways to overthrow "the mad man," as Eisenhower then called Castro. In March, five weeks after Soviet Deputy Premier Anastas Mikoyan visited Havana, the U.S. government began devising an elaborate scheme to oust Castro that included a proposed armed landing by a Cuban American paramilitary group. Castro learned of the project within two days and quickly established formal relations with the Soviet Union.

For the oil industry, May 1960 was the landmark month.[10] After Cuba reestablished diplomatic relations with the Soviet Union and signed a trade agreement, Cuba on May 23 ordered the operations of Texaco, Standard Oil Company, and Royal Dutch Shell to refine shipments of Soviet crude. Within a month, the U.S. companies refused.[11] Nationalization was imminent. The Cuban Council of Ministers, reacting to the increased tensions, met to rewrite the Cuban constitution and the transitional Fundamental Law.[12] The ground was set for the U.S.-Cuba break. Contributions to the compensation fund for expropriated property consisted of 25 percent of foreign exchange proceeds of sugar sales to the United States at a price not below 5.75 cents per pound. Cuban bonds would serve as compensation. There were no appeals. All previous law was revoked.

Cuba expropriated much more than the refineries. The government took all transportation, storage, and marketing facilities. The value of the oil companies' operations far exceeded the $750 million that Cuba offered.[13] On June 28, Castro ordered the Texaco refinery to process Soviet crude oil under the threat of expropriation by the Cuban government. The following day, as Soviet oil shipments arrived, the U.S. employees of Esso and Shell Oil left, and on June 30 the Cuban government nationalized their refineries.[14]

On Capitol Hill, the debate was heated. Whether the president should cut Cuba's sugar quota was the topic of floor debate and hearings. On the day that Castro issued his order to the Texaco refinery, the U.S. House of Representatives voted to authorize the Eisenhower administration to reduce the sugar quota. One week later, the vote in the U.S. Senate vote made the bill law. In July President Eisenhower authorized the suspension of Cuba's sugar quota. Cuba was by then broadening its expropriations in all areas of the private sector. The Hilton Hotel and the Hotel Nacional were expropriated. By the end of August 1960 most foreign private property was in the hands of the Cuban government.

By the summer of 1960, more than a year after the overthrow of Fulgencio Batista, the Eisenhower administration had become deeply distressed with bilateral relations. When the Organization of American States met in August 1960 in San José, Costa Rica, U.S. Secretary of State Christian Herter called for a condemnation of Cuba. The OAS passed a resolution declaring "totalitarian states to be inconsistent with the continental system." Castro withdrew from the meeting and denounced the organization.

Castro's next move came as the January 1961 New Year's celebrations were ending, when he demanded that the U.S. Embassy cut its staff to a handful of U.S. foreign service officers within forty-eight hours.[15] With tensions at an all-time high, the U.S. broke diplomatic relations on January 3, 1961.

Within three weeks the newly elected John F. Kennedy took over Cuba policy from Eisenhower. On April 3, 1961, two weeks before the failed Bay of Pigs invasion, the State Department issued a report on Cuba.[16] The regime of Fidel Castro, it began, "offers a clear and present danger to the authentic and autonomous revolution of the Americas."[17] The report concluded with an urgent call for Cuba to reverse its course and return to the inter-American alliance.

While the State Department did not intend the document to be justification for the invasion of Cuba that would take place two weeks later, the report called on regional allies to reject "the seizure by Communist movements" of Cuba. Cuba had been sending "large sums of money" to finance procommunist student groups plotting to overthrow the government of El Salvador. The "considered judgment of the Government of the United States," the report maintained, was that the danger threatened "all the republics of the hemisphere." It was not until year's end in 1961 that a clear statement of ideological direction emerged from the Cuban leadership. "Do I believe in Marxism?" Castro asked rhetorically in a December 1 speech, and he answered, "I believe absolutely in Marxism."

President Kennedy abandoned Eisenhower's step-by-step pressure but not the CIA's invasion plans. Crushed by Castro's forces within forty-eight hours, the Bay of Pigs landing in 1961 precipitated the final break in relations. Kennedy authorized "Operation Mongoose," a six-phase effort designed to "help Cuba overthrow" Castro. The goals did not even come close to realization. The culmination was to be an "open revolt" in Cuba in October 1962, which was instead the month of the missile crisis.

On January 31, 1962, at Punta del Este, Uruguay, the eighth meeting of foreign ministers of the Organization of American States passed a resolution declaring that Cuba had excluded itself from the inter-American organization because of its belief in Marxism-Leninism, a position that was incompatible with the principles of the OAS; Cuba was suspended from active participation. The next month, Kennedy imposed a comprehensive embargo and by 1964 the OAS had established a region-wide embargo.

In October 1962, Nikita Khrushchev, fearing another U.S. invasion of Cuba, had shipped forty-two medium-range ballistic missile (MRBMs) to the island—triggering the well-documented great confrontation.[18] In short, the U.S. faced off against the Soviet Union over the placement of offensive nuclear missiles in Cuba. The crisis ended in October 1962 when the Kennedy administration imposed a naval blockade. Ahead lay the tragic events in Dallas, which changed the entire course of U.S. history. Four days before he was assassinated, Kennedy sent a message informing Fidel Castro that he wanted to normalize relations between Washington and Havana.[19]

The theory at the time was that if the sanctions were eliminated, "Cuba would no longer be totally involved with the U.S.S.R. since important trade would have developed between our two countries."[20]

After the 1965 exodus of rafters from the port of Camarioca, the Congress began to debate issues related to the Cuban government and U.S. immigration. In 1966 Congress enacted the Cuban Adjustment Act, which gave the U.S. attorney general the right to grant permanent resident status to Cubans who had been admitted or paroled into the U.S. after Castro came to power on January 1, 1959, and who had been living in the United States for at least one year. The atmosphere surrounding détente between the United States and the Soviet Union had a significant impact on U.S. negotiations with Cuba. In the first three years of the decade, there was a growing movement in Congress to permit Americans to travel to Cuba and explore the possibilities of a rapprochement. Under President Gerald Ford, the embargo was modified to permit subsidiaries of U.S. corporations to trade with Cuba on a case-by-case basis. In February 1973, the U.S. and Cuba signed an antihijacking agreement. By the early summer of 1974, Secretary of State Henry Kissinger was growing impatient with the intransigence of those responsible for the U.S.-Cuba impasse. His diplomatic largesse in U.S.-China relations had paid off. During the month of June, Kissinger took several initiatives toward normalization that were significant, though unsuccessful. First, in the last days of the Nixon administration, Kissinger approved a trip to Cuba by Senate Foreign Relations Committee staff, dispatched a message to Castro via U.S. journalists, and appointed William D. Rogers, who had advocated normalization, to the post of Assistant Secretary of State for Inter-American Affairs.[21]

Public statements of a possible opening matched the private shuttle diplomacy of Henry Kissinger. He signaled in a speech in Washington that he saw "no virtue in perpetual antagonism" toward Cuba, and Assistant Secretary of State Rogers said that even the future of Guantanamo Bay Naval Base, leased "in perpetuity" since 1901, could be negotiated.[22]

A January 2, 1975, checklist that Rogers sent to Kissinger reveals how substantially the balance sheet of bilateral issues has changed in twenty-some years. Today, only a handful of the twelve points on the list are major issues on the bilateral agenda. Rogers's balance sheet included six economic and six political points.

In economic matters, the United States was seeking compensation from Cuba for (1) U.S. private property that Cuba had expropriated, (2) the takeover of the U.S.-owned Nicaro Nickel Mine, (3) unreturned ransom monies, (4) the Cuban postal debt, (5) defaulted bonds, and (6) improvements to the U.S. Embassy building (now the U.S. Interests Section).

Among the political issues were (1) release of U.S. political prisoners held in Cuba and return of hijackers then in Cuba, (2) improvement in Cuba's record on human rights, particularly for Cuban political prisoners who had relatives in the United States, (3) permission for dual-nationality American citizens to leave Cuba for the United States, (4) an end to Cuba's "mischievous" involvement in the Puerto Rico issue, (5) restraint in Cuba's support for terrorist insurgents in Uruguay, Chile, and elsewhere in Latin America, and (6) permission for U.S. citizens to visit families in Cuba.[23]

Several of these issues have been taken off the agenda since 1975, and others have been added. In economic affairs, the list no longer includes ransom monies, postal fees, or improvements to the U.S. Embassy building, which in 1977 was reoccupied by the State Department as the U.S. Interests Section, under the sponsorship (and flying the flag of) the government of Switzerland.

Regionally, Cuba's isolation was beginning to end, and in 1975 the OAS approved a resolution, with U.S. support, that lifted its overall embargo and allowed individual countries to determine their political and trade relations with Cuba.

In 1975 the Ford administration modified the embargo and allowed U.S. subsidiaries in third countries to trade with Cuba. The efforts of the Ford administration were suddenly reversed in the fall of 1975, when the civil war in Angola began to heat up. In October 1976 an Aviacion Cubana flight en route to Venezuela was bombed, killing all seventy-three passengers. Reported CIA involvement and the U.S. refusal to extradite accused terrorists involved in the bombing led the Cubans to abrogate the antihijacking agreement since the provisions of the antiterrorist sections had been violated. Bilateral relations again went into a tailspin.

Attempting to pick up the pieces, the Carter administration undertook extensive negotiations, broadening bilateral relations in several areas. Unlike the previous record, however, the Carter years reshaped the method of negotiations in a way that has lasted for almost two decades: serious negotiations as part of an incremental process. Simply stated, the Carter approach was "One step at a time." The framework that would later orient the "carefully calibrated steps" of the Cuban Democracy Act emerged during the Carter years, although the goals shifted several times during the following two decades, from possible normalization to increased hostility. As expressed by one of the Cuban negotiators, Roman Sanchez Parodi, "Carter wanted serious talks but the talks should be about small steps. Kissinger had something much more dramatic in mind: the full normalization of relations." Sanchez was Cuba's ambassador to Brazil and later represented the Ministry of Foreign Affairs at the United Nations.

In 1977 a big step toward normalization was taken with the establishment of mutual "Interests Sections" in lieu of embassies in Washington and Havana, albeit flying flags of Czechoslovakia and Switzerland, respectively. In April Assistant Secretary of State Terence Todman went to Havana to sign fishing and maritime boundary agreements. The large U.S. team, the first diplomats to travel to Cuba in over sixteen years, included Rozanne L. Ridgway, Frank Willis, Robert Hodgson, Wayne Smith, Culver Gleysteen, Stephanie Van Reigersberg, and Terence Todman. The Carter administration eased currency restrictions and permitted charter flights.

Although polls continued to show Americans to be highly critical of Castro, several U.S. businesses began tentatively to support the possibility of doing business in Cuba, including Dow Chemical, the Florida East Coast Railway, and Burroughs Corporation. In an early speech, Carter declared it time to end an "inordinate fear of communism": Cuba no longer presented a threat to U.S. national security. The U.S. ambassador to the UN, Andrew Young, even argued that Castro's troops in Angola brought "stability and order." Senate Foreign Relations Chairman Frank Church (D-Idaho) visited Havana. Wayne Smith, head of the Interests Section during the Carter years, recalled that full relations seemed destined to follow "in short order."

As part of the reason for the perspective that there was movement, the Carter administration had scheduled a secret meeting in New York City on May 25, 1978, between Secretary of State Cyrus Vance and Cuban Vice President Carlos Rafael Rodriguez.[24] The agenda was a clarification of the disagreements about Cuba's Africa intervention.

As during the Ford administration, movement toward full diplomatic relations halted because of developments in Africa, this time in Ethiopia, known later as Shaba II. In 1977 a major invasion of Ethiopia by Soviet troops dashed expectations of a further dialogue.

Regardless of the tensions mounting over Africa, two rounds of secret U.S.-Cuban talks did occur in the spring of 1978, before the crisis escalated. The talks had been initiated—as during the Kissinger period—through a nongovernment intermediary. This time, a Cuban American banker who had served with the Castro government, Bernardo Benes, had delivered a message to the Carter administration from Castro. Benes had passed on Castro's suggestion that the talks be secret and that the participants be from only the highest level of administration officials to avoid "speculation" and "media hype."[25] The talks were arranged by Peter Tarnoff, from the National Security Council. The participants were Viron P. Vaky, Assistant Secretary of State for American Republics Affairs (the predecessor to Inter-American Affairs); Under Secretary of State David A. Newsom, who personally conducted the first two rounds of talks; and David Aaron, deputy to National Security Adviser Zbigniew Brzezinski.[26] Aaron met in May in a New York hotel with Jose Luis Patron, a member of the Cuban Communist Party Central Committee and later minister of tourism. On the U.S. agenda was Cuba's withdrawal from Africa, but what Castro proposed, both in this meeting and in a later private meeting with Newsom in his home in Washington, was a release of political prisoners. The U.S. agenda was simple. Stated in a State Department briefing paper, it included three major points: (1) the moderation of Cuban foreign policy and the withdrawal of troops from Africa, (2) compensation for U.S. citizens whose goods and properties had been nationalized, and (3) the establishment of human rights in Cuba, including the release of political prisoners.[27] Several rounds of talks were scheduled for Newsom and Aaron in Atlanta in August 1978, but events in Africa again became divisive. The Carter White House thought it had an understanding that the Cubans would not expand their involvement in Africa. In May 1978, for a second time, the Katanganese invaded Zaire's Shaba province using Zambia as the launch point; Castro denied to the chief of the U.S. Interests Section, Lyle Lane, that Cuba had incited or supported the invasion.

Early in 1979, Cuban troops arrived in Ethiopia to aid its Soviet-backed Marxist regime in a quarrel with Somalia (which had just expelled its Soviet and Cuban advisers) over the Ogaden region. The result was a split within the Carter administration, primarily between Secretary of State Cyrus Vance and National Security Adviser Brzezinski. The latter felt that the "SALT lies buried in the sands of the Ogaden"—meaning that Soviet-Cuban adventurism in the Horn of Africa would kill the Soviet-American SALT II arms control treaty in the Senate. In a statement on the day that Vance was to have met secretly with Rodriguez, President Carter blamed the Cubans for not restraining the Katanganese from invading.

Nonetheless, talks continued, and in 1979 the Cuban government approved Cuban American family visits, an issue on the agenda since the secret Kissinger negotiations, and a sizable group of exiles began to visit the island regularly.

By the fall of 1979, the coup de grace was the discovery of a Soviet combat brigade in Cuba. With a presidential election year approaching, a debate in the Congress regarding SALT II and the Panama Canal Treaty, crises in Nicaragua and Iran, and good faith in relations between the United States and Cuba wearing thin, the highly publicized revelation that a new combat brigade was in place in Cuba was enough to quash the effort. In 1979 the Carter administration confirmed an account by Senator Frank Church of the presence of a Soviet combat brigade of two thousand to three thousand men. The "brigade" furor—what Under Secretary of State David Newsom called a "bizarre and instructive" episode—began.

A U.S. intelligence study commissioned by Brzezinski found signs of a brigade-sized Soviet unit on Cuba. Senator Church, battling for reelection to the Senate, argued that SALT II's ratification would require the troops' removal. But the brigade was neither new nor in violation of U.S.-Soviet agreements. Neither the Kennedy-Khrushchev agreement banning offensive nuclear weapons and delivery systems in Cuba nor the 1970 prohibition of Soviet submarine bases covered the presence of ground forces. The "brigade," as specialists knew, had been in Cuba since 1962. To Washington's requests that the brigade's weapons be removed, Leonid Brezhnev replied that it was a training unit and that there was "no intention of changing its status." Any remaining chances for Senate ratification of SALT II ended with the late-1979 Soviet invasion of Afghanistan.

Plans to open relations with Cuba were stalled. Carter even dropped plans to establish relations with Angola. "As a nation," Vance later wrote, "we seemed unable to maintain a sense of perspective about Cuba." Castro made maintaining a sense of perspective even more difficult. Angered by a crowd of Cubans at the Peruvian Embassy in Havana seeking asylum in early April, 1980, he offered anyone who wanted to leave the island the chance to go to the United States. Unprepared, the Carter administration neglected to foresee the impact. It was the first of the major exoduses from Cuba of refugees, fleeing in small wooden makeshift boats or *balsas*, composed of inner tubes and small rafts. No fewer than 125,000 people showed up at the Mariel embarkation port in a major boatlift that continued for two months and that had a significant negative impact on Carter's failed reelection bid in November.

Several rounds of negotiations, including a June trip to Havana by National Security Council (NSC) staffer Robert Pastor along with Peter Tarnoff, failed to resolve the crisis. Cuban refugees continued to come through the summer while U.S. military began maneuvers in Guantanamo Bay Naval Base. Nothing stopped the exodus. In early July, the Cuban government began loading more than three hundred refugees onto a passenger ship scheduled to land in Florida at the time of a campaign visit by President Carter, whose secretary of state had just resigned. The Iran crisis, problems in Nicaragua, and the boatlift were plaguing the administration. Arkansas Governor Bill Clinton felt the impact as well, when a few thousand of the recent Mariel exiles rioted at the holding base in Fort Chafee, Arkansas, by most accounts costing Clinton reelection. In September Tarnoff returned to Havana to continue talks, but not until late September did the Castro government agree to halt the exodus. The administration continued negotiating on improvement of bilateral negotiations to the very last days of the term, even into January 1981—days before the inauguration of President Ronald Reagan. No change was forthcoming from the Cubans and time had run out for the Carter team.

By the time Ronald Reagan moved into the White House in January 1981, Cuban troops were established in Ethiopia and Angola. And Havana was sponsoring the new Sandinista regime in Nicaragua, assisting Marxist rebels in El Salvador, and helping to furnish an airport suitable for jet transport for the Marxist regime on the tiny island of Grenada. Reagan put some emphasis on the neighbors to the south that the United States had neglected. The first visiting foreign leader he welcomed was Edward Seaga of Jamaica, Cuba's southern neighbor. Within short order Edward Seaga had arrested and expelled a Cuban diplomat and a *Prensa Latina* reporter, and Cuba's relations with Jamaica, as well as with other countries in the Caribbean, had deteriorated.

Reagan also sent secret emissaries to Cuba, and in March 1982 Gen. Vernon Walters arrived in Havana to meet with Fidel Castro. Walters's list of concerns was substantially longer than Carter's: (1) Cuba's involvement in Central America, (2) Cuba's involvement in Africa, (3) the return of U.S. criminals fleeing prosecution in Cuba, (4) compensation for American properties, and (5) human rights and democratic processes. The same month, Reagan's Assistant Secretary for Inter-American Affairs, Thomas Enders, told Congress that the administration's negotiations on the larger issues would be more difficult. The administration tightened the rules on American travel and on April 19 added new restrictions on trade because of Cuba's support of armed violence in the hemisphere.

Whereas the 1970s began for Cuba with renewed efforts to mend fences in Central America and the Caribbean region and to reestablish diplomatic relations (culminating in the OAS embargo being lifted), by 1979 and into the 1980s Cuba's foreign programs increased geometrically, with large-scale assistance to Nicaragua and El Salvador. Within the hemisphere, Cuba was committed to expanding its influence by diplomatic as well as military programs, particularly through the Non-Aligned Movement.

For Cuban foreign policy, 1979 was a pivotal year. In March 1979 the election of Maurice Bishop and his New Jewel Movement in Grenada set the stage for Cuban support for the new international airport there and, ultimately, for the Reagan administration's invasion in October 1983. Although Reagan did not "go to the source" in the phrase of his first Secretary of State, Alexander M. Haig, he made it clear that further Cuban meddling would carry risks.

The 1980 exodus of refugees from Cuba seriously undercut Castro's credibility in the region and strained Cuba's relations with allies such as Costa Rica, Venezuela, and Peru. The election in 1980 of conservative Edward Seaga in Jamaica and the prompt removal of Cuba's attaché signaled that Cuba's advances in the Caribbean would be impeded. In May 1980 Cuban aircraft strafed Bahamian naval vessels, and by that time Cuba had begun to lose much of the ground it had gained in the region during the early 1970s. In December 1980, Costa Rican President Rodrigo Carazo cautioned that the two greatest threats to Central American democracies were the worldwide economic crisis and communist penetration.

Nicaragua became a point of antagonism with the Reagan administration. When in July 1979 Nicaragua's Gen. Anastasio Somoza Debayle was overthrown by the Sandinista National Liberation Front (FSLN), Cuba gave strong support to Nicaragua's revolution. In view of its successful involvement in Nicaragua, Cuba turned to the opposition in El Salvador in late 1979 and early 1980. From the standpoint of Cuban foreign policy, the conflict between Washington and Havana reached a crisis when the United States early in 1981 accused Cuba of sending large shipments of arms to El Salvador. The accusation was made in a State Department white paper released on February 23.

Even after detailed reports of inconsistencies in the white paper had been produced by the State Department and published by the press, the Reagan administration continued to accuse Cuba of sending arms, not only to El Salvador but to the opposition movement in Colombia as well.

Despite its anti-Castro rhetoric, however, the Reagan administration subsequently concluded agreements with Cuba on immigration as well as the exchange of technological information. On December 14, 1984, the Reagan administration signed an agreement on immigration procedures that established the current U.S. ceiling of twenty thousand visas per year for Cubans in addition to visas granted to close relatives of U.S. citizens. For its part, Cuba agreed to accept the return of 2,746 Cubans excludable or not admissible as refugees (mostly convicts and mental patients) under U.S. law. These Cubans, who had arrived during the 1980 Mariel exodus, were being held at a U.S. federal prison. The agreement also provided for the release of three thousand former political prisoners still in Cuba.

Remarkably, during the Reagan years, a delegation from Cuba's atomic energy commission, headed by Castro's son, Fidelito, visited a North Carolina nuclear plant, and Castro released several political prisoners in a gesture of good will.

In the heat of the 1992 presidential campaign, both Democratic Party candidate Bill Clinton and President George Bush sought the support of the Florida Cuban American vote. Shortly after Clinton's endorsement of a draft version of the Cuban Democracy Act of 1992, President Bush voiced support for the bill. On October 23, President Bush signed the legislation into law,[28] tightening the embargo by restricting trade by third-country subsidiaries of U.S. corporations and opening up telecommunications. Several of the law's provisions had been put into effect in April 1992 by an executive order signed by President Bush, in order to show support for a bill that the administration saw as problematical. Part of the executive order prohibited ships from entering a U.S. port if the ships had entered a Cuban port during the previous six months. The Cubans reacted angrily but privately expressed hope that a new era was about to begin.

When Bill Clinton was elected president in November, he did not carry the state of Florida, whose Cuban American vote he had courted, but he carried Dade County and got 40 percent of the statewide vote, to Bush's 41 percent.

Overall, the Clinton administration's early Cuba policy was oriented by the Cuban Democracy Act's two-track approach: tightening the trade provisions of the embargo—particularly third-country subsidiary trade—and opening the door to communication with the Cuban people. By its first summer in office, the Clinton administration had issued guidelines, provided for by the bill, for improvement of telecommunications and for adding human rights organizations and clearly defined educational and religious organizations to the categories of authorized travel.

In Cuba the economy continued its downhill slide: in 1992 the Cuban economy declined 11.6 percent and in 1993, 14.9 percent. By early summer, trouble signs on the Cuban horizon signaled a major migration crisis. The Cuban port of Cojimar, east of Havana, became the site of raft building, and on July 1 Cuban border guards fired on a boat leaving Cuba, leading to a small but angry protest.

Cuban economic reformers responded with the first legalization of the U.S. dollar, in July 1993, and with economic reforms the following fall, including self-employment, but nothing could stop the downward spiral of the economy. On July 13, a seminal event took place when the Cuban border guard vessel rammed a tugboat fleeing Cuba, the *13 of March*, killing forty Cubans, including women and children.

Relations became increasingly tense between Washington and Havana and a vocabulary of escalation began. The Clinton administration warned that Castro could not dictate U.S. migration policy, and Castro threatened to open the floodgate of illegal migration. On August 4 a Cuban ferry was hijacked and a Cuban police guard killed, and the next day one of the largest demonstrations in the postrevolutionary period occurred. Thousands of Cubans gathered on the Malecon seawall, throwing rocks at Cuban police and protesting the sinkings. The following week Castro announced on Cuban radio that Cubans who wanted to leave were free to do so.

For previous U.S. administrations, the focus had been Africa and the cold war, relations with the former Soviet Union, and intervention in Central America, but the Clinton administration had little choice but to focus on immigration issues in its negotiations with Cuba. A severe economic crisis in Cuba and an open-door policy in Washington had come together to shape events.

Between late 1992 and 1993, increased activity at the United Nations brought U.S. and Cuban diplomats into contact, but neither the U.S. Mission nor the Cuban Mission to the UN was able to win straight diplomatic victories. In early March 1992, the UN Commission on Human Rights approved a resolution expressing concern about human rights violations in Cuba. Eight months later the General Assembly voted overwhelmingly that the United States should lift its bilateral embargo on Cuba. The following March the General Assembly repeated a call to allow the U.S. Special Rapporteur to assist in the improvement of human rights conditions in Cuba. The dual mandate of the General Assembly—to the United States, lift the embargo; to Cuba, improve human rights—was repeated in votes in November and December 1993.

In the summer of 1994, coming on the heels of a U.S. anti-immigrant wave, tens of thousands fled Cuba on leaky rafts headed for U.S. shores beginning in May and June. Florida Governor Lawton Chiles declared an immigration emergency, and the issues of massive refugee flows, domestic politics, and foreign policy merged. By August the fear of another Mariel mass migration had set off the alarm bells. In the absence of negotiations with the Cubans, the Clinton administration called in a group of Cuban American political and community leaders and formulated a plan to deter some rafters (*balseros*). The result was a policy shift by President Clinton, the interdiction of the balseros, and the granting of temporary safe haven to the fleeing Cubans and Haitians at Guantanamo Bay Naval Base and in Panama.

The moving stories of harrowing escapes at sea by the rafters underscored the humanitarian issues and thrust the issue of U.S. immigration policy to the forefront of the American policy agenda and the nightly news. In an election year, the financial burden on state governments became the first question, and the U.S. ability and willingness to absorb large numbers of undocumented immigrants was the second. The experience of the Mariel exodus in 1980, when 125,000 Cubans came to the United States, including almost two thousand prisoners and mental patients, shaped the fear that countries might dump unwanted citizens on American shores. The perception that the August crisis was encouraged by the Cuban government increased the hostility.

As the numbers increased, the need for a policy response became clear. The result was the announcement on August 19 of Operation Safe Haven, in which 32,000 Cubans were granted indefinite safe haven on the U.S. naval base at Guantanamo Bay and a six-month stay in Panama. On schedule, the following February, 7,500 "bitter and angry" Cubans began their return from Panama to Guantanamo. Migration talks between Washington and Havana culminated in an agreement on September 9, 1994. In order to persuade the Cuban government to stop the exodus of rafters, the administration agreed to accept a quota of twenty thousand Cubans yearly through legal migration procedures, whereas it emphatically insisted that the balseros that had arrived at Guantanamo would not be allowed into the United States. Several administration spokespersons, including Michael Skol, deputy assistant secretary of state; Doris Meissner, commissioner of the Immigration and Naturalization Service, and Janet Reno, the attorney general, testified to Congress that not one Cuban in Guantanamo would be allowed into the United States. The September agreement, which resulted from almost two weeks of intense negotiations, also called for the United States and Cuba to facilitate safe, legal, and orderly Cuban migration to the United States. Under the agreement, the United States agreed to accept a minimum of twenty thousand Cubans annually, not including the relatives of U.S. citizens.[29] The 33,000 Cubans picked up at sea were brought to Guantanamo Bay Naval Base as a temporary safe haven and any Cubans arriving in the United States were allowed to be paroled in, under the Cuban Adjustment Act of 1966, which continued in effect.[30]

The most extensive secret U.S.-Cuban negotiations since the Kissinger period took place in April 1995 on the subject of immigration. Meeting in Toronto and New York City, the negotiators were Under Secretary of State Peter Tarnoff and Cuba's National Assembly President Ricardo Alarcon. They reached an agreement, announced on May 2 by the Clinton administration, to allow the twenty thousand Cuban refugees from the Guantanamo camps to come to the United States. The accord marked the end of thirty-five years of virtually automatic admission of Cuban refugees. The agreement reflected a reversal of the position that the administration had taken since the August 1994 exodus: previously Cubans who made it to Guantanamo had not been allowed into the United States. The reaction by the Cuban American exile community was mixed, with polls showing about half of the community in support of the policy. The political landscape had changed dramatically since the Mariel boatlift during the Carter administration, and the Clinton administration, at least for the summer of 1995, was the beneficiary of the calmed waters.[31]

The history of the accord is worth noting: On August 8, 1994, after several days of rioting, Fidel Castro stated that he would no longer prevent emigration from Cuba, effectively opening the door to a flood of refugees. To stem the flow—and, in fairness to the accords, to prevent the loss of life at sea—on August 19 the Clinton administration announced it would intercept rafters and transfer them to the U.S. naval base at Guantanamo Bay as a temporary safe haven. Under the September 1994 immigration agreement by the United States and Cuba, a minimum of twenty thousand Cubans are allowed to migrate legally, but the Cubans at the base were not allowed to apply for asylum in the United States. The subsequent May 2 migration agreement allowed the Cubans at the base to enter the United States but cut off further rafter entries except for refugees—establishing a new policy of repatriation.

The forced repatriation of Cubans was the primary factor in stemming the flight of Cubans to U.S. shores. Several Cuban academics and non-Cuban diplomats attribute the calming of the migration crisis to the accords, which also grant more than twenty thousand visas a year (the largest single-nation group in the world) to eligible Cubans who apply in Havana to emigrate to the United States.

Both the September 9, 1994, and May 2, 1995, immigration agreements have reduced the option of fleeing Cuba and created an atmosphere of greater acquiescence within Cuba by potential migrants. A slightly improved Cuban economy, economic reforms, and the availability of consumer products have added to the shift.

Five rounds of immigration talks had taken place by November 1995, when tensions increased. While both Washington and Havana have firmly backed the migration accords, other events took precedence.

In September 1995, the administration revealed that it had proposed supervision of the accords by an international organization, a proposal the Cubans rejected. The Cuban argument: There would not be reprisals against repatriated balseros. At the same time, Richard Nuccio, the White House special adviser to the president and to the secretary of state on Cuba, repeated the harder line of the administration: There would be no "calibrated" responses to the release of six high-profile political prisoners at the request of two prominent human rights groups in the spring of 1995, or after the promulgation of Cuba's Foreign Investment Law that the National Assembly had passed in early September, which allowed 100 percent foreign ownership of businesses and permitted some real estate sales.[32]

The Clinton administration held several rounds of negotiations to review and implement the immigration agreement of September 9. The first round of negotiations took place October 24–26 between Dennis Hays, the head of the Cuba Desk at the Department of State, and Cuba's Alarcon.

Negotiations in the short term had to take into account recent economic shifts that deeply affect the Cuban government. The economic downturn between 1989 and 1994, after the collapse of the Soviet Union and the loss of substantial Soviet subsidies, has increased Cuba's interest in opening its economy to Western markets. It has also increased the Cuban government's antagonism to a comprehensive approach to the settlement of Cuban claims.[33]

Cuba's centrally planned socialist economy has been oriented to the export of sugar since the time before Fidel Castro but has been geared to bartering and sale to the Soviet Union since the United States cut Cuba's sugar quota. From 1962 until 1991, Cuba signed five-year agreements with the Soviet Union to sell approximately 3 million to 4 million tons annually of its production of 7 or 8 million tons for prices well above the world price. In exchange, the Soviets delivered 12 million or 13 million tons a year to the Cubans for domestic use, the excess of which was sold on the world market for hard currency. During the three decades since the revolution, sugar has continued to be Cuba's main source of export earnings, accounting for 75 percent to more than 85 percent of all export earnings.

The economic landscape changed with the collapse of the Soviet Union, and by 1992 sugar exports accounted for less than half of Cuba's foreign exchange. In the years following the Soviet collapse in 1991 and for three years of Soviet decline preceding it, Cuba's gross domestic product (GDP) shrank by 50 percent. In 1993 the Cuban government initiated free-market reforms that began an evolution of the Cuban economy away from its three-decade model of socialist development. In July 1993 the Cuban government declared that the dollar would be legalized—a surprising reversal of more than three decades of rejection of the U.S. currency by the island. Reforms included more than two hundred joint ventures worth about $2 billion dollars, allowing Cubans to be self-employed and legalizing the small family-run restaurants called *paladares*.[34]

In 1994 the economy began to turn the corner, as reported first by the UN Economic Commission for Latin America and confirming the expectations of Cuban economic planners.[35] The 0.7 percent growth was achieved through unemployment, higher prices, and incentives for foreign investment. Although the improvement of the government's internal account was achieved by layoffs and increased prices, the small rise in economic activity, including a tacit approval of the burgeoning informal economy, was enough in the short term to act as a pressure valve for the Cuban government, crippled during the previous summer by the desperation that led to the mass exodus of rafters. Cutting expenses and taking excess pesos out of circulation helped the peso rise in the summer of 1995 to 35 to a dollar from its low in August 1994 of 150 to a dollar. The passage of the Foreign Investment Law in the fall of 1995 also gave rise to increased European investment, and a debate on the merits of the embargo returned to the forefront of the U.S. policy in the region.[36]

With bilateral migration issues on track, 1996 held out the promise of increased communication, as several prominent congressional delegations planned trips to Havana. On January 16 Representative Joseph Moakley (D-Mass.) hosted one such trip to Cuba, and on January 17 Representative Bill Richardson (D-N.M.) secured the release of several political prisoners. With moral support from the international community, particularly the European Commission and the United States, an umbrella organization of Cuban dissidents, Concilio Cubano, announced a meeting to be held on February 24. A European Commission group that had begun discussions of aid packages to Cuba encouraged the Cuban government to allow the meeting to occur.

Nonetheless, in mid-February the Cuban government began a crackdown on members of the group, including arrests and prison sentences. Tense diplomatic messages went back and forth between Washington and Havana. Washington criticized the crackdown, and Havana shot back with several letters complaining of violations of Cuban airspace, particularly by a January 13 flight of Miami-based Brothers to the Rescue, a boat rescue group, which flew over Havana and dropped leaflets.

On February 24 Cuban MiG-23 and MiG-29 fighter jets shot down over international waters two small U.S. Cessnas flown by Brothers to the Rescue. Although Cuba argued that the planes were shot down within Cuban airspace, President Clinton condemned the downing as a violation of international law and imposed immediate sanctions: (1) support for passage of embargo-tightening legislation sponsored by Senator Jesse Helms (R-N.C.) and Representative Dan Burton (R-Ind.), (2) travel restrictions on Cuban diplomats within the United States, (3) suspension of charter flights to Cuba out of Miami, and (4) support for legislation permitting compensation for victims' families from blocked Cuban accounts. On February 27 the UN Security Council requested the Montreal-based International Civil

Aeronautics Organization (ICAO) to investigate and report on the downing of the planes.

The administration and the Congress moved quickly to support the legislation, and on February 28 a House and Senate conference committee approved H.R. 927, the Cuban Liberty and Democratic Solidarity (Libertad) Act.[37]

Within a month, both the House and the Senate approved the conference version of the bill, and on March 12, 1996, President Clinton signed it. The law allows U.S. nationals to sue in federal court to recover money damages from an individual or country that traffics in property confiscated in Cuba; denies admission to foreign nationals involved in the trafficking of U.S. property; and codifies previous legislation and regulations regarding the embargo, taking much of U.S. policy regarding the embargo out of the hands of the president.

With the intention of reducing the tensions and proving to the Cuban government that the U.S. aircraft had been over international waters, on March 2 John P. Gannon, the Central Intelligence Agency's deputy director, sat across a table at the Cuban Mission to the United Nations from the chief of Cuba's air force. Accounts differ on the objectives of the meeting. The White House says it was intended to prove definitively to the Cuban government that the Cuban American pilots shot down in unarmed Cessnas by Cuban MiGs were over international waters. The Cuban government says the purpose of the meeting was to give the United States assurances that during the flotilla that would take place later that day, March 2, there would be no further provocations. The only point of agreement between the United States and Cuba in convening a secret and unprecedented meeting of the CIA and Cuban military intelligence was to avoid a military confrontation, which both agreed was possible.

During the summer of 1996, the Clinton administration was presented with its first test on the Helms-Burton legislation, which set an August 1 deadline for determining whether or not a provision of the law would take effect, thereby creating a private right of action by U.S. claimholders. In order to satisfy the conflicting interests of claimholders and the anger at the United States by U.S. allies in Western Europe, Mexico, and Canada, President Clinton chose to allow the provision to go forward but suspended the lawsuits for six more months. As a follow-up to the decision, the administration appointed a special envoy, Stuart E. Eizenstat, under secretary of commerce for international trade and former U.S. ambassador to the European Union, to meet with U.S. allies that would be affected by the decision. Nonetheless, by late September, Mexico had passed legislation to block the impact of the law, and Canada's parliament had proposed an amendment to its 1984 Foreign Extraterritorial Measures Act to include Helms-Burton.

The context was an election year, when any major foreign policy confrontation—particularly one involving Florida and New Jersey and their large Cuban American votes—was a particular consideration for a presidential contender. Cuba policy remained highly contested not only between the Congress and the administration but also within the administration: White House, State Department, and Pentagon.

In the days following the downing, quiet meetings further reminiscent of the Kissinger-era contacts took place. The Pentagon dispatched two-star Air Force Gen. John Sams to secret talks with Cuban Armed Forces Brig. Gen. Carlos Manuel Perez at the Gitmo gate of the U.S. naval base at Guantanamo Bay. The pretext was that a Cuban freight plane had strayed over the U.S. base. The case was dropped, even though a videotape of the meeting was leaked, causing a brief uproar in the exile community.

Several other military-to-military meetings had taken place in the months before. On January 18, as Joint Chiefs of Staff Chairman Gen. John Shalikashvili flew to Guantanamo Bay Naval Base to officially close the refugee camps, Nuccio and Gen. John Sheehan, head of the U.S. Atlantic Command, met quietly with Cuban Armed Forces Brig. Gen. Ulises Rosales del Toro.

The administration argued that it had done what it could to stop the unauthorized flights that had passed over downtown Havana. The FAA issued a warning to 33,000 pilots in South Florida not to stray into Cuban airspace and threatened to revoke licenses, as it did to Jose Basulto, head of Brothers to the Rescue, for two overflights.

In June the ICAO report was published and distributed to a divided UN Security Council. The report, entitled "The Shooting Down of Two U.S.-Registered Private Civil Aircraft by Cuban Military Aircraft on 24 February 1996," was not formally endorsed by the Security Council. Rather, a less strongly worded resolution circulated by the United States was passed in July 1996, condemning the use of weapons against civil aircraft but making note that U.S. planes had flown unauthorized into Cuban airspace in the months preceding the shootdown.[38] The issue of U.S. citizens who have sought asylum in Cuba also came to the forefront during the election summer of 1996, when U.S. financier Robert Vesco went on trial in early August for fraud and economic crimes and was convicted in Cuba.

CONCLUSIONS

Every U.S. administration in office since the embargo was imposed has conducted negotiations with Fidel Castro, none with any degree of success in moving relations toward normalization, although negotiations have succeeded in moving the ball forward in areas as diverse as nuclear energy and immigration. Most of the negotiations, in their turn, began as part of a larger scheme of bettering relations between the United States and Cuba. In the end, each fell apart with acrimony and accusations. Negotiations, however, have to overcome an antagonism that is more "normal" than normalization would be: The roots of U.S.-Cuban antipathies go back at least ninety years, to the time when Teddy Roosevelt led his Rough Riders up San Juan Hill. Nonetheless, all nine U.S. presidents who have been in office since Fidel Castro came to power have negotiated agreements, including the Reagan administration, under which tensions were at their height. Cuba has in fact been a focus of U.S. administrations for well over a century. John Quincy Adams commented in 1823, before his presidency, that Cuba would "gravitate" toward the "North American Union," and four subsequent presidents—Polk, Buchanan, Grant, and McKinley—tried to buy Cuba from Spain.

An evaluation of U.S. diplomatic efforts, as well as the usefulness of policies of pressure, is instructive in evaluating both the process and substance of negotiations that could return democracy to Cuba and resolve the outstanding issues between the two countries.

NOTES

1. Pamela S. Falk, "Washington and Havana," *Wilson Quarterly*, Winter 1988, 12: 64–74.

2. One of Jose Martí's most well-known quotes refers to his years of exile from Spain, which he spent in the United States. Years after, in his treatise about colonialism, *Inside the Monster: Writings on the United States and American Imperialism*, trans. Elinor Randall, Luis A. Baralt, Juan de Onis, and Roslyn Held Foner, ed. Philip S. Foner (New York: Monthly Review Press, 1975), he wrote, "I have lived inside the monster and I know its entrails, and my sling is the sling of David."

3. More than six hundred documents relating to the fall of Batista and Castro's rise to power, as well as the U.S. Embassy's involvement, are published in John P. Glennon, ed., *Foreign Relations of the United States, 1958–60: Cuba* (Washington, D.C.: Government Printing Office, 1991). An analysis based on the documents is found in Mark Falcoff, "Cuba and the United States: Back to the Beginning," *World Affairs* 156, no. 3 (Winter 1994): 111–23. The declassified documents from the Kissinger negotiations, obtained under the Freedom of Information Act, are the basis of an article by James L. Blight and Peter Kornbluh, "Our Hidden Dialogue with Castro," *New York Review of*

Books, October 6, 1994: 45. It includes interviews with the participants in the secret negotiations.

4. William D. Rogers, confidential memorandum to the White House, 1975.

5. Of the six demands of the economic "balance sheet" of the Kissinger days, only one—payment of property claims by Cuba—is central to the current policy debate. (See n.23.)

6. Falk, "Washington and Havana," pp. 64–74.

7. See Pamela S. Falk, *Cuban Foreign Policy: Caribbean Tempest* (Lexington, Mass.: D.C. Heath/Lexington Books, 1986), pp. 41–56.

8. For a list of the largest registered U.S. claims, see the Atlantic Council's *Road Map for Restructuring Future U.S. Relations with Cuba* (Washington, D.C.: Atlantic Council of the United States, 1995), appendix A.

9. Manuel Urrutia Lleo, interview by author, New York City, October 15, 1975. Before Urrutia fled Cuba, he wrote about the transition he hoped he had not witnessed in *Democracia falso y falso socialismo: Pre-castrismo y castrismo* (False democracy and false socialism) (Englewood Cliffs, N.J.: Vega Publishing Company, 1975), but thereafter he rarely spoke about the revolution. I encountered Urrutia when he was teaching Spanish at Hunter College, where I was also teaching, and a few years before his death he became willing to talk about the revolution that he felt had failed him.

10. International Commission of Jurists, *Cuba and the Rule of Law* (Geneva: ICE, 1962).

11. On May 24 the Cuban National Bank notified Royal Dutch Shell to prepare to process 300,000 tons, or 2.2 million barrels, per year of Soviet crude.

12. Articles 24 (conditions of property expropriation with compensation), 30, and 147 (concerning the courts and the expropriation process) were amended to broaden the use of expropriation and expand the definition of compensation. The amendments authorized the president and prime minister to expropriate oil companies owned by U.S. citizens, to provide for caretakers to take charge of the properties, and to designate the value of the company for compensation. See Pamela S. Falk, "Cuba," in *Constitutions of the Countries of the World,* ed. Gisbert H. Flanz and Albert P. Blaustein (Dobbs Ferry, N.Y.: Oceana, 1975).

13. Shell was the only oil company to take steps immediately to test the constitutionality of the seizure in the Cuban courts. *Wall Street Journal,* June 30, 1960.

14. Emilio Collado, Shell Oil Company, interview by author, July 14, 1982; for a detailed history, see Hugh Thomas, *Cuba: The Pursuit of Freedom* (New York: Harper & Row, 1971) p. 1289.

15. U.S. Senate, Select Committee to Study Government Operations, *Alleged Assassination Plots Involving Foreign Leaders: An Interim Report of the Select Committee to Study Governmental Operations with Respect to Intelligence Activities,* 94th Congress, 1st sess., November 20, 1975, S. Rept. no. 94–465. "We have found concrete evidence," the Senate study begins, "of at least eight plots involving the CIA to assassinate Fidel Castro from 1960 to 1965" (p. 71).

16. For an extensive discussion of the role of the Central Intelligence Agency and the influence of analyst Richard Bissell on Kennedy, see "Wayward Spy," *Civilization* 2, no. 5 (Sept.-Oct., 1995), pp. 36-46.

17. U.S. Department of State, "Cuba," White Paper no. 7171, Inter-American Series no. 66, pp. 2, 26, 28, and 34.

18. Among the dozens of books on the history of the missile crisis, recent works are especially enlightening, being based on declassified documents and on interviews with the participants. They include James G. Blight, Bruce J. Allyn, and David A. Welch, *Cuba on the Brink: Castro, the Missile Crisis and the Soviet Collapse*, (New York: Pantheon, 1993), and Arthur M. Schlesinger Jr., "Four days with Fidel," *New York Review of Books*, March 26, 1992, pp. 22–29.

19. Pierre Salinger, letter to Michael Skol, U.S. Department of State, March 31, 1994. Salinger's letter lays out the chronology clearly: "[But] it was Kennedy who sent a message to Fidel Castro four days before his assassination telling him the United States wanted to normalize relations with Cuba."

20. Ibid.

21. For an extensive discussion of the secret negotiations from June 1974 through 1975, including a discussion over coffee in a crowded cafeteria at La Guardia Airport between Kissinger's deputy, Lawrence Eagleberger, and Cuban diplomats, see Blight and Kornbluh, pp. 45–49.

22. Falk, "Washington and Havana."

23. Briefing memorandum, "Meetings with Cuban Emissary," U.S. Department of State, January 2, 1975, declassified August 18, 1993.

24. Wayne S. Smith, *The Closest of Enemies: A Personal and Diplomatic Account of U.S.-Cuban Relations since 1957* (New York and London: W. W. Norton, 1987), p. 140; Carlos Rafael Rodriguez, interview by the author, June 17, 1982.

25. Smith, p. 146.

26. The history of the talks was conveyed to Smith by Vaky, who apologized for excluding him from the information; Smith, p. 146.

27. Department of State, GIST, in Smith, 149.

28. *Cuban Democracy Act, Title 17 of the National Defense Authorization Act for Fiscal Year 1993*, PL 102–484, 106 Stat. 2315.

29. See *A Road Map*, pp. 5–7, and C. Richard Nelson and Kenneth Weisbrode, eds., *U.S. Relations with Cuba: Compendium of Laws, Regulations and Policies* (Washington, D.C.: Atlantic Council of the United States, 1994), for the text of the September and May accords.

30. Cuban Adjustment Act, Pub. L. No. 89-732, @ 1, 80 Stat. 1161, 1161 (1996), as amended by Pub. L. No. 96-212, @ 203(i), 94 Stat. 102, 108 (1980), reprinted as 8 U.S.C. @ 1255 note (1994).

31. In testimony to Congress on May 18, 1995, Under Secretary of State Peter Tarnoff felt the heat of the decision regarding repatriation. In two days of testimony and in the subsequent 129 questions that he answered for the record, Tarnoff was grilled on every aspect of the secret talks in Montreal and New York. See U.S. House of Representatives, International Relations Committee, May 18, 1995, *U.S. Policy toward Cuba*, (Washington, D.C.: Government Printing Office, 1995). Also testifying were Doris Meissner, commissioner of immigration and naturalization, and Norman Saunders, admiral, U.S. Coast Guard.

32. Pablo Alfonso, "EU firme en las sanciones impuestas a Cuba," *El Nuevo Herald,* September 10, 1995, p. A1.

33. See *A Road Map,* pp. 13-19.

34. Douglas Farah, "Cuba Learns New C-Word: Capitalism," *Philadelphia Inquirer,* September 16, 1995. For a more extensive discussion of the informal economy, see "On the New Economic Geography of Havana's Food and Paladar Markets," by Joseph L. Scarpaci, paper presented at the fifth annual meeting of the Association for the Study of the Cuban Economy, University of Miami, August 11, 1995; Jose F. Alonso, "The Path of Cuba's Economy Today," *ASCE Newsletter,* Spring 1995, pp. 18–23.

35. Pamela S. Falk, "Cuban Growth," *Wall Street Journal,* July 7, 1995, p. A11.

36. Christopher Marquis, "Foreign investors' money talks—and Cubans are listening," *Miami Herald,* September 18, 1995, pp. 1, 10A; Douglas Farah, "Foreign Investors Finding Cuba More Comfortable—With U.S. Away," *Washington Post,* September 12, 1995; Mireya Navarro, "Cuba Passes Law to Attract Greater Foreign Investment," *New York Times,* September 7, 1995; Jose De Cordoba, "Cuba Will Allow Foreigners to Own 100% of Firms," *Wall Street Journal,* September 5, 1995.

37. PL 104–114, 110 Stat. 785 (1996), known as Helms-Burton Act.

38. International Civil Aeronautics Organization, *Report of the ICAO Fact-Finding Investigation* (Montreal: ICAO, 1996), appendix to C-WP/10441.

SELECTED BIBLIOGRAPHY

Arnson, Cynthia J. *Crossroads: Congress, the President, and Central America, 1976–1993*. University Park: Pennsylvania State University Press, 1993.

Barnett, A. Doak. *China and the Major Powers in East Asia*. Washington, D.C.: Brookings Institution, 1987.

Blight, James G., Bruce Allyn, and David A. Welch. *Cuba on the Brink: Castro, the Missile Crisis and the Soviet Collapse*. New York: Pantheon, 1993.

Carter, Jimmy. *Keeping Faith: Memoirs of a President*. New York: Bantam Books, 1982.

China: U.S. Policy since 1945. Washington, D.C.: Congressional Quarterly, 1980.

Conroy, Michael E. "Economic Aggression as an Instrument of Low Intensity Conflict." In *Reagan versus the Sandinistas: The Undeclared War on Nicaragua*, ed. Thomas W. Walker. Boulder, Colo.: Westview, 1987.

Davis, Paul K., and John Arquilla. *Deterring or Coercing Opponents in Crisis: Lessons from the War with Saddam Hussein*. Santa Monica, Calif.: Rand Corporation, 1991.

Dickey, Christopher. *With the Contras: A Reporter in the Wilds of Nicaragua*. New York: Simon and Schuster, 1985.

Falcoff, Mark. "Cuba and the United States: Back to the Beginning." *World Affairs* 156 (Winter 1994).

Falk, Pamela S. *Cuban Foreign Policy: Caribbean Tempest*. Lexington, Mass.: D. C. Heath/Lexington Books, 1986.

———. "Washington and Havana." *Wilson Quarterly*, Winter 1988.

———. "Cuba." In *Constitutions of the World*, ed. Gisbert H. Flanz and Albert P. Blaustein. Dobbs Ferry, N.Y.: Oceana, 1975.

Friedman, Alan. *Spider's Web: The Secret History of How the White House Illegally Armed Iraq*. New York: Bantam Books, 1993.

Gaddis, John Lewis. "The Long Peace." *International Security* 10 (Spring 1986).

Galtung, Johan D. "On the Effects of International Sanctions, with Examples from the Case of Rhodesia." *World Politics* 19 (April 1967).

Garthoff, Raymond. *The Great Transition: American-Soviet Relations and the End of the Cold War*. Washington, D.C.: Brookings Institution, 1994.

George, Alexander L. *Bridging the Gap: Theory and Practice in Foreign Policy*. Washington, D.C.: U.S. Institute of Peace Press, 1993.

George, Alexander L., and Richard Smoke. "Deterrence and Foreign Policy." *World Politics* 41 (January 1991).

————. *Deterrence in American Foreign Policy: Theory and Practice.* New York: Columbia University Press, 1974.

Gilbert, Dennis. *Sandinistas: The Party and the Revolution.* New York: Basil Blackwell, 1988.

Glennon, John, ed. *Foreign Relations of the United States, 1958–60: Cuba.* Washington, D.C.: U.S. Government Printing Office, 1991.

Gutmann, Roy. *Banana Diplomacy: The Making of American Policy in Nicaragua 1981–1987.* New York: Simon and Schuster, 1988.

Harding, Harry. *A Fragile Relationship.* Washington, D.C.: Brookings Institution, 1992.

Hiro, Diliip. *Desert Shield to Desert Storm: The Second Gulf War.* London: HarperCollins, 1992.

Hoffman, Bruce. *The Ultimate Fifth Column: Saddam Hussein, International Terrorism and the Crisis in the Gulf.* Santa Monica, Calif.: Rand Corporation, August 1990.

Houtart, Francois. "Crisis in the FSLN: Class Conflict." *Envio* (Managua, Nicaragua) 13 (September 1994).

Huth, Paul, and Bruce Russett. "Deterrence Failure and Crisis Escalation." *International Studies Quarterly* 32 (March 1988).

————. *Extended Deterrence and the Prevention of War.* New Haven, Conn.: Yale University Press, 1988.

International Commission of Jurists, eds. *Cuba and the Rule of Law.* Geneva: ICE, 1962.

Jentleson, Bruce W. *With Friends Like These: Reagan, Bush and Saddam, 1982–1990.* New York: W. W. Norton, 1984.

Kaplowitz, Noel. "Psychopolitical Dimensions of International Relations: The Reciprocal Effects of Conflict Strategies." *International Studies Quarterly* 28 (December 1984).

Karsh, Efraim, ed. *The Iran-Iraq War: Impact and Implications.* New York: St. Martins, 1989.

Karsh, Efraim, and Lawrence Freedman. *The Gulf Conflict: Diplomacy and War in the New World Order.* London: Faber and Faber, 1993.

Kennan, George F. *American Diplomacy, 1900–1950.* Chicago: University of Chicago Press, 1951.

————. ("X"). "The Sources of Soviet Conduct." *Foreign Affairs,* July 1947.

Kober, Stanley. *Appeasement and the Gulf War.* Washington, D.C.: Progressive Policy Institute, 1992.

Kornbluh, Peter. *Nicaragua: The Price of Intervention.* Washington, D.C.: Institute for Policy Studies, 1987.

Kornbluh, Peter, and Malcom Byrne, eds. *The Iran-Contra Affair: The Making of a Scandal, 1983–1988.* Alexandria, Va.: Chadwyck-Healey, 1990.

LeoGrande, William M. "The United States and the Nicaraguan Revolution." In *Nicaragua in Revolution,* ed. Thomas W. Walker. New York: Praeger, 1982.

————. *Public Opinion and Central America.* Washington, D.C.: Washington Office on Latin America, 1984.

————. "The United States and Nicaragua." In *Nicaragua: The First Five Years,* ed. Thomas W. Walker. New York: Praeger, 1985.

————. "Rollback or Containment: Nicaragua, the United States, and the Search for Peace." *International Security* 11 (Fall 1986).

————. "The Contras and Congress." In *Reagan versus the Sandinistas: The Undeclared War on Nicaragua*, ed. Thomas W. Walker. Boulder, Colo.: Westview, 1987.

Li, Victor. *Derecognizing Taiwan: The Legal Problems.* Washington, D.C.: Carnegie Endowment for International Peace, 1977.

Lowther, William. *Arms and the Man: Dr. Gerald Bull, Iraq and the Supergun.* Novato, Calif.: Presidio Press, 1991.

Luard, Evan. "Conciliation and Deterrence: A Comparison of Political Strategies in the Interwar and Postwar Periods." *World Politics* 19 (January 1967).

Macaulay, Neil. *The Sandino Affair.* Chicago: Quadrangle Books, 1971.

Miller, Judith, and Laurie Mylorie. *Saddam Hussein and the Crisis in the Gulf.* New York: Times Books, 1990.

Millet, Richard. *Guardians of the Dynasty.* Maryknoll, N.Y.: Orbis Books, 1977.

Nelson, C. Richard, and Kenneth Weisbrode, eds. *U.S. Relations with Cuba: Compendium of Laws, Regulations and Policies.* Washington, D.C.: Atlantic Council of the United States, November 1994.

Normalization of Relations with the People's Republic of China: Practical Implications. Report of the Subcommittee on Asian and Pacific Affairs of the House Committee on International Relations, U.S. Congress. Washington, D.C.: U.S. Government Printing Office, 1977.

Oberdorfer, Don. *The Turn: From the Cold War to the New Era.* New York: Poseidon Press, 1991.

Oksenberg, Michael, and Robert B. Oxnam. *Dragon and Eagle.* New York: Basic Books, 1978.

Pastor, Robert A. *Condemned to Repetition: The United States and Nicaragua.* Princeton: Princeton University Press, 1987.

Pollack, Jonathan. *The Lessons of Coalition Politics.* Santa Monica, Calif.: Rand Corporation, 1984.

Procedimiento para establecer la paz firme y duradera en centroamerica. (Procedure for establishing a firm and durable peace in Central America.) San Jose, Costa Rica: Oficina de Apoyo de la Presidencia de la Republica, 1987.

The Property Issue in Nicaragua: Advances and Challenges. Managua, Nicaragua: Ministry of Finance, 1995.

Reilly, John E. "America's State of Mind." *Foreign Policy* 66 (Spring 1987).

Report of the Congressional Committees Investigating the Iran-Contra Affair. Washington, D.C.: U.S. Government Printing Office, 1988.

Report of the National Bipartisan Commission on Central America ("Kissinger Commission"). Washington, D.C.: U.S. Government Printing Office, 1983.

Report of a Property Issues Conference. Working Paper Series, Carter Center of Emory University. Atlanta: Carter Center, 1995.

Restoring the Balance: U.S. Strategy and the Gulf Crisis, Initial Report of the Washington Institute's Strategic Study Group. Washington, D.C.: Washington Institute on Near East Policy, 1991.

A Road Map for Restructuring Future U.S. Relations with Cuba. Policy Paper Series. Washington, D.C.: Atlantic Council of the United States, 1995.

Roshco, Bernard. *When Policy Fails: How the Buck Was Passed When Kuwait Was Invaded.* Harvard University, John F. Kennedy School of Government, Discussion Paper D-15, December 1992.

Sciolino, Elaine. *The Outlaw State: Saddam Hussein's Quest for Power and the Gulf Crisis.* New York: John Wiley, 1991.

Selser, Gregorio. *Sandino.* New York: Monthly Review, 1981.

Serafino, Nina M. *Nicaragua Chronology since the February 25, 1990 Elections: The Transition and President Chamorro's First 100 Days.* Washington, D.C.: Congressional Research Service, 1990.

———. *Nicaraguan Elections and Transition: Issues for U.S. Policy.* Washington, D.C.: Congressional Research Service, 1990.

Shevardnadze, Eduard. *The Future Belongs to Freedom.* New York: Free Press, 1991.

Shultz, George P. *Turmoil and Triumph: My Years as Secretary of State.* New York: Scribner's, 1993.

Sifry, Micah L., and Christopher Cerf, eds. *The Gulf War Reader: History, Documents, Opinions.* New York: Times Books, 1991.

Smith, Wayne S. *The Closest of Enemies: A Personal and Diplomatic Account of U.S.-Cuban Relations since 1957.* New York and London: W. W. Norton, 1987.

Stein, Janet Gross. "The Wrong Strategy in the Right Place." *International Security* 14 (Winter 1988/89).

Storrs, K. Larry, Mark P. Sullivan, and Maureen Taft-Morales. *Congress and Policy Toward Latin America in 1992.* Washington, D.C.: Congressional Research Service, 1993.

Sutter, Robert G. *China Watch: Toward Sino-American Reconciliation.* Baltimore: Johns Hopkins University Press, 1978.

Sutter, Robert G., and Larry Niksch. "China's Role in U.S. Security Policy." *Issues and Studies* (March 1984).

Thomas, Hugh. *Cuba: The Pursuit of Freedom.* New York: Harper & Row, 1971.

Timmerman, Kenneth R. *The Death Lobby: How the West Armed Iraq.* Boston: Houghton Mifflin, 1991.

Urrutia Lleo, Manuel. *Democracia falso y falso socialismo: Pre-castrismo y castrismo* (False democracy and false socialism). Englewood Cliffs, N. J.: Vega Publishing Company, 1975.

U.S. Overseas Grants and Loans and Assistance from International Organizations: Obligations and Loan Authorizations, 1945–1993. Washington, D.C.: U.S. Agency for International Development, 1994.

Vickers, George R., and Jack Spence. "Nicaragua: Two Years After the Fall." *World Policy Journal* 9 (Summer 1992).

Watts, William, et al. *Japan, Korea and China: American Perceptions and Policies.* Lexington, Mass.: D.C. Heath, 1979.

Woodward, Bob. *The Commanders.* New York: Simon and Schuster, 1991.

———. *Veil: The Secret Wars of the CIA.* New York: Simon and Schuster, 1987.

Contributors

Richard T. Childress is president of Asian Investment Strategies, a consulting firm in Washington, D.C. He is a former director of Asian affairs and political military affairs at the National Security Council (1981–89). A Vietnam veteran, he led or participated in every policy level delegation to Vietnam and Laos from 1982 to 1989.

Pamela S. Falk is a lawyer and authority on international relations, Latin America, and immigration issues. She is a former staff director of the Subcommittee on Western Hemisphere Affairs of the U.S. House of Representatives (1993–94) and is currently professor of international trade and commercial transactions in the City University of New York School of Law.

Bruce W. Jentleson is director of the University of California–Davis Washington Center and professor of political science and from 1993–94 served as special assistant to the director of the policy planning staff, U.S. Department of State.

Robert Legvold is professor of political science at Columbia University and former director of the Harriman Institute. He has written extensively about Russia and the former Soviet Union.

William M. LeoGrande is professor of political science in the Department of Government in the School of Public Affairs at the American University. He has published widely on Central America, Cuba, and U.S. foreign policy, and served as a consultant to a variety of congressional committees, executive branch agencies, and private foundations.

C. Richard Nelson is director of the Program on International Security at the Atlantic Council of the United States.

James N. Rosenau is one of America's premier political scientists and author of several important works on U.S. foreign policy and international relations. He is university professor of international affairs at the George Washington University.

Burton M. Sapin is professor emeritus of political science and international affairs at the George Washington University and former dean of the School of Public and International Affairs. He is the author of numerous books and articles on U.S. foreign policy and civil-military relations.

Stephen J. Solarz is director of the Foreign Policy Forum at the George Washington University and serves on the boards of several corporations and nonprofit organizations. For twenty-four years he served in public office, both in the New York State Assembly and in the U.S. House of Representatives, where he sat on the House Foreign Affairs Committee.

Robert G. Sutter is a senior specialist in international policy with the Congressional Research Service, where he has been since 1977. He served previously with the Central Intelligence Agency, the Senate Foreign Relations Committee, and the Department of State.

Kenneth Weisbrode is deputy director of the Program on International Security at the Atlantic Council of the United States.

About the Atlantic Council

History

Within a few years of the signing of the North Atlantic Treaty in 1949, voluntary organizations emerged in the member countries of the Alliance to promote public understanding and support for the institutions that would put into practice the lessons of the turbulent years 1914 to 1945. The international network of citizens' associations was bound together formally in 1954 with the creation of the Atlantic Treaty Association.

In 1961 former Secretaries of State Christian Herter and Dean Acheson, with Will Clayton, William Foster, Theodore C. Achilles, and other distinguished Americans, recommended the consolidation of the proliferating citizens groups supporting the Atlantic Alliance under the Atlantic Council of the United States, incorporated as a bipartisan, educational, and tax-exempt organization.

Today the Atlantic Council continues as a bipartisan network of private individuals who are convinced of the pivotal importance of transatlantic and transpacific dialogue in promoting the effectiveness of U.S. foreign policy and the cohesion of U.S. international relationships. To those ends the council has remained committed to enhancing U.S. initiative and leadership through sound and skillfully administered policies that identify and pursue national interests in a framework of global interdependence and through the education of future generations.

Purpose

The council accomplishes these goals through action projects that address the challenges facing U.S. leaders in the midterm future. Dedicated to this task, the council:

- assesses policy options and develops bipartisan policy recommendations for consideration by the U.S. government and private sector;

- brings to bear on these issues the judgment of its widely experienced and rigorously bipartisan roster of directors, councillors, sponsors, academic associates, and corporate leaders, together with resident senior fellows and independent specialists;

- engages counterparts throughout Europe, Asia, and the Americas in dialogue through joint consultations about common problems and opportunities;

- disseminates information, sponsors public debate, and promotes the education of future leaders about key international issues.

RECENT ACCOMPLISHMENTS

Through its diverse network of committed volunteers, the council is able to build broad constituencies prepared to impact directly on the formulation and implementation of U.S. foreign policy. Examples of recent contributions by council working groups include laying the groundwork for:

- NATO's Partnership for Peace;

- bipartisan consensus on U.S. relations with China, Japan, and the Pacific Rim;

- comprehensive energy policies for Russia and Ukraine;

- important reductions in nuclear arsenals by the major nuclear powers;

- U.S. government contingency planning for Bosnia, Cuba, and Panama.

In all its efforts, the council is dedicated to integrating the views of experts from a wide variety of backgrounds, interests, and experience.

Atlantic Council of the United States
Suite 1000
910 17th Street, N.W.
Washington, D.C. 20006

INDEX

DATE DUE